CULTURE SHOCK!

Ecuador

Nicholas Crowder

·K·U·P·E·R·A·R·D·

In the same series

Argentina	*Egypt*	*Laos*	*Sri Lanka*
Australia	*Finland*	*Malaysia*	*Sweden*
Austria	*France*	*Mauritius*	*Switzerland*
Belgium	*Germany*	*Mexico*	*Syria*
Bolivia	*Greece*	*Morocco*	*Taiwan*
Borneo	*Hong Kong*	*Myanmar*	*Thailand*
Britain	*Hungary*	*Nepal*	*Turkey*
California	*India*	*Netherlands*	*UAE*
Canada	*Indonesia*	*Norway*	*Ukraine*
Chile	*Iran*	*Pakistan*	*USA*
China	*Ireland*	*Philippines*	*USA—The South*
Cuba	*Israel*	*Scotland*	*Venezuela*
Czech Republic	*Italy*	*Singapore*	*Vietnam*
Denmark	*Japan*	*South Africa*	
Ecuador	*Korea*	*Spain*	

Living & Working in Barcelona	*Living & Working in London*	*Living and Working Abroad—*
Living & Working in Chicago	*Living & Working in New York*	*A Parent's Guide*
Living & Working in Havana	*Living & Working in Paris*	*Living and Working Abroad—*
Living & Working in Jakarta	*Living & Working in Rome*	*A Practical Guide*
Living & Working in Kuala Lumpur, Malaysia	*Living & Working in San Francisco*	*Living and Working Abroad—*
	A Student's Guide	*A Wife's Guide*
	A Traveller's Medical Guide	

Culture Shock! Ecuador
First published in Great Britain 2002 by
Kuperard
311 Ballards Lane, Finchley, London N12 8LY.
Tel: 0208 446 2440 Fax: 0208 446 2441
Email: kuperard@bravo.clara.net

Kuperard is an imprint of Bravo Ltd.

All rights reserved. No part of this publication may be
reproduced, stored in a retrieval system, or transmitted
in any form or by any means, electronic, mechanical,
photocopying, recording or otherwise, without the prior
permission of the copyright owner.

© 2001 Times Media Private Limited

Illustrations by TRIGG
Front cover photograph from David Simson
Back cover photograph from Pietro Scozzari
All inside photographs from Nicholas Crowder

Printed in Singapore
ISBN 1-85733-289X

*I would like to dedicate this book to my Ecuadorian wife
and our children. I feel the same way as a good friend
of mine, who also married an Ecuadorian—
"Isn't it wonderful how the two cultures blend
to produce wonderful children who understand
different points of views!"*

*This book is also dedicated to my mother and father
who made it possible for me to attend the American
Graduate School of International Management
for advanced studies. That opportunity exposed
me to numerous cultures and it was there that
my passion for travel and to understand people
from distant lands was honed.*

CONTENTS

Culture   92

Language   118

Customs and Etiquette   129

Cuy, Caldos & Chicha   150

ACKNOWLEDGMENTS

When I began my experiences in Ecuador, over 20 years ago, I never expected that I would have had the good fortune to meet so many individuals who have provided me such valuable insight into this small and immensely complicated country. Numerous people have helped me in the writing of *Culture Shock! Ecuador* and I regret that I only have the space to thank some of them here.

Phone numbers, addresses, and so on, seem to be in a constant state of flux here. Just before this book went to print, the whole telephone numbering system changed! I have tried my best to ensure this material is as accurate as possible and take full responsibility for all the facts in this book.

I wish to offer my special thanks and deepest appreciation to the following people: Marc Becker, Mercedes Crowder, Jenny Estrada Ruiz, Michelle O. Fried, Amalia V. Garzón, Dr Angel Gustavo Guevara, Angela Hamilton, Rodolfo Perez Pimentel, Milly Rivadeneira, Professor John Schechter, and Tim Virnig.

ECUADOR

INTRODUCTION

As a young man, my father always encouraged me, in a lighthearted manner, to take a banana boat down to South America. He probably did not realize that that thought stayed in my subconscious and determined my future.

In my early twenties, when working in a department store, I met a wealthy Ecuadorian by chance. He was visiting the States and had lost his passport. With my Spanish 101, I did my best to help him and he explained to me that he was a banana farmer and was in Arizona studying water resources to help combat some of the droughts in Ecuador. A stout muscular man with a genial smile, he had a very attractive wife with bronze skin and eyes who looked as if she were descended from an Indian princess. Later, I had a Spanish professor from the Sierra (mountain area) region of Ecuador who did not look like or speak like my newfound acquaintance from the coastal plains of Ecuador in the city of Guayaquil. My professor was slight in build and had a distinct accent, sounding very different from the man from Guayaquil.

It was on a jet that I finally made my first trip to Ecuador in the early 1980s, not on a banana boat. Ecuador captured my soul. In this small country I found a dose of all that was good and bad in life. Within its borders, it is a country steeped in the human spirit and every human experience. If James A. Michener had lived long enough, he would probably have discovered the tiny jewel of Ecuador and found more then enough material to write a number of epic novels.

If you are lucky enough to have the opportunity to move to or visit Ecuador, you are in for an adventure. Despite its small size, it is not a homogeneous country. It possesses many divisions socially, culturally, and geographically. A constant factor about Ecuador is that it always seems to be in transition. Whether it is suffering from natural catastrophes or expanding substantially due to oil exports, it is always changing.

Superficially, however, much of the country does not appear to have changed from the time the Spanish conquered it. On the surface, it appears similar to other Latin American countries. Ecuador, however, has a unique way of conducting life. One of the most profound statements I have ever seen regarding Ecuador can be found in Walker Lowry's rare masterpiece—*Tumult at Dusk: Being an Account of Ecuador*. During his visit to Ecuador, he and his companions became aware of a murder at a ranch named *Ila*. They were concerned, as many North Americans would have been, and thought something had to be done. But a colonel offered this advice: "That is right Señores. Whatever you do you will only make things worse. Forgive me for saying it but you do not understand this country. You do not understand its people. You think that because we have houses, cars and clothes like yours, because we talk of democracy and freedom, because we read your books, borrow your money, buy your goods, we are like you.

"But we are not. We look like you, sometimes we talk like you, but we do not think like you. The difference, Señores, is not great but it is important. If you do not see it, the things you do in this country will be wrong. You will only make trouble. Your motives will be good but you will always be misunderstood. You will try to make friends and find only enemies. You will be disappointed. You will condemn this country. Or you will make fun of it. You will go home and say this country is ridiculous, that everything is hopeless.

"But who are you to say, you who have never understood us? Señores, try to understand. Look at this country with open eyes believing only what you see. Look at our people. Look at our history. Look at our land. Do this, Señores. Do not worry about Ila. Ila is no your affair. Adiós, Señores."

What about you, my dear visitor friend? Do you wish to understand Ecuador? Do you wish to look at this country with open eyes? If you do, it is for you that this book has been prepared. It will guide you through the maze of cultural differences and help you understand its people, history, and land and believe what you see.

ONE COUNTRY, FOUR FACES

"The geography of Ecuador has always dominated the humans who have come to make their homes on her soil."—Albert B. Franklin, *Ecuador: Portrait of a People*.

In your quest to understand Ecuador, you will find that it is one of the most unique geographical places on Earth. It is a very small country with lots of geography. Imagine being near glaciers, hours later tromping in the rain forest, then a few hours later boating through the mangroves on the Pacific coast. If Walt Disney were looking for a location for a nature park this would be the ideal place. (They might have to add a number of restrooms, however.)

In an area about the size of Colorado, with an area of 103,930 miles (269,178 square kilometers), Ecuador's geography has been a major factor in the development of the cultures that have resided there. It is also a virtual mosaic or museum of almost every type of terrain, flora, or fauna to be found on our planet. There are so many types of flora that many have not even been described or catalogued to date. This is a very special place, which is under increasing stress from human and commercial pursuits.

Ecuador is one of the smallest Andean countries located in the northwestern corner of South America. It is bordered with Colombia on the north; Peru on the south and east; and the Pacific Ocean to the west. The mainland is comprised of three unique geographical regions. These areas are referred to as the Costa (coastal lowlands in the west), the Sierra (central mountainous region), and the Oriente (eastern region, also known as the Amazon region, which slopes easterly from the Andes Mountains). There is a fourth geographic zone called the Galápagos Islands or Archipiélago de Colón, lying about 620 miles (998 kilometers) off the Pacific coast.

The Costa and Sierra make up about 60% of Ecuador's land area and the Oriente the remaining 40%. The Costa and Sierra regions are home to most of the population, with slightly more people living in the Costa. Only about 5% of the population live in the Oriente. The population was about 12.9 million in July 2000, with about 60% between 15 and 64 years of age and about 36% younger than 14 years of age.

COSTA

The Costa is an alluvial plain on the west coast, as wide as 100 miles (161 kilometers) in some places, or as narrow as 12 miles (19 kilometers) across. Its main rivers are the Esmeraldas to the north, and the Guayas to the south, forming a fertile delta in between. This is the food basket of Ecuador, producing crops such as bananas, cacao, rice, sugar, coffee, and toquilla palm (from which the inaccurately named Panama hat is made). Some petroleum and gold is also produced here. This used to be the center of oil production but the oil has largely run out and the Oriente is where about 85% of Ecuador's oil is now pumped. Guayaquil, on the banks of the Guayas River, is Ecuador's largest port and a major source of economic capital.

The northern and eastern Costa is covered with tropical rain forest, including lianas, epiphytes, balsa, and cinchona trees. Moving south, the rain forest gives way to deciduous and semi-deciduous woodland. Here, palms which provide nuts for buttons and fiber for the Panama hat can be found. The swampy coast and river floodplains were once covered by dense mangroves which have now been cleared for shrimp farms.

The Costa is a populous region of Ecuador. Most of the country's agriculture production and industry take place in this region, the focus being Guayaquil, one of Ecuador's largest seaports. The Costa also holds a tremendous amount of opportunity for tourism, which has not been fully exploited to date. Much of the original mangroves have been eliminated to make way for shrimp farms. Economics, unfortunately, always seems to rule over conservation. The streams and the rivers in the Sierra flow to the sea through the lowlands of the Costa through soil which makes its basins rich for agriculture. I remember my first time in Guayaquil: I was amazed to see mangoes and papayas there the size of large cantaloupes in the United States!

The temperature is generally high throughout the year here. Temperatures average between 76°F to 90°F (24°C–32°C). The rainy season (December–May) is warmer and more humid than the dry season. The Costa's dry season takes place during the second half of the year. Humidity can be quite high and stifling. Much of this depends on the wind patterns and rainfall.

The southern Costa near the border with Peru receives very little rain and is quite arid. The northern Costa, comprised of rain forest and mangroves, receives between 50–80 inches (1,270–2,032 milimeters) of rain annually. Guayaquil receives about 40 inches (1,016 milimeters) of rain per year. The southern Santa Elena Peninsula is a dry area, rainfall averaging 4 inches a year.

Every four to seven years, during the rainy season, the infamous El Niño phenomenon may occur, resulting in torrential rains. I have experienced two El Niño seasons, over the last eight years, and have witnessed the amount of damage they can wreck. During the 1982–1983 season, there was much loss of life and billions of dollars in damages. During the 1997–1998 season, numerous dead blue-footed boobies washed up along the Ecuador coast, about 600 miles (966 kilometers) from their Galápagos Islands habitat. I also heard that Ecuadorian bananas and aquatic reptiles were found in Peru. Deadly floods and mudslides washed away towns and destroyed highways. Unusually warm waters caused coral near the Galápagos Islands to bleach. A terrible drought also hit the Amazon region, resulting in raging forest fires.

SIERRA

The Sierra is the central mountainous region, consisting of the Andean highlands which run north to south along the entire length of the country. The world's highest active volcano is found here— Cotopaxi, standing at 19,347 feet (5,897 meters). The slope to the west is quite steep but more gradual to the east toward the Oriente. There are two distinct Andean ranges—the Eastern and Western Cordilleras. The fertile valley between them is called the Avenue of the Volcanoes. The Sierra has more than 12 peaks higher than 16,000 feet (4,877 meters), most capped with snow. Ecuador's highest peak is Chimborazo (20,702 feet or 6,310 meters), an inactive volcano.

Ecuador has a long history of volcanic explosions and earthquakes. Tungurahua, an active volcano, is known locally as *The Black Giant*. On November 10, 1999 explosions of ash and incandescent material occurred some 25–35 times per day from The Black Giant, and loud bangs could be heard as far as 12 miles (19 kilometers) away.

The Cotopaxi Volcano—a photographer's dream.

Ecuador's major rivers and streams begin in the Sierra, making deep trenches in the landscape and causing much erosion. This has limited the amount of land available for agriculture in the highlands.

Much of the Sierra feels as if it were in an eternal spring. Temperatures average around 60°F (16°C) and the sun sets at almost the same time every day. North of Quito there is a range on the way to Otavalo where you would think you are in the mountains of Arizona. However, rainfall patterns can be quite varied, decreasing toward the centers of canyons and valleys. The interior plateau and slopes are very dry and cold. The rain here is often very fine, producing misty conditions. Some basins in the Sierra are comparatively arid. Rainfall reaches a maximum during the equinoxes. The rainy months are from October to November and February to May.

Quito is nestled in the Andes Mountains, at an altitude of 9,350 feet (2,850 meters). Having limited contact with the outside world until recently, Quito, and the other Sierra cities of Cuenca and Loja, have developed into bastions of conservative Spanish culture. Even today, alongside modern office buildings and apartments, stand some of the finest examples of colonial art and architecture in all of Latin America.

ORIENTE

Slowly descending from the Sierra into eastern Ecuador, you will enter the mystical jungle region of the Oriente. Comprising the eastern slopes of the Ecuadorian Andes and the lowland areas of rain forest in the Amazon basin, the Oriente takes up about 40% of Ecuador's land area. There are three principal waterways in the region—with the slow and wide Amazonian rivers and their tributaries—Río Napo, Río Pastaza, and Río Santiago.

Fantastically colored birds, such as long-beaked toucans, noisy macaws, and flitting humming birds, share this land with exquisite butterflies, 28-foot anacondas, and ferocious howler monkeys.

The Quito skyline on a cloudy day.

Largely undeveloped, only about 5% of Ecuadorians live here. Most of the people here are Indians, the largest Indian community being the Jíbaros, who live on the banks of the rivers in the southeastern jungles. A fiercely independent people, they successfully fought off the Spanish by killing them, abducting their women, and setting fire to their settlements. Headhunters and skillful warriors, they can blow poisoned darts with deadly accuracy. Other communities found here include whites and mestizos from the highlands, the nomadic Aucas, the Quichua-speaking Záparos and Yumbos, the tunic-wearing and ornamented Cofáns.

Petroleum and timber (formerly gold) are the major economic resources of the Oriente. Oil was discovered here around 1970. Plantains and cassava are important staple food crops here, and corn (maize) and oranges are also cultivated. Cattle are left to graze.

The Oriente is very hot all year round and experiences continuous and abundant rainfall. Temperatures range from a high of 84°F–91°F (29°C–33°C) during the day to a low of 68°F–75°F (20°C–24°C) at night. This region has a poor drainage system because of the low gradient of the topography.

GALAPAGOS ISLANDS

The fourth geographical region of Ecuador is the Galápagos Islands. American novelist Herman Melville described these islands as such: "Take five and twenty heaps of cinders dumped here and there in an outside lot, imagine some of them magnified into mountains and the vacant lot the sea; and you will have a fit idea of the general aspect of the Encantadas, or Enchanted Isles." These heaps of cinders consist of 13 major islands (ranging in area from 5.4 to 1,771 square miles or 14 to 4,587 square kilometers), six smaller islands, and scores of islets and rocks lying west of the mainland of Ecuador. The islands have a total land area of 3,093 square miles.

The government of Ecuador designated part of the Galápagos Islands a wildlife sanctuary in 1935. In 1959 the sanctuary became the

Galápagos National Park. This archipelago is Ecuador's main tourist magnet. When I first visited Ecuador in the early 1980s, it still seemed to be an exotic destination reserved only for the scientists and the rich. Tens of thousands of tourists arrive every year now. The value of the Galápagos Islands tourism to the Ecuadorian economy is estimated to be more than US$55 million a year.

Only five islands are permanently inhabited, San Cristóbal being the most populous. Some 80% of the islanders live on the islands of Santa Cruz, San Cristóbal, and Isabela. Many Ecuadorians try to move to the Galápagos Islands to cash in on the tourism. Every few years you will notice efforts by the government to restrict migration to these islands. Tourism and migration places severe pressures on the ecosystem and great care should be taken to preserve the qualities that the Galápagos Islands such a unique destination.

Underwater volcanoes formed the islands millions of years ago. The first historical report of these islands dates from 1535 when it was discovered by accident by the Bishop of Panama, Tomás de Berlanga, when his ship drifted off course. He did not name the islands but reported tortoises or *galápagos* "so big that they could carry a man on their backs." This was probably what led the Flemish cartographer Ortelius to name the islands *Insulae de los Galopegos*. A seafaring Spaniard, Diego de Rivadeneira, visited the islands after Berlanga and named them *Las Encantadas* (The Enchanted Isles) after strong currents threw his ship mysteriously off course, giving the impression that the islands could move out of his reach at their own will.

It was, ultimately, Charles Darwin who drew international attention to Las Encantadas, or Archipiélago de Colón as they are known locally. Arriving in 1836 and staying for five weeks, it was here that Darwin gathered evidence for his momentous study—*On the Origin of Species by Means of Natural Selection*. His study of the Galápagos finch (or Darwin's finch) gave him evidence for his thesis that "species are not immutable."

Numerous species of plant and animal life are endemic to the Galápagos Islands. There are approximately 625 plant species and subspecies found here, of which 36% are endemic. There are approximately 1,000 insect species present (including 50 spider species), and more than 60 species of snails. Some 298 fish species have been recorded.

One animal endemic to the Galápagos Islands is the famous giant tortoise (*Geochelone elephantopus*). Whalers and sealers have decimated the tortoise population and now only 15,000 remain. The small-winged flightless cormorant (only 700–800 are still in existence), the dark-brown Galápagos hawk with a 4-foot wingspan, the small and scurrying Galápagos rail, the hideous and prickly-pear-eating iguanas, the drab and non-poisonous Galápagos snake, and the luxuriously coated Galápagos fur seal are just a sampling of the local inhabitants.

The climate here is influenced by the ocean currents. January to May is the typical hot or rainy season. June to December is the dry or cool season. There is minimal rainfall, which often forms a mist.

Two of the most interesting islands are San Cristóbal and Santa

Cruz. San Cristóbal is the eastern-most island. The first permanent settlers arrived here in 1869. Many of the cruise tours of the islands begin in San Cristóbal.

Santa Cruz is where the National Park headquarters and the Charles Darwin Research Station are located. A number of tours also begin from this island. The U.S. Navy had a small installation just off this island during World War II.

VEGETATION

Ecuador is one of the richest places in the world for flora. Ten percent of the world's vascular plant species is located within an area that covers just 0.2% of the Earth's surface. Ecuador houses some 25,000 species of vascular plants. (All of North America only has 17,000 species.) This is largely due to the diverse ecological conditions created by the great altitudinal differences in this small land. The vegetation varies from xerophytic scrub to rain forest.

This land is one of the largest growers of roses in the world. More than 10% of all the orchid species in the world grow here. Forests from which many exotic woods are derived cover much of the country, such as cedar, ebony, cyprus, and myrtle. Other plants include vanilla, cinnamon, and chicle. Montane rain forest covers the eastern slopes of the Andes. The soils in the Sierra are porous and there is poor forest coverage except for the eucalyptus, which was imported from Australia. The lower levels of the Sierra are comprised of scrub brush and cacti. The higher levels consist of tufted grass, just before the glaciers begin.

WILDLIFE

Ecuador's wildlife is just as impressive. In the Sierra, llamas exist alongside pumas and jaguars. The Costa and Oriente are populated by many varieties of parrots and monkeys, which you might see for sale on the streets of cities such as Guayaquil. There is a wide variety of rodents, bats, alligators, turtles, and iguanas.

If you are a bird-lover, Ecuador is also the place for you! There are about 1,500 species to be found here, a number endemic to Ecuador. In 1998 a new species from the Antpitta family was discovered—a bird which barks like a dog and hoots like an owl! There are also over 115 species of hummingbirds that add a lot of color to the geography.

Frogs and butterflies are also abundant here. I remember seeing, during my first trip from Guayaquil to Cuenca, places in the lower Andes which were just covered with blue butterflies. There are also more than 450 marine species and 800 freshwater species in Ecuador's teeming waters.

PROVINCES

Understanding the names of places in any country can give you substantial insight into the local culture. The country of Ecuador is divided into 22 *provincias* (provinces). These provinces are divided into *cantones* (regions), which are in turn divided into *parroquias*

Llamas at play, watched over by the Cotopaxi Volcano.

(parishes). Very small villages, where there may be just a few homes, are called *caseríos*.

A number of places have older names that were changed by the local government. While officially having a new name the locals would continue to refer to the place by the older name. One example is J. Gómez Rendon, a small city, which was originally called *Progreso*. The locals still refer to it as Progreso even though going through town it is marked J. Gómez Rendon. A number of towns are named after saints such as San Miguel de Salcedo. Towns named after male saints outnumber towns named after female saints.

In the Sierra many town names were originally in the Quechuan language. A number of town names have aquatic associations, named after nearby bodies of water. Examples are Los Encuentros where two rivers meet or La Bocana which refers to the mouth of a river. A number of provinces and towns have taken on the names of volcanoes. Examples are Cotopaxi and Cotocachi. Towns within certain provinces use names of lesser-known volcanoes such as El Altar and Toacaso.

In the Costa region you will see names of cities which refer to the elevation of the area or of certain vegetation. Some examples are Lomas de Sargentillo, which refers to the hills, and Zapotal, which is named after the Zapote tree.

Other cities may have use the last name of the founder such as Rivera or Mariano. Some townships use the name of a large land owner or of a ranch. Often a feminine name will be used, as in *La Hacienda Mercedes* (Plantation Mercedes). Names may also refer to a certain ideal or concept. Examples are El Progreso (*progreso* means progress), La Paz (*paz* means peace), or El Paraíso (*paraíso* means paradise). Houses are often named, no matter how humble. You may also see a home or small home with the name of the female occupant over the front door. An example is Villa Rosa.

23

GHOST TOWNS

Villages and cities come and go with time. Acts of nature and man contribute to the death and change of communities.

In Ecuador, both earthquakes and volcanoes have a tremendous impact on both geography and societies. A potent combination of lava and ice has caused significant mud and river flooding, aggravated by deforestation. Riobamba and Ambato have been destroyed three times. The most serious earthquakes and volcano explosions have had their major impact in the Sierra.

Humans have also played their part. Many of the initial Spanish settlements in the Oriente were wiped out by Indians. Other settlements such as Tomebamba and Mocha also suffered similar fates. During colonial times Guayaquil, Manta, and Portoviejo were attacked by pirates and their locations shifted. Since many of the earlier houses were built from cane, fires burnt down many towns, especially in the Costa region. Guayaquil burned down a total of three times prior to the 20th century. Babahoyo, Esmeraldas, and Vinces have also been damaged by fire.

CHALLENGES IN THE 21ST CENTURY

Ecuador's main challenge in the 21st century is maintaining the balance between man and geography. Planning, discipline, and the curbing of greed will be indispensable in keeping Ecuador a beautiful natural location. Ecuador is considered ecologically unique, with an unrivalled variety of ecosystems and diversity of species. Its breadth of ecological variation is largely attributable to the biodiversity on the Galápagos Islands.

The engines of economic development and enterprise (such as petroleum exploration, lumber production, and agricultural cultivation) is putting this delicate ecosystem under threat. Unsound environmental practices have contributed to considerable environmental degradation and given rise to these main environmental problems— deforestation, as a result of petroleum exploration and lumber production; soil erosion, as a result of over-grazing, poor agricultural cultivation practices and deforestation; desertification; water pollution; and deterioration of biodiversity.

There is a huge demand for shark's fin around the world, in particular Asia, with its insatiable appetite for shark's fin soup. A bowl of shark's fin soup can cost up to US$100 in some Hong Kong restaurants. World Heritage Sites and Marine Reserves, like the Galápagos Islands and the Cocos Island (in the Indian Ocean southwest of Java), are increasingly raided by illegal fishermen, as shark populations in outside reserves decline. Some fishermen take only the fins, dumping the maimed sharks back into sea, often still alive. At 50 dollars a pound for the fins, local fishermen also have no qualms about killing sea lion pups for bait. Sea turtles and sea birds (such as the rare-waved albatross and blue-footed boobies) are also often casulties that sadly get caught in nets meant for sharks.

Sea cucumbers lack an advantage that other sea creatures have, i.e. the ability to scurry or swim away from attackers. Due to their profitable return (up to 25 times their cost), this sea slug is particularly susceptible to over-fishing. Due to the alarming decrease in the early 1990s and an Executive Decree in 1993, all fishing of sea cucumbers in the Galápagos Islands was banned.

The government of Ecuador has committed itself to an environmental agenda called Agenda 21. In accordance with this, there is an urgent need to replace exploitative practices with sustainable development. The aims of Agenda 21 includes establishing a program to conserve and preserve the biodiversity of the Galápagos Islands; strengthening its system of protected areas; and applying strategies for reforestation. Ecuador must also formulate a legal framework, based on public policies, to address and regulate these suggested measures.

The regulation and protection of the environment in Ecuador is controlled by the Ministry of the Environment and the Dirección General del Medio Ambiente (General Directorate for Environment).

The non-governmental environmental organizations and entities that are active here include the Amigos de la Naturaleza de Mindo, EcoCiencia, and the Fundación Charles Darwin para las Islas Galápagos.

Galápagos Islands

Most scholars of the Galápagos Islands agree that the human population here has reached unsustainable levels.

The growing number of visitors that have come to witness the natural wonders of the Galápagos Islands have the potential to endanger them. The Park Service has found it difficult to limit the number of visitors to the islands but does regulate the licensing of guides required for disembarkation to the islands as well as the designation of low-impact landing sites. The National Park has to deal with the conservation problems that motor yachts and their trash (often dumped in the waters off Park limits) bring. Although responsible tourism is a sustainable means for preserving the park, its negative effects have to be closely monitored.

— *Chapter Two*—

THE SOMBER HISTORY
OF A DIVIDED LAND

"Ecuador is a somber land."—Walker Lowry, writer of
the classic *Tumult at Dusk: Being an Account of Ecuador*.

Several years ago, on a flight from Ecuador, a young American
woman sitting next to me commented that she regretted not having
read more about Ecuador's history prior to her visit. She felt, as she
looked in the residents' eyes and at the colonial architecture, that there
was much she had missed.

She was right. History is the golden key that will help you unlock

27

the mind of the Ecuadorian. So we should start by trying to unravel some of the threads of this small country's intricate past.

ECUADOR'S ANCIENT HISTORY

Pottery figures have been discovered that date from 3,000 to 2,500 B.C. This indicates that Ecuador was inhabited as early as 5,000 years ago. Apparently, a great variety of tribes (nearly 50) had settled along the coast, in the Sierra, and in the Amazonian hinterland. However, unity was not achieved among these Indians. The greatest divisions existed between the tribes of the coast and of the mountains.

Some of the earliest civilizations included the Valdivia, the La Tolita, and the Manta cultures, which settled along the Pacific coast.

THE INCAS

The Incas invaded and dominated Ecuador's groups before the Spaniards. They would have a substantial impact on local history, despite reigning supreme in the region for only a hundred years.

The Incas first established themselves in the 12th century in Cuzco, now part of modern-day Peru. Their main period of territorial expansion came during the reign of Inca Pachacuti Yupanqui (1438–1471). They moved south to the Titicaca Basin and north to Quito, ruling over the Chancas, the Quechuas, and the Chimús.

Cleverly resettling the locals, the Incas practiced the divide and rule principle, making organized revolt difficult. The Inca Topac Yupanqui (1471–1493) extended the southernmost border to central Chile, and his successor, Huayna Capac (1493–1525), northwards to the Angasmayo River, obtaining power in what is now southern Colombia.

Quito became a vital administrative and military center for the Incas. Huayna Capac divided the empire for his two sons with Atahualpa governing the north (including Quito) and Huáscar ruling the south. Huayna Capac's death set off a struggle for succession, which was still unresolved when the Spanish arrived in Peru in 1532.

At its height, the Incan civilization controlled about 12 million people in more than 380,000 square miles (980,000 square kilometers) of territory. They introduced taxes, the Incan religion, and the Quechua language. An extensive network of roads and bridges was laid—15-feet-wide (or 4.6-meters-wide) in some places. (This network ironically aided the Spanish conquest.) Llamas were used for transport and runners were used to relay messages, covering hundreds of miles in a day.

Incan society was highly stratified. The emperor ruled with the aid of an aristocratic bureaucracy, exercising authority with harsh and often repressive controls. Indians were at times forced into labor but the Incas did not tax them on the production of their own fields.

Incan technology and architecture were highly developed, although not strikingly original. Their irrigation systems, palaces, temples, and fortifications can still be seen throughout the Andes. The economy was based on agriculture, its staple crops being corn (maize), white and sweet potatoes, squash, tomatoes, peanuts (groundnuts), chili peppers, cocoa, *yuca* (cassava), and cotton. They raised *cuy* (guinea pigs), ducks, llamas, alpacas, and dogs. Much clothing was made from llama wool and cotton constructed from stone or adobe mud. Practically every man was a farmer, producing his own food and clothing.

The Incan religion combined features of animism, fetishism, and the worship of nature gods. The pantheon of gods was headed by Inti (the sun god), and included Viracocha (a creator god and culture hero), and Apu Illapu (the rain god). The Incan religion was a highly organized state religion, but, while the locals were required to worship the sun god, their native religions were tolerated. Incan rituals included elaborate forms of divination and the sacrifice of humans and animals. Much of their religious institutions were destroyed by the Spanish conquistadors in their campaign against idolatry.

The descendants of the Incas are the present-day Quichua-speaking indigenous Indians of the Andes. They combine farming and herding with simple traditional technology. Rural settlements are of three kinds: families living in the midst of their fields, true village communities owning fields outside inhabited centers, and a combination of these two. Towns are centers of mestizo communities. An Indian community is usually close-knit, and intermarriage within families is common . Much of the agricultural work is done cooperatively. Their religious beliefs are a form of Roman Catholicism infused with the pagan hierarchy of spirits and deities.

THE CONQUISTADORS

After the discovery of the New World, stories spread about the fabled wealth and riches of the Incan dynasty. A number of Spanish expeditions set out from Panama in search of gold. It is the view of some that it was the Spanish conquest that brutalized the region and put in place a rigid class structure. The area of Ecuador was first discovered by the Spaniards on an exploratory voyage around 1526, landing at Esmeraldas.

Francisco Pizarro departed from Panama in 1531. He ventured further south, landing in 1532 at Tumbez, on the present-day Peruvian coast. At that time, at least four culturally related Indian groups occupied the coastal lowlands who possessed gold and jewels: the Esmeraldas, the Mantas, the Huancavilcas, and the Punáes. The highland peoples included the Pastos, the Caras, the Panzaleos, the Puruhás, the Cañaris, and the Paltas. The Esmeraldas worked with gold and platinum and were hunters. The Mantas lived south of the Esmeralda and worked in gold jewelry and with emeralds. They were extensive traders and sailed up and down the coast.

Pizzaro continued down the coast to what is now Isla Puná (Puná Island) which is in the Gulf of Guayaquil. He had heard of gold in Tumbez but found it in ruins as a result of an Indian battle. He traveled into what is now Peru to Cajamarca where he planned to take Inca King Atahualpa into custody and hold him for ransom (a common tactic of the Spanish). When he arrived in Cajamarca he found that Atahualpa was not there but had moved himself and many of the residents to the surrounding hills. The Spanish pressed Atahualpa to visit and he foolishly accepted. He was taken captive and promised his freedom only if he could fill a room with gold. Atahualpa did so once and twice with silver. The Spanish still executed him. It was from here that they tightened their noose around the region. The Inca did not put up much resistance, weakened by internal division and defenseless against Spanish horses, canons, guns, and swords.

One of Pizarro's lieutenants, Sabastián de Benalcázar, headed north with a band of 200 men. Forming an alliance with the local Cañari people, they fought their way along the inter-Andean valley to Quito. Even the great Incan tactician, Rumiñahui, was finally forced out of Quito, but not before razing it to the ground. Benalcázar would

31

initiate one of the first municipal governments and became a lieutenant governor to Pizarro. (Benalcázar's home still stands at calle
Benalcázar y Olmedo in Quito.) He conquered most of Ecuador,
including Guayaquil in 1533. This was a brutal time when the Indians
were basically beaten into servitude.

The half-brother of Francisco Pizarro, Gonzalo Pizarro, was made
governor of Quito in 1539. In 1541, with about 200 Spanish troops,
some 4,000 Indians, horses, and other animals, he made an expedition
into the unexplored region east of Quito. The expedition ran into
trouble when supplies dwindled. The Indians did poorly in the tropics
and died. The Spanish were also not accustomed to such difficult
terrain. They had previously obtained supplies by stealing them from
the locals but the Indians they encountered in the new areas escaped.
Gonzalo's lieutenant, Captain Francisco de Orellana, left with some
men down the Napo River in search of provisions. Pizarro waited and
waited and waited for Orellana. After his men had eaten their dogs,
horses, shoes, and saddles, realizing that Orellana and his men were
probably not coming back, Gonzalo and the survivors stumbled back
to Quito. Only to find it in upheaval. Francisco Pizarro had been
assassinated by the Almagristas and another Spanish faction was
seeking control of the region. Something good did come out of this
expedition, however—the discovery of the Amazon River!

The Spanish Crown was upset with the situation and specifically
with the enslavement and maltreatment of the Indians. The Crown
ruled that the Indians be set free. It was also declared that the land
acquired by the conquistadors, after their death, was to be returned to
the Crown for management. This caused an uproar since many of their
widows and children would be reduced to poverty. In 1544 a new
viceroy was sent to try to manage the local administration. Blasco
Nuñez had a short and violent career. It started with him trying to
impose the New Laws of Bartolomé de Las Casas to the letter. He
stepped hard on many important toes and either ordered a murder or
committed one himself. Opposition grew against him and he was

arrested and packed off home to Spain. On the way home, however, he was killed by troops loyal to Gonzalo Pizarro.

The crown then sent Pedro de la Gasca, a priest and lawyer, to try to calm things down in 1547. He succeeded by granting amnesty to the rebels and repealing many of the most hated laws. Pizarro had planned an attack against Gasca, refusing all offers of a peace accord. Pizarro was grossly outnumbered and his troops deserted him, professing allegiance to Spain. When Pizarro was taken into custody, he knew his time had come. Before being beheaded in 1548, he asked the executioner to make it quick and clean.

COLONIAL PERIOD

The colonial period of Ecuador continued to be a difficult time for the inhabitants. It is important to understand that Ecuador's history at this time was really one of Peru's. At the same time, it is was during the colonial period that the seeds of nationalism were sown, starting a long but painful gestation that would bear fruit with independence in 1830. This identity crisis explains in some degree the persisting problems between Ecuador and Peru and the regional divisions within present-day Ecuador.

In 1563 the northern region acquired the status of audiencia and came under the auspices of the viceroy of Lima in Peru. The audiencia was the highest tribunal of justice and a general administrative board for the region. The hierarchy of authority was absolute and began with the King of Spain. Under the king and governing the new colonies of America was the Council of Indies established in 1524 and residing in Spain.

Under the council were four viceroys who resided in the new Americas. The viceroy of Peru was based in Lima and was founded in 1544. The area of Ecuador and Quito reported to Lima. The audiencia or judicial body of Quito was formulated in 1563. Under the audiencia were provinces with a *corregidor* (governor) also appointed by the king. In what is modern-day Ecuador there were five provinces, consisting of Cuenca, Guayaquil, Loja, Quito, and Zamora. In 1739 Ecuador became part of the new Spanish Viceroyalty of Nueva Granada, which included Colombia and Venezuela, with its capital in Bogotá (Colombia).

Colonial cities were governed by a city council, its councillors appointed by the king. This was very likely a position for life. The councillors were referred to as *regidores* and would select a city leader or judge called an *alcalde*. In some instances there could be two *alcaldes*. The management style was quite onerous and the sole reason for the existence of these positions was to handle the king's affairs. Spain had no system in place to handle the conflicts in its new territories. All decisions had to be approved by Seville and answers could take longer then a year to obtain.

While Spain's primary interest was to expand its wealth, it professed a desire to convert the indigenous population to Catholicism. The Church became extremely important in the development of what is now Ecuador and became powerful and wealthy. In many ways the Church became more powerful then the government organizations. There was much bickering between the bishop and president of the audiencia as to who held the higher social status. The people of Quito found themselves constantly battling sickness, droughts, earthquakes, and volcanoes.

In the 1580s there were attacks by pirates along the Ecuadorian coast. In 1591 Spain realized that they needed numerous ships to protect its interests and a tax was levied to raise money for shipbuilding. The residents of Quito were upset with this and felt that the coast and Guayaquil should take care of itself. They revolted. A number of rebels were jailed and troops were sent from Lima. A representative was sent from Spain and a number of people were hung.

Caste System

It was during colonial times that Ecuador developed a strict social or caste type system. These social divisions have endured until today and one's place in society is often determined by the shade of one's skin. The social levels in colonial Ecuador were basically divided into five different levels:

Blacks

Blacks were among the lowest echelon of society. In fact they were not considered human and had no rights. The clergy made no attempt to convert or care for the blacks. They were originally brought to Ecuador along the northern coast in the late 16th century to work the sugar plantations. However, in present-day Ecuador, blacks are considered a step above the Indians in society.

Indians

Indians provided most of the labor in colonial Ecuador. In general, they were passive and did as they were told. They were usually attached to a large *hacienda* (plantation) and would be called from time to time to work on large public projects. The Church made efforts to teach the Indians to read and to convert them to Catholicism.

Mestizos

Mestizos claimed the next level of society and were often fathered by a Spaniard and had an Indian mother. They had very little access to positions of power or prestige. There was some movement by mestizos into the Church culture.

Criollos

The criollos were of Spanish descent and officially had the same rights of the Spaniards. However, it was the Spaniards who received the best positions and the favor of the courts. There was a great deal of quarrelling and hatred between the criollos and the Spaniards.

Spaniards

The Spaniards clearly held the highest places in society. There were approximately 1,000 Spaniards at that time. Most of the early Span-iards were conquistadors. They believed that the Indians were there to do their manual labor, having a distaste for working with their hands. This is still the case in Ecuador where it is believed that only the lower classes work with their hands.

Some Spaniards married Indian women because there were few Spanish women then. Their children had little opportunity of moving into the higher circles of society and were often regulated to managing groups of Indian laborers. Many became artisans and contributed significantly to much of the beautiful architecture of Quito.

The lower classes had literally no representation at that time and were perceived to exist to serve the higher classes. Greed and ambition existed among the higher classes.

INDEPENDENCE

Ecuador's independence from Spain took similar lines to the unrest spreading across the South American continent. The first rumbles started in Quito in 1592, recurred in 1765, and erupted in the events which took place between 1770 and the end of the 18th century.

One of the strongest proponents for independence for Ecuador was Francisco Javier Eugenio de Santa Cruz y Espejo, a mestizo medical doctor. A well-regarded scholar, he had a wide range of interests and a grand vision for Ecuador's future. Advocating com-plete freedom from Spain, autonomous government for each colony, and nationalization of the clergy, he was persecuted, imprisoned, and exiled for his ideals. Eugenio Espejo published the first newspaper in Ecuador (*Primicias de la cultura de Quito*) that was heavily critical of the Spanish government. This newspaper only made seven issues. He died in 1795, but not before he had planted the hope of independ-ence in many Ecuadorian hearts.

The independence of North America, the French Revolution, and the invasion of Spain by Napoleon fed existing anti-Spanish senti-ments. The Spanish government had tried to dominate all aspects of economic and political life and many locals found their rule unjust and oppressive, bringing more negative consequences than benefits. They blamed the Spaniards for establishing hateful racial, economic and cultural castes; stealing land from those who depended on it for their livelihood; forcing the poor into slavery; bringing with them infectious diseases such as smallpox and syphilis; and stripping Indians of their self-respect.

A group of Quito elites formed a junta on August 10, 1809. Successful for a year, it collapsed due to a lack of support from other Ecuadorian cities. Further plans for rebellion were held in check by the locals' fear of the Spanish Pacific fleet. But the military's abuses caused much of the population to side with the rebels, resulting in riots in 1810. After an agreement for a troop withdrawal, the junta was told it could exist, but only under the leadership of the audiencia. The viceroy of Peru opposed this plan. The Spanish remained in control for the next 10 years.

By 1819, the Spanish threat had lost its teeth. Another movement for independence had begun in Guayaquil. Leaders were able to enlist the assistance of Simón Bolívar from Venezuela and José de San Martín from Argentina who were marshalling independence struggles on either sides of the continent. Simón Bolívar (nicknamed *The Liberator*) had a grand vision of several large independent countries across the continent—Gran Colombia. He had soon entered Bogotá, the capital of Colombia, taking the Spanish by surprise in the Battle of Boyacá on August 7, 1819. In 1821 troops were sent from Colombia under the command of Antonio José de Sucre. The liberators foiled the Spanish troops in Guayaquil and then focused on the Sierra. General Sucre defeated the royal troops in the mountains above Quito at the Battle of Pichincha. Venezuela was freed from Spanish rule in 1821 and Ecuador in 1822.

It was in Quito that Bolívar won Ecuador's independence, and it was also in Quito that he won Manuela Sáenz's heart. Sáenz was an ardent revolutionary who united her life with Bolívar's cause. She

Simón Bolívar's monument in Parque Bolívar, Guayaquil.

saved him from conspirators in 1828 in Bogotá and attempted suicide when he died in 1830. Exiled to the small Peruvian port of Paita, she spent her last days eking out an existence selling sweets and tobacco.

Bolívar's goal at that time was to combine Colombia, Ecuador, and Venezuela into the Viceroyalty of New Granada. Bolívar and San Martín met from July 26–27, 1822 in Guayaquil on the banks of the Guayas River, where there is now a statue of the both of them. San Martín's campaign was to liberate Peru but Bolívar wanted it as part of his Gran Colombia. What was said between the two was not recorded but they parted quickly neither promising aid to the other. Guayaquil was divided and had three options to determine its existence:

a) Unite with Bolívar and become a part of Gran Colombia

b) Unite with Peru

c) Become self-governing

Bolívar made option a) come true, delivering the final blow to the Spanish colonial regime in South America two years later.

As a part of Gran Colombia, Ecuador became embroiled in military campaigns to liberate Peru. Ecuadorians resented the 30% tax Bolívar had levied on Guayaquil's cacao exports to finance his Peruvian campaign.

The Guayaquil elites agitated for self-rule and on May 13, 1830, the independent republic of Ecuador was proclaimed. Juan José Flores was appointed president five months later. Venezuela and Quito both withdrew from Gran Colombia in 1830. Bolívar died, soon after his dream, of tuberculosis in the house of a Spaniard near Santa Marta, Colombia. His last words were "(South) America is ungovernable. Those who have served the revolution have plowed the sea."

BABY REPUBLIC

While Ecuador gained its independence, it in no way lost the tremendous and deeply entrenched culture of Spain. The divisions between the social classes continued, and power remained in a few aristocratic hands. The lower classes had no say and little influence. The distinct geographical divisions also played a considerable factor in dividing the three distinct regions (Costa, Sierra, and Oriente) into one country. The main divide lay between the Sierra's wealthy landowners and the coastal merchants, centered around Quito and Guayaquil, respectively. They had contrasting economic and social attitudes. The inhabitants of the Sierra were conservatives, devout Catholics, and supporters of Church-sponsored education for all. Their economic interests revolved around the close management of native labor. In contrast, the coastal peoples were liberals who favored free enterprise, the development of agricultural exports and other trades. They opposed the Church's involvement in matters of state.

Juan José Flores was a general in Simón Bolívar's army. A Venezuelan by birth, he married into an influential Quito aristocratic family and became a national hero during the fight for independence. Flores was merciless in his pursuit for power. He called an assembly to declare the Republic of Ecuador a new nation and himself president. Flores' autocratic rule, poor administrative ability, his support of entrenched privileges, especially those of the Church, and his perceived favoritism towards the Sierra provinces, fed opposition against him.

Based in Guayaquil, Vicente Rocafuerte headed opposition to Juan José Flores. In 1834, at the close of Flores' first term as president, civil war broke out between Quito and Guayaquil. To quell this dangerous unrest, Flores cleverly installed Rocafuerte as president from 1834–1839. Flores retained a great deal of power from behind the scenes, however, by keeping a strong hold on the army.

Vicente Rocafuerte's term in office was a productive one. He promoted civil liberties and established public schools. Many reforms were carried out to protect the rights of native Indians and to advance and secularize education.

Once Rocafuerte's term ended in 1839, Flores resumed control with the support of Venezuelan and Colombian soldiers loyal to him. The tussle between these two strong leaders continued, but with Flores as president up until 1845. Rocafuerte went into self-exile in 1843 in protest against Flores's unsavory dictatorial practices, including inviting the Spanish to return. A young student, Gabriel García Moreno, made a failed assassination attempt on Flores. The coastal liberals finally forced Flores into exile. Even then, Flores stirred up trouble in Ecuador, attempting to overthrow the government from abroad.

CHAOS AND CATHOLICISM

The period 1845–1860 saw Ecuador in chaos, with a string of weak leaders jostling for power. For example, in 1859 a general controlled Guayaquil, both Loja and Cuenca declared themselves independent, and Quito had a provisional government. During this time of vulnerability, Peru invaded southern Ecuador and placed a blockade on Guayaquil. There was discussion with Colombia about dividing up the country.

Even as Ecuador seemed to be torn apart politically and wrecked economically, some saw this as a time of emancipation. The first laws to the advantage of the indigenous population were passed at this time, many slaves were liberated, and three centuries of compulsory tribute payments by Indians were ended.

Gabriel García Moreno was watching and waiting in the wings. He was repulsed by the chaotic violence that liberalism and self-interested factionalism had brought about. Careful analysis of Ecuadorian society convinced him that the country was hopelessly divided by regional interest, class, race, and language. Convinced that the only thing that could unify Ecuador was religion, García Moreno, himself a devout Roman Catholic, saw religion as the only means to create nationalism and foster social cohesion. To achieve this, Ecuador needed a period of peace and strong government.

In 1859 Peru took possession of Ecuador's southern provinces. Drastic action was needed. Courting the help of the man he wanted dead in the 1840s, García Moreno joined forces with Juan José Flores, forced the Peruvians out and began uniting the country.

García Moreno has been described by liberals as one of history's worst tyrants and by conservatives as a great nation-builder. Ruling from 1860–1875, he made Roman Catholicism the exclusive state religion and no other religions were tolerated. Education, welfare, and government policy came under the Church.

García Moreno's presidency inaugurated many public works projects. Schools (from primary to polytechnic level) and hospitals were built. Construction started on the Quito-Guayaquil railroad to link the Costa and the Sierra, and road were built. Eucalyptus trees were even brought in from Australia to alleviate erosion in the Sierra. Agricultural reforms improved production. Cocoa exports grew from approximately $1 million to $10 million dollars annually. Guayaquil developed as the key port for Ecuador and a rising middle class.

The object of countless assassination attempts, García Moreno was said to have had an indefatigable confidence in the future, allegedly declaring: "The enemies of God and the Church can kill me but God does not die." Not long after his third term, his presidency was abruptly ended when he was hacked to death on the steps of the presidential palace.

LIBERALS TAKE THE LEAD

After García Moreno's death, the liberals and conservatives jostled for power. Due to the increasing economic importance of the coast, the Guayaquil-based liberals began to take the upper hand. General Eloy Alfaro, a magnetic liberal hero emerging from the lower classes, became the constitutional president for two terms (1897–1901 and 1906–1911).

Under Alfaro, the affairs of the state were separated from those of the Church. Commercialism was promoted, as was freedom of religion and speech. Divorce was permitted as was civil marriage and burial. The Church tithe was abolished and many large estates confiscated by the state or liberal leaders. Alfaro continued and completed many of Moreno's road and railroad projects—the Quito-Guayaquil railroad was completed in 1908.

Alfaro was as heavy-handed as his predecessors, making little impact on the impoverished lives of the Indians and peasants. His growing unpopularity and relentless attempts to hold on to power led to his overthrow by a coalition of conservatives and dissident liberals. He and his lieutenants were dragged, dismembered, and burnt by a lynch mob in 1912.

DARK TIMES

During World War I and the short boom which followed, power shifted into the hands of the wealthy merchants and bankers of Guayaquil. This clique made attempts to take control of the agriculture of the coastal plain. The 1920s brought economic depression, the devaluation of the sucre, and a fungal epidemic which destroyed cacao crops. This precipitated urban discontent, the formation of trade unions in Guayaquil, riots, and even massacres conducted by the army. Riots broke out in November 1922, killing hundreds.

The army stepped in and seized power in 1925. They were unable to unite Ecuador, however, and the country entered a period of instability. Twenty-two presidents, dictators, or juntas were catapulted in and out of power over the next 25 years.

The 1930s were horrendous for the country. It would not be until the late 1990s that Ecuador would experience such difficult times. During the 1930s a number of new political parties evolved and presidents came and went. Border disputes were frequent during this time.

Ecuador–Peru Border Dispute

In 1830 there was a signed agreement with Peru designating the Marañon–Amazon River as the border. However, Peru had continuing and deep disagreements with this accord. During the mid-1930s Colombia turned over part of territory that Ecuador had claimed in exchange for Colombia's access to the Amazon River. In the mid-1930s Peru would continue to contest the eastern border without any success.

On July 5, 1941 Peru invaded Ecuador while President Carlos Arroyo del Río was still trying to work this dispute out diplomatically. With thirteen thousand Peruvian troops aligned against them, the 1,800-strong Ecuadorian troops in the affected areas in the eastern Amazon and sections of the southern provinces of Ecuador were unable to put up much resistance.

43

In 1942 a meeting was held among numerous countries in Brazil discussing the entrance of the United States into World War II. The issue of Ecuador and Peru was debated. Ecuador ceded more than half of its territories to Peru and four countries (Argentina, Brazil, Chile, and the United States) guaranteed that this new border would stand. In exchange, Peru promised to remove its troops from the southern provinces of Ecuador. This treaty was called the Protocol of Río de Janeiro and was signed on January 29, 1942. Thus far, 400–500 Ecuadorians and just over a hundred Peruvians have been killed over this border conflict.

An interesting fact about this conflict is that paratroopers were used for the first time in Latin America by Peru. More significantly, the Peruvian invasion and the outcome of the Protocol of Río de Janeiro brought about the political demise of Arroyo del Río. Violence erupted across the country. José María Velasco Ibarra would be president for four years, operating as a dictator.

THE FORTIES AND BEYOND

In 1948 Galo Plaza Lasso was elected president. He was an influential landowner from the Cotopaxi region. He didn't have the support of the military but he took some progressive measures. He brought in a number of outside experts to assist in the development of the country. However, Ecuador had limited funds and many of his plans never came to fruition. During this period, agriculture developed and a number of new road were constructed.

But the presidents played musical chairs and Velasco Ibarra returned from exile and was re-elected. Velasco Ibarra had a propensity towards socialism and kept close contact with Russia and Cuba. However, he never turned down aid from the United States. He made significant promises to the poor but little happened. He only lasted fourteen months this time. Velasco Ibarra was president five times but only completed one term of office.

In 1961 the vice-president Carlos Julio Arosemena was made

president. He, too, had strong socialist or communist leanings. Fearing a communist takeover, the military took control of the country. A number of the communists were exiled.

In 1964 the government introduced numerous agrarian reforms. However, regionalism remained a constant thread through the sixties, the people from the coast (*costeños*) often felt cheated that the people from the Sierra (*serranos*) received the best share of everything, including the fruits of the *costeños'* labor. There were numerous riots in 1965.

The military performed a coup in 1972, claiming that it would be better for the military to run the oil deposits for the country so that the elite would not get all the benefits. Money had started to roll in from oil exports by this time. Significant oil reserves were discovered in Ecuador in the 1960s and with it the promise of changing fortunes. Modernization programs were begun and the debt began to pile up with the belief that oil revenues would make all the difference. A middle class developed and many would start businesses. For example, there were only a handful of automobile parts importers in the mid-1970s but, by the 1980s, there were several hundred.

In 1979 Jaime Roldós Aguilera from Guayaquil became president. He was a technocrat and inherited many of the problems that came with a country deep in debt. He was killed along with his wife and several military leaders in a plane crash in 1981. Ecuador's economy suffered tremendously during the 1980s and much of the middle class disappeared. Ecuador went through a number of presidents including socialist Rodrigo Borja Cevallos from Quito. Inflation went out of control and the indigenous problem continued.

In 1995 Ecuador had a brief battle with Peru again over their border. At that time I was in Guayaquil and my nephew was called into military service. It was a tense time as many young men from both Ecuador and Peru were placed into action against each other. After dozens of troops were killed and hundreds were injured, a ceasefire was called. Thousands of troops were withdrawn from the Cenepa

Valley where most of the conflict was lodged and more than 140,000 troops were demobilized. Negotiations began immediately and lasted for the next several years until a peace accord was signed in 1998. Peru was granted a 48-mile section in the eastern Amazon. Ecuador was granted, in the middle of this area, a 250-acre hill called *Tiwintza*. Ecuador defended this area during the conflict. A new treaty was drawn up around four major themes:
- Securing a land boundary between the two countries.
- Establishing a commerce and navigation treaty.
- Defining and resolving security issues.
- Providing a comprehensive accord as to the integration of the borders.

I feel that there will be tremendous growth and development over the next 50 years along the border of Ecuador and Peru. There are numerous restructuring projects being planned, including highway

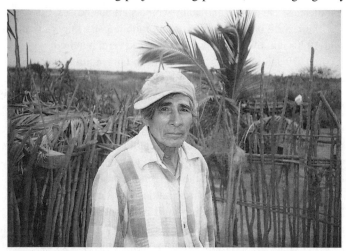

The care-worn face of an indigenous farmer. Originating from Manabí province but driven by need, he has moved south to Chanduy, an ancient fishing village on the coast south of Salinas.

connections and human development projects. Two negative aspects of the peace accord involve land mines that remain in the area and the rights of indigenous groups not consulted during the settlement process. At least 60,000 land mines remain, threatening to maim and kill residents. Chile entered into an accord to assist Ecuador and Peru in the removal of these mines over a 8–10 year period.

In 1996 Abdalá Bucaram was elected president and made many promises to the poor. However, corruption and mismanagement led to him being voted out by congress and exiled to Panama. From the late 1990s to 2000, Ecuador went through several more presidents. It would also suffer its worst financial situation in nearly 70 years. So bad was the situation that between 1999 and the end of 2000, nearly a million Ecuadorians left their homeland for economic opportunity. Please refer to the Society chapter for more details on the exodus of the 1990s.

There was much dissentient opposition to the government and President Jamil Mahuad in the late 1990s. He had proposed that Ecuador remove the sucre as the official currency, to be replaced by the U.S. dollar. Inflation was at over 60% and the gross domestic product had shrunk at least 7.3% primarily because of low oil prices. Unemployment had jumped from 12% to 17%. There was much opposition to Mahuad's proposal and, on January 22, 2000, thousands of indigenous people and middle to lower level military members walked into congress (which was unoccupied) and placed a three-man junta in charge of the country.

The United States placed pressure on this group and the committee was disbanded. Vice-president Gustavo Noboa was instituted as president to fulfill the remaining three years of office. Noboa vowed to continue with the dollarization plan and attack corruption. In his early 60s, he is an educator and is viewed by many as intelligent and honest, not appearing to have acquired material wealth for himself. Noboa does not belong to a political party and his priorities are modernizing the state and economic reform.

Yet another transaction is concluded at the Saquisilí market using the new U.S. dollars.

The indigenous community felt betrayed by the military as the government was put back in the hands of those sympathetic to the oligarchy. I agree with Walker Lowry who said in his book *Tumult at Dusk:* "Ecuador means equator. It ought to mean Indian." The Indians are now more organized than ever before and are committed to controlling their destiny and Ecuador's. There has been increasing activism from indigenous groups. The Confederation of Indigenous Nationalities (CONAIE) are leading the struggle for representation in Ecuador. The CONAIE President, as of October 2001, is Leonidas Iza. (Related material can be found on CONAIE's website: http:// www.CONAIE.org or http://www.CONAIE.org/ecu14.htm.)

Here is an extract from a statement by the former President of CONAIE, Antonio Vargas:

"If they want to find the coup participants, they should look for them in the corridors of the oligarchies, the parliament, the corrupt courts and bankers who with their policies and holdups have deepened the misery, the hunger, unemployment, and the migrations from the countryside to the city....Again historical injustices are repeated. During 500 years of oppression, our towns rose up demanding justice and the respect to the human rights which were cruelly violated again and again. But when there were uprisings, leaders like Rumiñahui, Tupac Amaru, Jumandi, Daquilema, and many others were taken prisoner, tortured and assassinated....But they must understand that there will be no wall nor any bars that can stop our ideas and our equitable and deeply participative fight, because with wrath and wisdom of centuries we are up building pressure like our sacred volcanoes to construct Ecuador as a just and participating Nation."

The deep-rooted contrasts of Ecuador's varied peoples and the divisive powers of external influences have been dominant threads in Ecuador's history. This author feels that Ecuador is on the verge of tremendous change. In thinking about Ecuador's future, I fear that Ecuador could fall prey to ambitious dictators, drug lords, or guerrilla groups from Colombia in the next 50 to 70 years. Whatever the outcome, we can only watch anxiously as Ecuadorians forge their unique identity in these tumultuous times.

Chapter Three

ECUADORIAN SOCIETY

"Ecuador has a severe inferiority complex."—Ecuadorian State Department Officer to author Tom Miller in an interview for Miller's book *The Panama Hat Trail*.

IDENTITY CRISIS

Ecuador is a country rich in human and geographical capital but appears to suffer from an inferiority complex and an identity crisis. It is this which seems to keep the majority of the population from true social and economic change. There is perhaps a Malinche syndrome in Ecuador. Malinche was the name of an Indian slave girl who belonged to Hernán Cortes in Mexico. She became his lover and was seen by many as a traitor to her Aztec roots. Malinche-thinking is a term I use to describe a Mexican preference for things foreign rather than Mexican. I feel that Ecuadorians also prefer foreign things rather than their own unique and rich culture. I have found that store clerks push an imported item over a local brand as if the imported item were automatically superior. I once interviewed a president of a trade organization in Ecuador who commented that his country always views its products or itself as being inferior.

Tom Miller, acclaimed writer and author of the book *The Panama Hat Trail*, found that many Ecuadorians, especially those from the lower classes, expressed this same sense of inferiority. Some of these identity issues may be caused by the fact that Ecuador's history has been so much a part of Peru's and Colombia's heritage. Ecuador is also a country of numerous internal cultural differences, which have been magnified by geographical divisions. How, then, was it to establish a clear and consistent sense of identity?

CLASS STRUCTURE

Ecuador's social structures have also been indelibly marked by the caste system from colonial times. Wealth and human rights seem to belong to the upper class or oligarchs and the rest of the country remains in abject poverty. James Orton expressed this eloquently in his book *The Andes and the Amazon; or, Across the Continent of South America*, writing this about the white aristocracy: "This is the governing class; from its ranks come those uneasy politicians who make laws for other people to obey, and hatch revolutions when a rival party is in power."

While Saudi Arabia is not a democracy, a visitor can see that the oil wealth of the country has trickled down to a wide group of the populace and raised the overall standard of living. To my foreign eyes, however, Ecuador's hundreds of thousands of barrels of oil a day do not seem to have an impact on the spreading of wealth. Compared to the United States, there are also limited opportunities for movement to higher social classes. If one is poor in Ecuador, one usually accepts one's station in life and concentrates on the continual struggle for existence.

Much of the rigid class structure, which has been in place for nearly 500 years, still exists. It is almost like going back in time. This hierarchical social structure is similar to that found in other Andean countries, such as Peru and Colombia. Much of Ecuador, until the last century, remained in isolation from other parts of Ecuador and the outside world, due to the rugged terrain and the absence of a good national transportation system. Hence, much of the Spanish psyche lingers on.

REGIONALISM

Another unique aspect of Ecuador is the strong regionalism, most especially between the people from the Sierra (*serranos*) and the people from the Costa (*costeños*). Differences in region and social class can be observed in one's dress, physical appearance, language, title, and family name. After some time in Ecuador, you will be able to tell quite quickly where an Ecuadorian is from.

Serranos vs Costeños

Serranos are for the most part mestizo. There are also a few who would consider themselves white and of pure Spanish blood. These will tend to dress more conservatively in the Sierra than in the Costa. I have also found that *costeños* are stouter than people from the Sierra.

The original fortunes of the Sierra were made from large landholdings. Few *serranos* branched out to the Costa during colonial times, due to its harsh living conditions. Guayaquil, in the Costa, has more of an appearance of a frontier town, with inhabitants of many classes. Guayaquil has been seen as a place to make a fortune and move on. Quito and Guayaquil have developed independently and do not think they need each other. Guayaquil grew into a major shipping and economic center. Society here is more liberal and the classes less well-defined than in Quito. There is still a divide between the lower and upper classes, however.

THE CLASSES, AGAIN

The family you were born into and your skin color "class-ifies" you.

Upper Classes

The whiter members of society are usually from the higher classes. Whiteness seems to mark one out as from among the top tiers of society. This can be seen in the advertisements and the media, which feature white actors and actresses. There is a lower upper class in the smaller cities throughout the Sierra with family names like Riobamba and Ambato.

Middle Class

Ecuador's middle class evolved in the second half of this century when the country went through tremendous growth, largely due to oil exports. The middle class is made up of businessmen, professionals, bureaucrats, and military officers. Most middle-class members have at least a high school education and are not involved in any type of manual labor. Working with one's hands is viewed by the middle and upper classes as inferior work. This thinking is a by-product of Spanish colonial times. As a result, you are unlikely to see people from the middle or upper classes doing any sort of work around the house, even gardening or home repairs. Attention to dress, grooming, and manners are also important to the middle and upper classes.

Lower Classes

The lower classes often work as guards, factory workers, small or street merchants, and domestic helpers. In the rural areas, they work as laborers and farm workers.

The lower classes have divisions of their own. Blacks or negros

Mother and child tending to their flock of sheep near Cotopaxi.

are usually found in the lower classes, ranked just above the position of indigenous groups. It is believed that the first blacks to enter Ecuador did so with Diego de Almagro, the Spanish conquistador, in about 1534. They participated in the conquest and worked the mines. There are differing accounts as to why the blacks concentrated in Esmeraldas, on the northwestern coast of Ecuador, and in El Valle de Chota (the Chota Valley). It is believed by some that there was a shipwreck off the northern coast and that they settled in this area. Other blacks migrated here from neighboring Colombia. The community of blacks in the Chota Valley live in an Afro-Ecuadorian settlement called Chamanal, six hours from Quito and 34 kilometers north of Ibarra, on the Carchi–Imbabura border. This valley was once the principal holding area for slaves brought from Colombia and Panama and is also famous for sugar cane.

The blacks have maintained many aspects of their African heritage, evident in their native music, dance, and oral traditions. Their music has been their main contribution to the Ecuadorian culture.

Laura Hidalgo Alzamora, Ecuadorian literary critic and literature professor, has produced an excellent study of the oral traditions of the decimas of the Afroamerican culture in Esmeraldas. Her doctorial thesis of 1982 was called *Decimas Esmeraldeñas—Recopilacion y Analisis Socio-Lieterario*. The decima are compositions which were passed down orally and are often satirical in nature. Many are also quite comical and have double meanings, including sexual innuendo.

While most decimas contain about 44 lines, one of my favorites, which is shorter then a normal decima, is often used before the marimba and other instruments join in and a dance follows. Here it is in Spanish then in English:

El Hombre: !Ay por Dios!
               Cuando veo a la negrita
               bien vestida y peinadita,
               me dan ganas de abrazarla
               y besarle esa boquita.

La Mujer: !Ve!
               Amores habrás tenido
               como bardolada en playa,
               pero nunca encontrarás
               una negra de esta laya.

El Hombre: Qué bonita muchachita,
               si su mama me la diera
               sólo esta noche y mañana
               se la volviera.

La Mujer: Bolívar con su espada
               conquistó cinco naciones,
               y yo con mis caderas
               conquisto los corazones.

Coro, Los Hombres: Y vamo' a ver si eso es cierto,
                                    y que suene la marimba.

Man: Oh, my Lord!
When I see that little black woman well
Dressed and combed,
I want to kiss her little mouth.

Woman: Look
A lot of lovers you've had like the
bardolada plant
That grows on the beach,
But you're never going to find a black woman
of my kind.

Man: A good-looking little thing you are!
If your mother would give you to me
For just tonight and tomorrow
I would bring you back.

Woman: Bolívar with his sword
Conquered five nations
And me with my hips
I conquer all hearts

Group of Men: And we're going to see if
That's true—
Let the marimba play.

Indians

Nearly 25% of Ecuador's population is indigenous but they are at the bottom of the social ladder. However, they are growing in political power and the Ecuadorian government would do well to take their interests into consideration. Here are some brief descriptions of some of the indigenous groups that live in Ecuador. The other Indian groups include the Salasacas, Saraguro, Siona-Secoya, and Awá (Kwaiker).

Quechuas

The Quechuas are the largest indigenous group in Ecuador, numbering over 1.5 million. They are located throughout the Sierra and the Amazon. While they share a common language (Quichua), both groups differ in culture and practices. The Quechua in the Andes are primarily small plot farmers and tend to flocks of sheep and cattle. Textiles and weaving are also an important source of income. The Quechuan basic belief system revolves around the cosmos having four floors, being Ahua Pacha (heaven), Puyo Llacta (clouds), Cai Pacha (earth), and Ucu Pacha (inner world).

Aucas

Standing barely more than five-foot in height, the Auca are also known as the Huaorani or the Waorani and have been little influenced by the outside world. They are located east of Tena and south of Coca. They often marry by age 10 or 12 years old and the men are polygamous. They are communal in nature and everyone contributes to the group's interests. The men are hunters and use poisoned darts with blowguns.

Jíbaros

The Jíbaros are the infamous headhunters of the Amazon and include the Shuars and the Achuars. They are located in the southeastern jungle of Ecuador and are about 20,000 strong. Missionaries have influenced some of their lifestyle although they still believe in spirits and magic. They cultivate fruits and potatoes and hunt.

Cofáns

Situated in northeastern Ecuador, their communities straddle the Ecuadorian–Colombian border. The Cofáns paint their faces with achiote (a food coloring used throughout Ecuador) and often have large holes in their earlobes and noses that are adorned with feathers. When a Cofán wife passes away, she is usually buried in the house, which is never entered again. A new house is built for the remaining members of the family.

Cayapas

The Cayapas homeland is in the Esmeraldas province. They are river people and there are approximately 4,000 remaining. The Cayapas travel by canoe and live in homes made of palm fronds. They also paint their bodies using achiote. They are famous for the hammocks they make and grow cacao and fruits.

Colorados

The Colorados reside near Santo Domingo de los Colorados. They are best known for the painting of their hair using a paste made of achiote and slicking it down with Vaseline. The women often paint their teeth blue believing that it prevents tooth decay. There are just over a thousand Colorados remaining. Quite open to outside influences, the Colorados continue some of their traditional practices, not living in villages but separate houses divided by cultivated fields and forests. Girls will often marry just after puberty.

EXODUS

Ecuadorians began leaving their country in droves in the late 1990s. Friends would ask me for loans up to $2,000 in their quest to get out. With the recent collapse of the Ecuadorian economy, men and women from all over Ecuador have been leaving legally and illegally for destinations such as Spain and Italy, which have fairly lax entry requirements.

This is a human tragedy in the making. If you arrive in Quito and see a large group of people standing on the runway, you are witnessing the exodus. They are watching family members leave Ecuador for perceived greener pastures. It is believed that, as of 2001, as many as 1.3 million have left to make new lives for themselves.

This exodus has created a cottage loan industry where people borrow the money to leave and then pay it back to the lender. The lenders are often family or friends or a unique network of small businesspeople charging high interest.

Many of the emigrants work in Spain as caregivers, cooks, and manual laborers. A number of women have found work as prostitutes. This exodus has taken a human toll on families back in Ecuador and will have a permanent effect on society. The positive effect is an influx of foreign currency, which has helped families and made possible much new investment in homes and land. If a million people are sending a hundred dollars back each month to Ecuador it is not hard to imagine the significant boost to the economy that brings.

In the neighborhood of La Chala in the suburbs of Guayaquil where I visit my relatives every year, I have observed whole families leaving. It is hard not to find a family in the middle and lower classes that doesn't have a family member living in Spain or Italy.

PROSTITUTION

Although a far cry from other parts of the world, such as Thailand, prostitution is a real albeit unpleasant fact of life among Ecuador's lower classes. Many women resort to prostitution to survive. Many of these women were abused or abandoned by their husbands and have had to take on fulltime jobs and work as prostitutes to supplement their meagre incomes.

I once visited a bar in Guayaquil where sex workers had an arrangement with the owner of the bar, letting them leave with his customers. I frequented this bar to drink beer with my friends and because I didn't participate, the women would often jokingly accuse me of being a homosexual. I noticed that the drinking by the women seemed to increase significantly during Christmas. While they might have been celebrating, I perceived much sadness in their eyes.

Prostitution is legal in Ecuador. In Quito, there are several entertainment establishments where women are available for sex on the premises. Several of these places cater to the higher end clientele of wealthy businessmen, diplomats, and tourists. The cheaper places cater more for the locals. Establishments that provide massages are often just fronts for the sex trade. There are numerous streetwalkers in both Quito and Guayaquil, a number of which are transvestites. Most towns will usually have a house or street where the sex trade is conducted seven days a week. One of these is the infamous and rough Calle 18 (18th Street) in Guayaquil.

Sadly, there has also been a recent increase in child prostitutes. After the depression of the late 1990s, many children from the poorer barrios are recruited with the empty promise of a chance of a career or training in the city. It is distasteful for Ecuadorians to speak about this but, with more than half of the population living in poverty, this is a real social problem.

RECENT IMMIGRANTS

There are a number of ethnic groups which have settled in Ecuador relatively recently. The Lebanese have a history of several genera-tions in Ecuador and have become quite powerful in both the eco-nomic and political arenas. They have, for the most part, preserved their culture, are viewed as middle-class, and often possess signifi-cant monetary wealth. They are often referred to as *Turcos* (Turks).

The Chinese have also made their inroads into this society. The original immigrants arrived in the 1800s and were based primarily around the area of Quevedo. They make up the middle class and many have made it good here as middlemen and traders.

About a thousand Jews arrived in Ecuador during the 1940s to escape Hitler's regime. Some Arabs have also moved here. Most recently, many Colombians have immigrated to Santo Domingo de los Colorados, giving rise to the nickname *Santo Domingo de los Colombianos*!

While there has never been a large immigration of Germans in Ecuadorian history, there was a time when they were removed from society. During the signing of the Protocol of Río de Janeiro in 1942, the issue of the Germans in Ecuador was addressed. A number of Ecuadorians of German descent were identified by the government and were deported to the United States, forced to leave everything behind. There are still a few survivors left in the United States where they were housed for some time in Houston, Texas.

WOMEN'S ISSUES

Ecuador still lags behind much of the advancement in women's rights in most of Latin America. Generally speaking, up until the last 10 to 15 years, women were raised to find a husband and to play a subservient role. Except in the higher-middle and upper classes, even marriages are not the norm. The upper and middle classes often marry both in a civil ceremony and a church-sanctioned wedding. However, in the lower classes, many women are abandoned by their "husbands" and find themselves raising children by several fathers. This is especially the case in the coastal provinces.

The female's role in the marriage is commonly the running of the home and the raising of her children. Walker Lowry in his book *Tumult at Dusk* depicts the situation of Ecuadorian women as such:

"So little by little she gives him up, little by little she turns to another love, to the love of her children. She busies herself with the management of their affairs. She plots and prays for them. And the prayer in her heart is that somehow life for them will be better, more gracious and more glorious. For herself she has fallen into middle age and its endless, trivial bustling about. She is forever busy with the demands, the servants she must manage, the husband she must placate, the friends she must entertain. Her secret thoughts, when she has time for them, are mostly memories, memories of being seventeen with the world at her feet, memories of a dress or a kiss, of a few moments of adoration, flattery and a sense of importance, memories of her wedding day. The years lie ahead but her life, when she comes to think of it, is mostly behind her."

Ecuadorian poet Jorge Carrera Andrade expressed it more beautifully:

Mi madre, revestida de poniente,
guardo su juventud en una honda guitarra
y solo algunas tardes la mostraba a sus hijos
envuelta entre la musica, la luz y las palabras.

Or, in English:

My mother, clothed in the setting sun,
put away her youth in a deep guitar,
and only on certain evenings would she show it to her children,
sheathed in music, light and words.

Nowadays, women have moved ahead and there are many who are educated, have careers, and have become an integral part of this male-dominated society. I have met many women who will not tolerate the practice of infidelity or physical abuse, which is still prevalent and largely tolerated in Ecuador's lower classes. For the most part, however, the Ecuadorian woman still desires to please her children, spouse, and employer. This is part of her heritage that has been honed for nearly half a millennium.

MACHISMO

A common complaint Ecuadorian women voice about the men in their lives is: "*muy machista*." ("He is very macho.")

Machismo runs deep in the Ecuadorian man's soul. It affects both relationships between men and women and men and men, especially if there has been any slight to his manhood, which seems under constant threat. This behavioral pattern was introduced by the Spanish conquest when they dominated the Indian population. In turn this is said to originate with the Moors who invaded Spain.

Some of the strongest traits of machismo is a sense of male superiority manifested in refusing to back down from an argument and dominating one's wife and children. Machismo also includes being gallant and involves sexual conquests, the more the merrier in an attempt to prove his masculinity. Ecuadorian men can be very charming until they have made their conquest. You will even hear women referring to the man she has fallen in love with as having conquered her. It is almost as if she is his property and below his status.

Both men and women may refer to men who don't demonstrate machismo traits as homosexuals or as weak. Machismo behavior also tends to place women into black-and-white roles as good or bad, especially if the woman in question decides to have more than one relationship. A European woman once remarked to me that she has had to be careful about her relationships with men in Ecuador. She believed that if she had a short relationship with a man that included sex, she would be perceived as being promiscuous, whereas this would not be the case in her home country in Europe. She said that she would never marry an Ecuadorian man because of their *machista* attitudes.

CHILDREN

When a woman is pregnant in Ecuador, friends and family will refer to the unborn child as a *luz* (light). A common question is "*¿Cuando va a llegar el luz?*" ("When is the light going to arrive?") Children are regarded by most Ecuadorians as special and are given much attention. For the most part, they are doted on and coddled and may be considered by foreigners as somewhat spoiled. However, they are taught to obey their elders and to show a deep respect for their parents

Indigenous children near Cuenca.

and other family members, more so than in the United States. When they are young they can seem quite rambunctious, especially in public restaurants.

Most children remain at home until married, especially in the case of girls. Boys have more freedom of movement than girls. Being the father of three boys, I must say that they are a joy and have inherited some of the finest Ecuadorian traits, most especially the enjoyment of dancing.

DANCING

One aspect of Ecuador's society, which permeates all social levels, is dancing. Ecuadorians love to dance as much as they like to eat. Most social functions whether a baptism, birthday party, or dinner party is an excuse to celebrate life through dance. An old gringo (a common Ecuadorian term for an American) friend of mine that has lived in Ecuador for nearly 30 years commented to me that dancing "is part of the package of being Ecuadorian."

After attending hundreds of festivities over the years, I have noticed that Ecuadorians enjoy music and sway unconsciously to the rhythm of whatever is playing on the CD player. People of all ages can dance and there is no feeling of embarrassment or self-consciousness. Richard Poole, in his book *The Inca Smiled*, summed this up perfectly in his description of an Ecuadorian party: "At gatherings such as these everybody dances all evening. There is no division between the ages, no self-consciousness and no respite. It is a function as natural as breathing, and it embraces everyone—even babies are brought along."

Several years ago, at the height of the recession in Ecuador in the late 1990s, my Ecuadorian wife and I took two of our sons to visit her family. The neighborhood had decided to have a party in the street. There was laughter, drinking, fights, hugging, kissing, and most of all dancing! It was a moment of living to the fullest. My boys still recall this experience vividly and commented that they wished there were parties like that in the United States. I now understand why they are such fun at parties and can dance so well. It must be their Ecuadorian blood!

RELIGION

The Catholic Church arrived with the Spanish conquistadors. It played a critical role in Spain's conquest: as an excuse to abuse the Indians in the guise of converting the indigenous population to Catholicism and, more beneficially, as a foundation for the development of educational institutions. The Catholic Church became one of the largest landowners in the country and was closely allied with the Government, especially the political power in the Sierra.

After independence the Church continued to have a close relationship with the Government but continued as a spark of debate between the conservatives in the Sierra and the liberals on the Costa. When Eloy Alfaro seized power in 1895 that marked the beginning of the separation of the Church from the state.

While the Catholic Church is still the dominant religion in Ecuador, it has lost some of its power over the last 25 years. One of the earliest groups to enter Ecuador was the Christian group HCJB. This is a Christian organization that has one of the largest radio stations on Earth, broadcasting its Christian message to the world, its operations beginning in 1931. Mormons, Jehovah's Witnesses, Baptists, and Pentecostal groups have all made inroads. Much of this progress has been due to the increasing poverty of Ecuadorians. I remember seeing few other churches than Catholic and Mormon churches in the early 1980s. Now, numerous churches abound, especially in the Costa. The Protestant groups now account for about 10% of the population, and the Catholics are about 90%. There is also a small smattering of other religions in Ecuador.

Shamans and Herbs

One word that is loaded with mystique for visitors to Ecuador and much of Latin America is the word *shaman*. It is believed by some that the word originated from Russia and means someone who has powers over an individual's soul. Shamans play an active role in the medical field in Ecuador, using both the physical and spiritual world to treat maladies. They are also consulted to settle issues and provide solutions to problems. Many refer to themselves as *medicine men*.

Numerous tools such as dolls, beads, or other items may play a role in the shaman's efforts to help an individual. Dead animals and their body parts are sometimes also used. Shamans pass down their art from father to son. They are also highly skilled with the use of herbs. Herbs play a major part in Ecuadorian medicine. I was never a believer in herbs until one day I had a nasty stomach upset and my Ecuadorian wife pulled out some ugly twigs and dried flowers out of a bag. She used them to brew a tea, which was very soothing. Within half an hour my stomach was much better. Since then, I have turned to this tea rather than modern remedies for stomach upsets. Some of you might have heard of it. It's called *manzanilla* in Ecuador and *camomile* in English.

Godparents

Godparents play a very important role in Ecuadorian society. As it is primarily a Catholic country, the role of godparents is considered a important responsibility in helping to guide a child's spiritual life. The parents choose a married couple as godparents. They in affect become coparents with the female becoming a *comadre* and the male a *compadre*.

The godparents play an active role in the child's baptism. The godfather provides a gift to the child. The mother and father incur the cost of the baptism while the godfather will usually provide a small gift to the altar boys. The godmother will provide the dress for the godchild and small gifts for the people who attend the ceremony. These gifts are small ceramic pieces with the child's name inscribed on them. Such items are available in many party stores, which can be found at most of the major malls. After the baptism, there is usually a large party at the child's home. There will be loud music with lots of dancing. Baptisms are often filmed by professional cameramen on video to record the start of a lifelong relationship between godparents and godchild.

Godparents will usually give the child a gift on his or her birthday, first communion, graduation, Christmas, New Year, or any other important event in the child's life. The godchild also has an obligation to visit the godparents at least on New Year's Day. The godchild should also send an invitation or announcement of his or her first communion and wedding to his or her godparents.

Godparents also play the role of an extended family to the child. I once was with a friend in Quito when he received a call from his goddaughter in Guayaquil who was on a school excursion. She had become ill and didn't know what to do. He was there within a half-hour to check on her.

First Communion

The first communion often begins with a breakfast with the family, sometimes a new set of godparents, and maybe a few close friends. After the ceremony there will usually be a party at the child's home, beginning at about 5:00 pm and ending not too late in the evening. Acceptable gifts may include a bible, CDs or cassette tapes of classical music, a crucifix, rosary beads, watches, or jewelry. The child is obligated to provide a small gift or memento of the occasion to the priest who conducted the ceremony.

FUNERALS

Ecuadorian law requires that corpses be buried within 24 hours after death. Many Ecuadorians still adhere to several basic funeral customs. However, many of these customs have been relaxed over the years.

While many *velorios* (wakes) are conducted in *sala de velacion* (funeral parlors), it is just as common for the wake to take place in the home of the deceased. A wake in the home is the norm if the deceased passed away in his or her home or if the family doesn't have enough money for the funeral home. If there are not enough funds for a casket, a collection is often taken up. In most homes all the furniture is moved against the walls and windows are often shut. Many valuables are put away, including pictures and mirrors.

If the body of the deceased is lying at the funeral home, someone will stay with the body around the clock until it is buried. The wake will usually be in full swing by 10 pm, with the older people in the main living room and the others in the adjacent rooms.

Appropriate flowers for funerals include lilies and marigolds. *Rosquillas* (pastry shaped like horn shells) are usually served to the friends and family, who will also be offered *chicha* (corn beer) or cognac. Turkey or chicken broth is also served around midnight. People take this time to sit around and remember the deceased with fondness and respect.

The wake may last all night. The body is buried the next day between noon and 5:00 pm. The most common practice is a procession accompanying the casket to the graveyard. The priest will usually have a small mass in the home or the funeral home before the burial. Family and friends will then offer prayers for the deceased for nine days. Remembrance masses are held one, six, and 12 months after the funeral, and are often announced in the newspapers. After the first 12 months, a mass is usually held once a year.

Mourning or *luto* (grieving) is a very important part of Ecuadorian society. The general rule is that the spouse will mourn the deceased for two years. The mourning for children or grandparents usually last six months. Aunts and uncles are mourned for three months and cousins for three months.

Very young children wear white for mourning. Adults wear black and white clothes and black shoes. A black tie is appropriate. When half of the mourning period is over, subdued colors such as gray or burgundy are appropriate.

If you found out about the death only after the funeral you should stop by the home a few days later with a card, conveying your condolences. The remaining spouse will not socialize or visit others for about three months, and they should not attend parties or dances.

WEDDINGS

Many marriages in Ecuador are formed both by a civil ceremony and a church wedding. The civil ceremony is required for a marriage to be considered legal in Ecuador. The chief of the civil registry oversees civil marriages. Civil registries are located in the capital of each province. In rural areas the Teniente Politico, who is the local police head or official, oversees the marriage. Two witnesses are required, who must provide identification and proof of voting. The couple getting married should provide their birth certificate. The civil ceremony usually takes place prior to a church ceremony.

When a couple decides to get married in Ecuador, the parents of the man need to seek the permission of the woman's parents. This practice is known as *pedir la mano* ("to ask for her hand"). If both sets of parents know each other fairly well they will invite the prospective bride's parents to their home for dinner. If they don't know each other so well they will visit the woman's parents with her suitor to seek their permission for the marriage. If a commitment is made, the bride and her mother will visit the groom's parents' home within three days.

If you are invited to a wedding you are obligated to attend and to provide a gift. Many couples will have a gift register at one of the better department stores in Ecuador, such as Casa Tossi or De Pratti in Guayaquil. Your gift should be delivered at least three days before the wedding to the home of the bride or groom, depending on whom you are closer to. You shouldn't bring your gift to the wedding. Cash gifts are traditionally given only by the families of the bride and groom. However, a cash gift (averaging about US$40) is usually appreciated by the couple and is increasingly the practice. The bride's family is obligated to purchase most of her necessities for the wedding. This includes the banquet after the wedding and the flowers for the ceremony and banquet. Her family will pay for the invitations as well as the cake and wedding mementos. The groom pays for the ceremony including the services of the church and the priest. He also incurs the cost of the wedding rings and the honeymoon. Many rings will be inscribed inside with the names of the bride and groom and the date of the wedding.

In the coast, most weddings take place between 6:00 pm and 7:00 pm and in the Sierra at about noon. After the ceremony, the party proceeds to a banquet and dance. After dinner, the bride cuts the first slice of the cake. The bridesmaids then cut the rest of the cake for the guests and the waitresses serve it. Champagne is served and the toasts begin. The following people make toasts: the groom, the best man, a close friend of the family, and the father of the bride. Women usually do not make any toasts. After the cake and toasts, a dance will start.

The bride and groom will have the first dance together. The dance usually lasts until midnight. It is considered rude to leave before the bride and groom.

HOLIDAYS

Christmas

Christmas, as in other parts of the world, is a very important celebration here. This being wintertime in Ecuador, much of the country is on vacation. For schoolchildren in the coast, the winter break follows the South American system and is from December to April. Schools in the Sierra are like schools in the United States, vacationing from August to September. Christmas decorations, especially in commercial areas, start to appear by early November.

Christmas Eve

Christmas Eve is referred to as *Noche Buena* here. The typical celebration includes the preparation of a turkey, starting at midday. After the financial crisis in the late 1990s, ham or chicken may the primary dish in the Christmas festivities. The whole family takes part and the mood is quite festive. People are also doing a lot of shopping at this time. Many people will purchase a new set of clothes for Christmas. Children often write letters to baby Jesus and place these requests in their shoes by their bed.

Large nativity scenes are also very popular and there are contests for the most beautiful. Nativity scenes can occupy an entire corner of a home and can be quite extravagant. Christmas trees were first used in Ecuador in 1945 but now plastic trees made of cellophane are more common. At about ten o'clock in the evening, family members may eat *pan de yuca* (tapioca bread), *pan de pascua* (Christmas bread, a sort of fruit cake), white cheese cut in cubes, and hot chocolate. Dinner usually begins at midnight, as many families will stay up all night.

New Year's Eve

New Year's Eve is one of the most exciting holidays in Ecuador. Just before Christmas, you will see papier-mâché faces for sale all over Quito and Guayaquil. The traditional celebration of Año Viejo (Old Year) is still observed. This holiday is about getting rid of the old and celebrating the hope of a new year. Much of the partying began with the conquistadors when they would stuff dolls full of straw during fiestas on religious days and set them on fire. Explosives would also be stuffed inside the dolls, which would often be waved and twirled around. In 1842 there was a severe yellow fever epidemic and on the last day of the year, thousand of clothes would be burned from people with yellow fever in the hope of wiping out the illness. These clothes were even put on dolls designed to look like the people who had passed away.

This tradition has continued throughout the years and is spectacular. While the extravaganza is countrywide, Quito and Guayaquil

Boys playing with a Año Viejo doll in Guayaquil.

Año Viejo masks for sale in preparation for the New Year's Eve festivities in Guayaquil.

have the best celebrations. Guayaquil comes ablaze with an orange glow over the entire city. These Año Viejo dolls, often life-sized, are set on fire after being doused in gasoline at midnight, along with fireworks (often imported from Colombia). Many people will dress up as old widows and stand on the streets with the stuffed dolls crying and singing: "*Se va a morir mi viejo*" (literally translated "My old man is going to die"). Many participate in this tradition of dressing up as old women and children ask for money in the streets. Families gather and will often dance through the night until dawn. If you are faint of heart, the celebration can be a little intimidating.

The fires outside my house windows once got so close that I was afraid that my house would go up in flames. The neighbors thought I was crazy when I became concerned. My kids loved the Colombian rockets we bought for that evening. Ecuadorians take the celebration in their stride. It has become more dangerous over the years with heavy explosives being used and sometimes even nails. Numerous fires are set in the streets of Guayaquil and injuries have been reported.

Other New Year's Eve traditions include eating twelve grapes at midnight and setting luggage outside the house to bring good luck and much traveling in the forthcoming year.

Chapter Four

ECONOMY AND POLITICS

"We came back from (Ecuador) and we were writing our recommendation. We thought Ecuador was a very stable country. There hadn't been a revolution in 40 years....an Ecuadorian friend called to inform us a revolution had just broken out."—Melvyn N. Klein, founding partner of the investment partnership GKH Partners, L.P. (Quote taken from *Financial World,* October 21, 1996.)

ECONOMY

Ecuador's economy is one of the smallest in Latin America and heavily dependent on external markets. This has made it vulnerable to terms-of-trade (the relation between export and import prices) shocks. This vulnerability, as well as inadequate export diversification and structural reform in the public and financial sectors, has resulted in poor economic performance since the early 1980s.

The late 1990s found the economy shaking at its knees, resulting in its worst depression in 70 years. The economy has shrunk substantially with hyperinflation and the government has had to take the drastic step of replacing the country's currency, the sucre, with the U.S. dollar. The middle class has virtually disappeared and those with the means have left the country in search of better opportunities.

Much of Ecuador's economic past had revolved around agriculture. For many decades, Ecuador's largest export product was cocoa. Other agricultural products, primarily coffee and bananas, later increased in importance. Ecuador's economic landscape changed significantly when oil was found and exported. Almost overnight, Ecuador was flushed with oil earnings.

Oil is still Ecuador's largest export. This small nation is Latin America's fourth largest oil exporter and sixth biggest producer of oil. It produces an average of 380,000 barrels of crude oil daily. The government hopes to finance more than 30% of the state budget in 2001 with oil exports. In recent years, at least 50% of the country's budget is derived from oil revenue.

With the tremendous amount of new revenue from oil in the 1970s, the government tried to use this to finance the industrialization of Ecuador. This resulted in a fiasco when interest rates were raised and oil prices fell. Import substitutions were used in an attempt to promote development by using high import taxes to discourage the cheaper, and thus more attractive, imports. This contributed to increased corruption and tax avoidance by such methods as double invoicing by many import companies. Guarantees of future oil revenue provided financing that established large state-owned industrial companies that were lethargic and bureaucratic. This plan didn't produce results.

I tried to start a sales agency in Ecuador during this period in the early 1980s and the experience was horrendous. The requirements for importation were enough to kill my company. Companies with deep pockets were the ones that survived. Between 1984 and 1988 the government's import substitution program was wound down and some of the large state-owned companies were privatized.

Petroleum

Oil is a critical factor in Ecuador's economy. There is a long history of oil production in Ecuador, beginning in the first part of the 20th century along the coast of Ecuador. This was followed by major discoveries in the Amazon beginning in 1917. It was in the late 1960s and the early 1970s that oil became a significant export product and gradually replaced Ecuador's dependency on agricultural exports. Production began at about 78,000 BPD (BPD = barrels per day) and has increased to present-day levels of around 400,000 BPD. There remains about 2.1 billion barrels of proven oil reserves.

Oil exports produced a brief period of high growth for the country in the 1970s. But El Niño in 1998 led to widespread crop devastation. Then a sharp decline in world oil prices drove Ecuador's economy into a free-fall by 1999. This marked the beginning of the collapse of Ecuador's banking sector, and it defaulted on its external loans later that year. The currency depreciated by 70% throughout 1999, forcing a desperate government to replace its local sucres with U.S. dollars in 2000. This move stabilized the currency, but was followed by protests and riots, the deposits of some Ecuadorians having depreciated by as much as 400%. The new president, Gustavo Noboa, has yet to complete negotiations for a much sought after IMF accord.

Petroecuador (previously CEPE) is the state oil company and has begun to open up some concessions, operating joint ventures with many foreign firms. All oil is the property of Ecuador. The main pipeline in Ecuador is the Trans-Ecuadorian (SOTE), which starts in Lago Agrio and transports about 380,000 BPD of oil some 300 miles to a port north of Esmeraldas. It was built in the early 1970s and has experienced numerous problems. More recently, these have been attributed to sabotage. International experts believe that some of the problems with the pipeline is due to lack of maintenance and earthquakes. A new pipeline has just begun construction in July 2001 (expected to be completed by 2003) but is highly contested by a number of environmental and indigenous groups. This industry is susceptible to criticism due to the result of deforestation and pollution from the waste of oil products.

Wildlife and habitats have been devastated through pollution, including oil waste dumping, and accidents, such as oil spills. Oil exploration has contaminated water and land resources that the population depends on, ruining the indigenous lifestyles of hundreds of native communities. An environmental lawyer has blamed multinational oil companies for widespread skin, respiratory and other diseases; a rise in miscarriages; increased cancer rates for as many as 30,000 impoverished Indians and settlers; and widespread environmental damage. An Ecuadorian native has even launched a class-action lawsuit against Texaco in the United States on behalf of Oriente residents. His allegation is that "they poisoned the rivers, killed the fish and made the people sick."

The effects that oil pollution has had on human society has led to anti-government movements and uprisings in many areas. As a result of the damaging effect oil production has had on the Indians in Ecuador for the past 20 years, the Indians have resisted government oil exploration efforts, demanding rights to their ancestral lands.

Bananas

Ecuador is king when it comes to bananas. It is the largest exporter of bananas in the world. Approximately one-third of Ecuador's bananas are exported to the United States, one third to Europe, and the rest to other countries, including Russia, Argentina, Chile, and Japan.

Ecuador's largest exporter is a national producer—Noboa, the world's fourth largest banana company. While the big three U.S.-

Bananas for sale in the countryside between Guayaquil and Cuenca.

based companies of Dole, Fresh Del Monte, and Chiquita control nearly all exports in South American countries, Ecuador's banana export industry is unique in its domination by national producers. Although Ecuadorian bananas have to cross the Panama Canal in order to reach the European market, Ecuador's banana industry is not unionized, which keeps labor costs low.

Most farms are medium-sized (about 120 acres in land area) and giant trading houses control the distribution. About 10% of a population of approximately 13 million inhabitants is somehow connected to the banana industry. The mid-1990s saw a tremendous boom in sales, approaching a billion dollars a year. Everyone was planting bananas trying to make a quick dollar. A number of pesticides banned in foreign countries were permitted to be used in Ecuador.

Workers reported earning an average of US$56 per month, with few if any benefits. This compares to an average monthly wage of over $500 in Panama, $200 to $300 in Colombia, $200 in Costa Rica, $150 to $200 in Honduras, and $120 to $150 on Guatemala's Atlantic

Coast. In other banana-exporting countries, banana workers, even some non-union workers, typically receive social benefits such as housing, health care, potable water, electricity, and education for their children. In Costa Rica, even non-union banana workers get benefits left over from the time when unions were strong.

On many of these plantations, it is not uncommon to see warning signs telling workers that they must leave the fields when aerial spraying begins, and remain away for at least two hours after it stops. But at only one Ecuadorian plantation did workers report compliance with this norm, and only after the banana workers' union put up a fight. Where there is worker housing on the plantations, the houses are often located in the middle of the fields and are thus exposed to spraying. Workers know that exposure to these chemicals is unhealthy but complain that no one has ever informed them of the adverse effects of exposure. Packing workers report that they, especially women, are exposed to chemicals used to disinfect and clean the bananas prior to packing. They reported that they were not provided with any sort of safety equipment.

Banana workers have little power under the current structure and have expressed extreme distrust in the ability or the will of government authorities to protect their rights to free association and freedom of expression.

In the absence of social criteria governing world trade, consumers can play a strong role to support the rights of banana workers. Efforts are underway to organize unions in Ecuador's banana industry. Although this is a long-term project, it will need significant support from activists and consumers in countries like the United States that buy large quantities of Ecuadorian bananas. Ecuadorian banana workers are not calling for a boycott; but consumers can express a preference for "sweat-free" bananas to retailers. Likewise, we can pressure the Ecuadorian government to respect its citizens' labor rights.

Shrimp

Shrimp is Ecuador's third largest export after oil and bananas. Anyone visiting Ecuador will see and taste that shrimp is a staple and that some of the largest and best shrimps in the world are from Ecuador.

I first read about Ecuador's newfound wealth in shrimp farming in 1981. An American from the United States had been successful in other countries and began the shrimp farming process in Ecuador, making fortunes for some but taking a toll on Ecuador's beautiful mangrove forests. These forests have been decimated up and down the coast and significant intrusion has been made in the forests in northern Ecuador towards Esmeraldas. Ecuador is now the fourth largest producer of shrimp in the world and the largest in Latin America. There are at least 200,000 people with direct or indirect employment in the shrimp industry, and at least 105,000 hectares are dedicated to shrimp production.

Besides the destruction of the mangrove forests, many shrimp producers have significant problems with pesticide runoff originally used to fumigate bananas. As of 1999, shrimp farmers have contributed to the destruction of more than 65% of the Ecuador's mangrove habitat. This situation threatens to worsen, due to growing a demand for shrimps from the United States, Japan, and western Europe.

The arrival of the lucrative commercial shrimp farms and the clearing of mangroves to construct aqua-culture ponds started in the 1980s. The net profits of the farms were so high that the idea caught on and spread rapidly along the coast. A one-hectare shrimp farm could earn a gross income of US$5,000 to US$15,000 per year. Once cut, however, the mangrove cannot fully recover for more than a hundred years and many benefits to the ecosystem are lost. The waste water from the farms also pollute the surrounding area with antibiotics and chemicals used to prevent shrimp disease. There is growing conservation awareness among the local commercial farmers and foreign environmental organizations.

Flowers

Ecuador is home to literally thousands of species of plants that decorate the cities and countryside. In the last 20 years a significant business has developed in the export of its beautiful roses, and sales of orchids and exotic plants are on the rise, mostly to the United States, Russia, and Europe. In 1997, flower exports represented about 70% of non-traditional agricultural production.

Nestled in the deep valleys between the mountain ranges of the Andes you will notice large flower plantations throughout the Sierra. Eighty percent of the production of cut flowers come from the provinces of Cotopaxi, Pichincha (especially from Cayambe), and Imbabura. Ecuador is now producing over a billion roses a year and continues to produce good margins for the producers. Most of the Ecuadorian flower-growing companies are locally owned. It was in the late 1980s that many of the companies were started with an ever

TRIGG

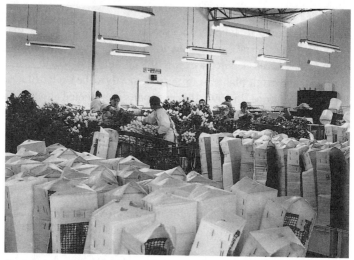

Roses being readied for export near Cotopaxi.

increasing world demand. In 1997 terms, each hectare required an investment of over $250,000. Net prices for roses have been as high as 25 cents in the last several years. A check with a large grower in Cotopaxi in 2000 revealed that their net sales price is often in the 10–11 cent range.

There are substantial margins between the sell price from the grower and the retail price for the end client primarily for transportation, storage, and marketing functions. Ecuador's competitive advantage has been that of labor. Flower growing is labor intensive, with between 10–12 laborers required per hectare for roses, for example. The marketing of flowers is done through specialist marketing companies, a number of which are foreign-owned. Contracts are not often the norm and business is often conducted on trust.

While Colombians and their influence in Ecuador is often depicted in a negative light by the press, this is one industry in which they have had a significant and profitable impact. Colombia, a major flower grower and exporter in its own right, has provided much of the technical know-how for developing the Ecuadorian flower industry. Flowers have officially been considered by the government as a non-traditional export as compared to such products as bananas or petroleum. However, the impact on the economy has been substantial especially in terms of offering employment opportunities in rural areas. Between 1990 and 1997 the number of flower producers jumped from 39 to 179 and from 286 to 1,549 hectares. Production has also begun in the lower Sierra. Flower production along the coast presents opportunities especially for orchids and other tropical varieties.

During the same period mentioned above, employment increased an average of 8% per annum. Women make up 70% of the labor pool for the flower industry. They are primarily involved in the cultivation and harvesting aspects. It is believed by most management that women are more adept at the growing of flowers, it being compared to child-rearing. Men are primarily involved in the maintenance, irrigation, and fumigation processes. Younger workers are often preferred with an average age of between 22–25. These jobs are highly desirable in rural areas and in 1997-terms paid about US$190 per month. Many new employees have been hired due to references from current levels using the *palanca* system, which is discussed in the Customs and Etiquette chapter of this book.

One of the major concerns of laborers is of getting ill or injured due to pesticides and chemicals. The Flower Label Programme, an organization comprised of flower importers and buyers from Germany, provides certification (The Green Seal) which promotes environmental consciousness and the good health of employees. In 1997 there were only a small number of firms certified in Ecuador but many were awaiting approval. Maintenance and harvesting are risk areas and cuts are common. The main physical complaints from workers are colic, blurred vision, and headaches. In November 2000 I visited a large plantation in Cotopaxi which clearly has responsible management. Workers seemed to be very well protected, from masks to full suits for fumigation. It was truly a first-class operation. This industry has a bright future in store for it.

Exports

I once spoke to a friend who said that if "Ecuador could get its act together that there could be thousands of millionaires." She was alluding to the economic potential of Ecuador's fruits, flowers, artisan crafts, and so on. While her statement may be somewhat true, Ecuador has some significant roadblocks to overcome before this Utopia can be reached. Some of these roadblocks include: the oligarchy present in much of Ecuador which wants to keep things as they are; low production numbers; a dependence on centralism by the government; the fragile nature of financial institutions; the lack of reinvestment or investment of capital (capital flight risk); and significant deforestation and environmental stress.

Unemployment

One thing about visiting or working in Ecuador is the amount of activity. It always looks bustling and as if there's lots of commerce going on. But the truth of the matter is that most people are working hard just to survive. More than 50% of the population lives under the poverty level and lead lives of quiet desperation. The rural areas for the most part are more impoverished then the urban sector.

Because of large migration patterns to cities such as Guayaquil and Quito, unemployment rates are usually higher. Men suffer a higher level of unemployment in the cities than women and the reverse is true in rural areas. During the 1990s the official unemployment rate was 9%. This has risen to 12% in 1998. But the real rates are generally much higher.

The economic situation of both unemployment and underemployment has contributed greatly to what is called the informal economy, to which thousands belong. This is evident throughout the country. Walk along any major street in Guayaquil and Quito and you will see hundreds of people camped out on sidewalks with a blanket spread or a cardboard box displaying their wares. These wares for sale can include batteries to watches and everything in between. What is really amazing is that these so called *ambulantes* are often parked right in front of a large store selling the same type of items and no one seems concerned about the so-called illegal operators. On almost every corner can be found small portable stands where the vendor sells different types of candies and small items.

For the most part, lower-class Ecuadorians live a sub-standard existence. I wanted to experience this and took to Ecuador some watches that I had bought at a liquidation sale. I took a blanket and walked down to 9 de Octubre in Guayaquil, parked my blanket, and laid out the watches. I attracted a huge crowd who seemed more interested to see a foreigner on the street than the watches. I spent several hours there and imagined how difficult it must be to do this every day with no protection from the heat or bathrooms available. I was surrounded by the lowest strata of society and members of all races who were just amazed that I was there at all. Luckily, traffic police who often chase street vendors away, unless they are paid a small bribe, did not approach me.

The streets are thronging with these vendors, especially during the Christmas holidays. I did manage to sell all the watches and moved on being grateful not to have to earn my living in such a manner. There are also thousands of *ambulantes* that sell juices or popcorn in the streets via pushcarts.

One of my most poignant memories of Ecuador are the popcorn-makers, who with a small cart roast up the delicacy with a small flame. There are also a number of vendors who cook food at home and visit stores and bars to hawk their food. Goods sold via vendors have often been obtained by legitimate means but a large number may have been stolen. Every year local governments declare that they will rid the streets of such vendors but they remain. There are also numbers of people who have a fulltime job and yet look for other sources of

Even foreign currency can be hawked on the streets.

income. I have met many people who sell goods such as jewelry from their homes, operate beauty shops, sell imported clothing, or who open up small stores selling small items such as soda, toilet paper, and necessities. There is not a block in Ecuador where you can't find such a set-up. Just look for signs that read: *Se Vende Colas.*

Jobs are highly prized in Ecuador as compared to in the United States where most people feel it is relatively easy to find some type of employment. Individuals keep jobs for longer periods of time and when jobs are advertised the competition can be very keen. I once had a friend who put an advertisement in the paper for a delivery person. The ad stated that interviews would start at 9:00 am. On that particular day, he heard a large commotion outside his office at about 8:00 am.

He discovered that a small riot had broken out with people fighting for a place in the line.

Many accounting or CPA firms, especially for large companies, act as an intermediary in hiring employees. The CPA firm will usually place anonymous advertisements requesting that a resume be sent to a post box. A survey of such ads might lead one to believe that there is age discrimination in Ecuador in terms of employment. Many advertisements will state that the applicant must be under a certain age (usually under 40). Also, most requests for resumes require a photograph of the applicant.

GOVERNMENT AND POLITICS

Instability is often the norm when it comes to Ecuadorian government and politics. This is partially evident by the number of constitutions (19) which have been instituted since 1830. The longest period of time between new constitutions has been from 1978 until 1998. Geographic regions play a significant role in politics and the differences have kept a cohesive front between political parties. No significant leader has yet been able to consolidate power. While democratic principles are espoused, regional issues seem to take precedence over national interests.

There are three main branches of the government, which are comprised of the executive, legislative, and judicial sectors. The executive branch position is to manage all sectors of the government. The legislative branch is responsible for running the congress. The judicial branch administers the justice programs. Voting is compulsory between the ages of 18–65 and the president is elected every four years, serving a single term.

The executive branch consists of the president and vice-president. His responsibility as head of the government is to manage the public administration, maintain internal order, public security, present a government plan, and inform the congress each year of the government's and country's status. He also coordinates the development of

89

new laws and selects ministers and diplomats. He is elected to take office on August 10 of the year following his election by the people. The president must be at least 35-years-old and born in Ecuador. If he becomes incapacitated, the vice president or a designated minister takes over. If both of them are not able to serve, the president of the national congress steps into place until congress selects a new president to serve the remaining term within 10 days. President Gustavo Noboa was elected to office on January 22, 2000, following a coup which deposed President Mahuad. Vice President Pedro Pinto has been in office since January 28, 2000.

The military exercises considerable power in Ecuador, reporting directly to the president. It is known to support labor unions which opposes the privatization of many of the country's state-owned companies. Many of the leaders in the military are from the Sierra. The military, during the early years of oil exports, took over the government. Profits from petroleum allegedly provide an unofficial source of funds for the military. It was a military-indigenous coup which toppled democratically elected President Jamil Mahuad.

In 1998 a new constitution was drawn up, largely as a response to the deep depression the country was in. Limits were placed on state intervention in the economy and rights were widened to all Ecuadorians, including the youth, Afro–Ecuadorians, and indigenous groups.

Here is a brief discussion of a few of the articles that were newly instituted or revised:

Article 16
The state has the obligation to respect the rights of human beings guaranteed by the Constitution.

Article 23
To protect the civil rights, liberties, and safety of its citizens. Citizens have the right to life, personal integrity, and liberty under the law. This includes the absence of a death penalty, cruelty of punishment, and

torture. This includes the state's responsibility of trying to prevent and eliminate violence especially to children, women, and the elderly. Everyone is to have the same rights without the distinction of age, gender, sexual orientation, color, religion, political party, state of health, or economic position.

Article 27
Voting is to be secret and is obligatory for those between from 18 to 65 years of age. If you're older than 65 it is optional to vote. Those that are in the armed forces or work for the government are barred from voting, as well as those who have a judicial order or who have been sentenced.

Articles 83–85
These articles specifically address those who are indigenous or black. Their ability to practice traditional medicine and to maintain cultural traditions is protected and this article also promotes the management of the ecological areas of such groups. The intellectual property rights of ancestors are to be retained and the quality of education improved. Their native languages are to be continued and taught.

Chapter Five

CULTURE

The ancient churches and monasteries, around which the people of Quito have grouped their lives in village-like cells, are treasure houses of the greatest collection of Spanish colonial sculpture, painting, and architecture in all the world."—Albert B. Franklin.

Although yet to be recognized on an international stage, Ecuador has a deep, varied, and unique culture.

Regional expression has also been a key factor in the arts since pre-Colombian times. Most arts prior to the Incan conquest developed along the coast. When the Spaniards entered the picture, there was significant and long lasting change, revolving primarily around Quito. There have also been significant contributions from all parts of Ecuador, the materials available in particular areas influencing the development of the arts regionally.

LITERATURE

Ecuador is not generally thought of as a country of readers, in comparison to Argentina or Colombia. When asked why Ecuadorians don't appear to read very much, an employee of a large bookstore in Quito once exclaimed, "*Todos son brutos.*" ("They are all ignorant.") He went on to explain that a significant reason was that books, especially imported ones, were expensive in Ecuador and that few people had the financial means to buy them. In my experience, Ecuador has a very small publishing infrastructure and market for books. Many writers here self-publish or try to sell books on consignment through bookstores, of which there are only a few.

There are a number of bookstores that use different marketing approaches to develop readers, such as small reading groups for children. I once published a small journal on Latin America and presented my journal to an agent to seek advertisers. She told me that many of the advertisers were not interested in the journal because it had too few pictures. Ecuadorians seem to be more attracted to publications that are filled with graphics and pictures. Another disincentive to read is the increasing popularity of television and video games.

The public also do not seem to hold much regard for writers. Most professional writers in Ecuador have to work other jobs to make a living. Despite the tremendous financial pressure, there is a significant number of books published in Ecuador in small press runs with modest sales.

If you read Spanish you will have a much wider range of books to choose from. My favorite bookstore in Guayaquil has several tables and shelves of books on Ecuador but this stack doesn't appear to grow very often. Books published in Ecuador are mostly paperbacks and the hardbacks don't appear to be of good quality. There don't appear to be many second-hand bookstores here. However, there is one dealer in Quito that stocks about 8,000 volumes (of mostly paperbacks) in English and a smattering of other languages. This is **Confederate Books**, located at Calama 410 y Juan León Mera, tel: (02) 2527 890.

Juan Montalvo (1832–1889)

Juan Montalvo was one of the greatest liberal thinkers in Ecuador's history. He was one of the biggest enemies of Gabríel García Moreno and after García Moreno was assassinated, Montálvo claimed that it was his pen that killed him. He wrote a number of anti-dictatorship essays and published an anti-establishment newspaper called *El Cosmopolita* in 1866. He believed that metaphors describing beauty would influence one to live a more virtuous life. Many of his works were written in exile, such as *Siete Tratados* (*Seven Treatises*, 1882) and *Capítulos Que se le Olvidaron a Cervantes* (*Chapters that were Omitted by Cervantes*, 1895).

Juan León Mera (1832–1894)

Juan León Mera wrote the national anthem and was a large collector of many Ecuadorian legends. He wrote a Romantic novel, *Cumandá, o, un drama entre salvajes* (*Cumandá, or, A Drama Among Savages*) set in the Ecuadorian jungle. About the oppression of the Ecuadorian Indians and published in 1871, it has been called *the* first important Ecuadorian novel.

Another famous work of his was a critical history of Ecuadorian poetry—*Ojeada Histórico-Crítica sobre la Poesía Ecuatoriana*, published in 1868. Ecuador, to him, was divided along Catholic, mestizo, and Hispanic lines. He was politically conservative but believed that the country should be united by one language and one religion. Some have said, however, that he didn't regard Indians as equals. *Cumandá* is about the doomed relationship between the son of a wealthy landowner and a young Indian woman. My personal view is that it actually demonstrates his allegiance with the upper classes and the Catholic Church, rather than the Indians.

Jorge Carrera Andrade (1903–1978)

Born in Quito and a diplomat for Ecuador, Carrera Andrade also wrote much about the Indians. His first book of poems, *Estanque Inefable* (*Indescribable Pond*), was published before he left university and was a voice for the destitute Indians, calling for social change. A number of his works have been translated into English including *Secret Country* (1946) and *Selected Poems* (1972). One of his earliest works, *The Perfect Life* was written when he was 18 and translated into French, German, Russian, and English. This was about a return to the common speech, favoring simplicity over ornamentation.

95

Jorge Icaza Coronel (1906–1978)

Jorge Icaza Coronel, also from Quito, was a civil servant and the director of the national library. A novelist and playwright, he has been called the father of indigenous literature in Ecuador. Icaza received international recognition for *Huasipungo: The Villagers* (1934), which has been translated into many languages. This book depicts, with brutal realism, the exploitation of the Indians at the hands of their estate landowner masters.

Demetrio Aguilera Malta (1909–1981)

Demetrio Aguilera Malta was one of Ecuador's most prolific and talented novelists. He was a self-educated writer, film director, and painter. His first novel, *Don Goyo,* was originally published in 1933 and translated into English in 1980. It is about a patriarch living along the mangrove forests of the Pacific coast near Guayaquil. *Don Goyo* is a social protest against the whites who were attempting to cut down the mangrove forests. That has sadly already happened in reality along most of the coast. A number of his other novels have also been translated into English, such as *Seven Serpents and Seven Moons* (1979) and *Manuela, La Caballeresa del Sol: A Novel* (1967), bringing Ecuadorian literature to outside markets.

José Joaquín Olmedo (1780–1847)

A poet, statesman, and spokesman of the liberation movement, Olmedo's odes commemorating South America's independence from Spain inspired a generation of Romantic poets and patriots. His most famous ode, *La victoria de Junín: Canto a Bolívar (The Victory at Junín: Song to Bolívar)*, was dedicated to Bolívar's military successes. Romantic in imagery and Neoclassical in form, it is considered by many the finest heroic poem to come out of Spanish America.

Luis Alfredo Martinez (1869–1909)

Writer, painter, and politician, Luis Alfredo Martinez's best work is a novel named *A La Costa* (*To the Coast*), written in 1904. This Realist novel portrays a man moving to the Costa from the Sierra for a new life. It is probably one of the best works that objectively describe the regional differences between the Costa and Sierra. An experiment with the Ecuadorian novel, it is also subtitled *Costumbres Ecuatorianas* (*Ecuador Customs*). Luis Martinez's paintings are prized possessions of some of the most important museums in Ecuador.

Gonzalo Zaldumbide (1883–1965)

Writing in the early part of the 20th century, Zaldumbide exuded a spirit of optimism in his writings. He was heavily influenced by Uruguayan Jose Enrique Rodó. One of his best known works was an essay entitled "De Ariel." Zaldumbide also published a Realist book entitled *Egloga Trágica* (*Tragic Eclogue*), in which he describes the emotion felt upon returning home after a long time abroad.

Jenny Estrada

Jenny Estrada began as a reporter in 1968, opening the way for feminine participation in the newspaper *El Universo*, where she consolidated her career through political editorials, interviews with a human perspective, and analytical articles. She has built a multifaceted career in public service and as a writer-historian. Her book, *Del Tiempo de la Yapa*, a chronicle first published in 1994, is about life and customs in Guayaquil, where she was born. She has penned over 10 books and written a remarkable history of the coastal cowboys called *El Montubio*. She continues her writings and is completing a large study of the oil industry in Ecuador. She believes that Ecuador still lacks well-defined objectives, hindering its progress. She feels that Ecuador would return to economic prosperity if it returned to its

Jenny Estrada, renowned historian and author of numerous books about Ecuador.

agricultural roots. In 1998 she won first prize in the *Concurso de Reportajes* (News Articles Competition) sponsored by Oderbrecht, a construction firm.

Michelle O. Fried

Michelle O. Fried is a good example of a self-published author in Ecuador who has supported herself from consulting and through her writing. Coming to Ecuador as an outsider when she was a young adult. Ms Fried has a Masters degree in nutrition from Teachers College–Columbia University. She has an intense desire to learn about Ecuador's culture and is very active in the development of both health and food studies. She has been associated for many years with the Centro Ecuatoriano para la Promoción y Acción de la Mujer (CEPAM) in developing numerous food and health programs throughout the country. She self-published *Foods of Ecuador: Traditional Recipes for Today (Comidas del Ecuador: Recetas tradicionales para gente de hoy)* in Spanish in 1986. This remains a bestseller in Ecuador. Available only in Spanish, it can be purchased in the United States through Kitchen Arts Center (http://www.kitchenarts center.com/index2.html) or the South American Explorers' Club. Look out for her latest book—*Food of the Andes*!

Rodolfo Perez Pimentel

The leading biographer in Ecuador is undoubtedly Rodolfo Perez Pimentel. He is a trained attorney and practices as a notary. He has published several books about Ecuador including *El Ecuador*

Rodolfo Perez Pimentel, author of numerous books on the history of Ecuador. He has published nearly 20 volumes of biographical information about Ecuadorians and foreigners who have had an impact on Ecuador.

Profundo—mito, Historica, Leyenda, Recuerdos, Anecdotas, y tradiciones del país (Deep Ecuador—myths, histories, legends, memories, anecdotes, and traditions of the country) in several volumes in 1988. His largest work is a seventeen-volume series (*Diccionario Biographia Del Ecuador*) featuring over 1,600 biographies on Ecuadorians and people who have influenced Ecuador. He is planning to complete up to 22 volumes. He loves his country deeply and the goal of this immense work is to "inform and develop a national identity."

Modern Poets

Ecuador has a number of fine poets who sensitively depict the soul of Ecuadorians. A very good anthology was published in 1997 called *Between the Silence of Voices—An Anthology of Contemporary Ecuadorian Women Poets*. Editors Alicia Cabiedes-Fink and Ted Maier did a fine job of editing and translating poems from nine women from different levels of Ecuadorian society and different geographical regions.

A prime example of such artistry is Ruth Bazante Chiriboga, born in 1942, who is one of Ecuador's preeminent poets. Editors Alicia Cabiedes–Fink and Ted Maier describe Ruth Bazante as "a poet of immense power and depth." They make note of her explorations into the soul and the eroticism in relationships. Bazante has published two major collections of her work in *Frito dentro, gritofuera* (1987) and *Manual de las cicatrices* (1988). "I Am" is one of my favorite poems by Bazante:

Estoy (in Spanish)

Estoy inundada de usted
hojarasca de sol,
humus febril.

Estoy con usted

en mis irrealidades
taladrándome;
con usted sobre mi piel
susurrándome
Sueño armonioso
sol adentro en mis ríos.

I Am (in English)

I am flooded by you
dead leaves of sun,
feverish humus.

I am with you
in my irrealities
boring into me;
with you
on top of me whispering.

Perfect dreams in chords
sun inside of rivers.

PAINTING

Painting runs deep in the soul of Ecuadorians. It is an expression of their spirit.

Quito School of Art

Ecuador's greatest gifts to the world in the realm of architecture, sculpture, and painting can be found in Quito. Quito is probably the only place in the world where you can find 30 churches within an area of eight blocks. With the conquistadors came Dominicans, Franciscans, Augustinians, and priests from other orders. Perhaps it became some sort of competition between the orders to venerate their respective saints with yet another church, cloister, or religious monument!

You will be mesmerized by the colonial ambience of the Old Town area. For a nearly 300-year period, Quito was the center of art production in Latin America. In the mid-1550s, Friar Ricke, a Franciscan, began the seedlings of what would become known as the Quito School of Art. Approximately 100 churches, monasteries, convents, and plazas were built during the colonial period in Quito.

The Catholic Church required a consistent supply of sculptures and paintings for its aggressive campaign of building churches. Ricke began the Colegio San Andrés in 1553 with limited materials. The indigenous population was taught numerous skills. When you explore the ancient streets of Quito much of the architecture and adornments were constructed by Indians. The Catholic Church also used the arts as a form of assimilating the Indians into the Catholic religion.

Magnificent wood carvings and sculptures were produced during this period. The great Quito sculptors were, in chronological order, Bernardo de Legarda, with his winged virgins; Pampite, whose crucified Christs invite meditation; and Manuel Chili "Caspicara," the artistic innovator. Many of Caspicara's sculptures can be found in The Cathedral and the Monastery of San Francisco. The movement and realism of the Caspicara's paintings and sculptures reveal much technical and aesthetic quality, attention to detail, and anatomical study.

The great Quito artists were Dominican Friar Pedro Bedon, who painted in the last quarter of the sixteenth century; Miguel de Santiago with his series of paintings dedicated to the lives of the saints; and Nicolas de Goribar, Miguel de Santiago's disciple.

Twentieth Century Art

Contemporary Ecuadorian artists include Manuel Rendon, considered one of the best Expressionists in the world; Enrique Tabara, famous for pioneering the use of pre-Colombian motifs and images;

and the Indigenous Expressionists Oswaldo Guayasamín, Eduardo Kingman, Guerrero, and Paredes.

Oswaldo Guayasamín

Guayasamín was born in 1919, the eldest in a family of 10 children, to an Indian father and a mestizo mother. Born to create, he began selling his sketches to tourists at age 10. His social realist work revolves around indigenous themes as well as mestizo and black issues. Guayasamín's first major exhibition was in 1942, after which he studied under the master muralist Orozco from Mexico. Oswaldo Guayasamín has exhibited his work internationally, including the Museum of Modern Art in Paris. *The Age of Ire*, a series of 250 paintings deserves special mention. He was also an active social protester and supporter of the Cuban revolution. Oswaldo Guayasamín passed away in 1999.

Eduardo Kingman

Eduardo Kingman was the other major social realism painter in the 20th century. Indian and Andean environments dominated his work. He was born in 1913 to an Ecuadorian mother and an American medical doctor from Connecticut. Ecuador's best known muralist, he was heavily influenced by the Mexican muralist Diego Rivera. Much of his work depicts the forced labor of the Indians and their suffering. With heart-rending and realistic scenes, this figurative artist revealed an interest in the human being and his internal drama. Dynamic forces are created with strong, sharp, and heavy lines used to draw the human figures. You will also notice a great deal of emphasis on the hands of the subjects. Kingman spent much of his career in the promotion and education of art both in Ecuador and in the United States.

Tigua Paintings

As if landing in Brigadoon (you know, that small misty town that only awakens one day in a hundred years), there is a small village of

Quichua-speaking Indians, called Tigua–Chimbacucho, located some 54 kilometers west of Latacunga on the Latacunga–Quevedo road. The Tigua are gaining recognition for their charming paintings.

In the 1970s Julio Toaquiza, a poor farmer in Tigua, was encouraged by a dealer of art in Quito to apply his talents to a sheepskin canvas, rather than on drums and masks, as his ancestors used to do. Painted with chicken feathers on sheephide stretched on decorated wooden frames, his paintings depict daily rural life in the Andean mountains. These colorful paintings were originally done with enamel paints but increasingly with oils and acrylics. They depict many facets

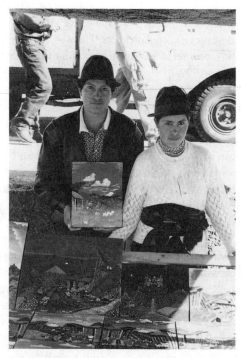

Tigua artist and his wife selling their paintings in the Sierra.

of festivals such as Corpus Christi and numerous indigenous rituals. Tigua paintings have been showcased around the world and have produced significant income for many residents of this small hamlet. Toaquiza now trains his children and others in his village to carry on his art.

CRAFTS

Ecuador possesses some of the most talented craftsmen in the world. I first realized this when I observed the number of seamstresses in Guayaquil and the immense patience they had with their work. When you see the beautiful colors of the clothes that are worn by many of the indigenous population, you will appreciate the tremendous creativity of Ecuadorians.

Andean cultures boast a long tradition of weaving abilities, far surpassing those of Europe in the same era. The best Andean weavers could produce material with as many as 500 two-ply woolen wefts per inch, as compared with just 100 in Europe before the Industrial Revolution. Weaving is a specialty for Ecuador and it is basically a family affair where weaving can vary dramatically from one township to another. The initiated can distinguish which region the weavers are from by the colors of the weave.

Materials such as cotton, llama, and alpaca wool were traditionally used to create complicated brocades, tapestries, double cloth, and gauze. With the arrival of the Spanish in the mid-1500s, new resources were introduced, such as silk embroidery yarns.

The Otavalo Indians north of Quito have successfully taken Ecuador's weavings to the world. While many indigenous groups in Ecuador remain in poverty, the Otavalos have been very successful in business and done much to keep their culture intact. There are certain areas of Ecuador where men predominantly do the weaving. Many of the woven products have become highly specialized. For example, *alpargatas* is a specialized shoe (which looks like a tennis shoe) that was introduced by the Spanish and is widely made in Imbabura.

Zuleta Embroidery

Ecuadorians seem to enjoy working with their hands and are good at intricate, detailed, and tedious work.

The women from the Zuleta area have long been known for their embroidery even before the Spanish arrived. Their original work showed a fondness for vibrant colors and was used mainly to decorate women's clothing. The Zuleta designs have not changed much over time and have become cultural icons, treasured as part of their unique heritage.

In the 1940s Zuleta embroidery would have its big international break. It was then that former president, Galo Plaza Lasso, and his wife, Doña Rosario, were inspired to start a workshop for women in Zuleta. This was the beginning of the Zuleta Embroidery Workshop. This workshop produced items for sale, promoting this craft further afield, giving the women an opportunity to supplement their income. The workshop in Zuleta proved a huge success, producing numerous articles such as exquisitely embroidered tablecloths, blouses, placemats, and towels, whilst significantly increasing family incomes. Some women have actually started their own independent workshops.

The Zuleta Embroidery Workshop is now managed by the Galo Plaza Lasso Foundation, benefiting over a hundred families in the Zuleta region. Their items are sold all over Ecuador. They have a small store in Quito at Veintemilla y 6 de Diciembre named *Bordados Zuleta*. You will be amazed at the attention to detail and the wonderful colors on show. You can find out more about the Zuleta Embroidery Workshop at http://www.ecuadorexplorer.com/zuleta/index.html.

Panama Hats

What did Teddy Theodore Roosevelt, Al Capone, and Winston Churchill have in common? The answer: the Panama hat. Before I first visited Ecuador, I knew that Panama hats were really from

Panama hat-making—meticulous work, but in good company.

Ecuador and not Panama. But when I asked locals where I could purchase a Panama hat, they looked confused. That was because the Panama hat here is called *sombrero de paja toquilla* (which means "hat of toquilla straw") or *jipijapa* (named after the town in the Manabí province where this hat was said to be have been first produced). So how did the name *Panama hat* come about? One story

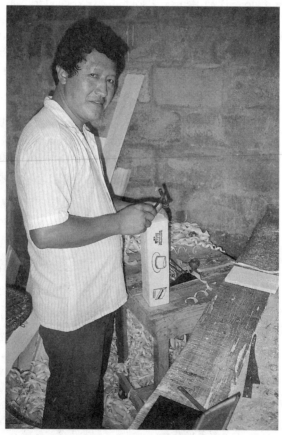

A craftsman preparing balsa wood boxes for Panama hats.

goes that U.S. President Teddy Roosevelt visited the Panama Canal, saw, and liked the hat, a favorite amongst the canal workers. He returned to the States wearing one and the newspapers coined the name which has stuck ever since. Other people say that it was at Panama that these hats were first shipped to every corner of the world, hence the name. No one knows for sure. What we do know is that they were originally manufactured in Jipijapa and Montecristi, both villages in the Manabí province on the coast of Ecuador. The Panama hat industry has now spread to Cuenca, Azuay, and Cañar, and each hat can sell for $400, $2,000, or even $30,000!

In the early 1900s the hat became a fashion statement around the world. Ironically, it was viewed as a lower-class accessory at home. During the 1940s these hats were a significant income-producer for Ecuador but this is less so over the last few decades.

A craft passed down from family to family, there are fewer craftsmen weaving the hats now. They make other products which sell better, such as baskets. One of the features I like about the hats sold here are the balsa wood boxes that come with them marked *Ecuador* on the outside. The family that manufactures these handsome boxes has been doing so for over 50 years and work out of their home in Montecristi. There seems to be a drop in the general quality and price of the Panama hats manufactured nowadays, and they are mainly sold to visiting tourists.

Tagua Ivory

Small coastal villages such as Curía San José, La Entrada, and El Saldo cultivate palm trees that yield the tagua nut. Growing from the seed *Phytelephas*, these trees can grow up to 20–30 feet (6–9 meters). Needing about 10 years to reach full maturity, the nut is cut and polished and is remarkably similar to the ivory of animals which are hunted and killed in different parts of the world, such as elephants, whales, and walruses. Ecuador is the world's largest producers of this nut, used to make some of the finest buttons in the clothing industry

Masapan-ornament-maker at work in Calderón.

from the late 1800s until World War II. Some of these buttons were even used on United States Army uniforms. The synthetics industry hurt this demand, however, and tagua ivory is now mainly used to make dice, dominoes, chess pieces, religious figurines, miniatures, and jewelry for tourists.

Masapan

I will never forget the first time I saw *masapan* ornaments. Better known as bread dough dolls, this is a craft unique to Ecuador. Bread dough figures are painted to produce fabulously beautiful and decorative dolls. They are very popular at Christmas and were said to have originated from a small suburb north of Quito called Calderón. Regardless of their origin they make lovely decorations and excellent gifts. I've noticed that the quality of the craftsmanship has improved dramatically over the last 20 years that I have been in Ecuador. *Masapan* ornaments are now exported all over the world.

MUSIC

It has been said that the haunting melodies from the Andes can make a grown man cry. When you hear the unique instruments and mournful vocals of Andean music, I think you might agree that it is difficult to remain unmoved. Quechuan poet June Ireland describes it better:

Andean Music

Andean music
is a waterfall
encountered in a quiet forest:
playful and powerful at the same time.
Andean music
is the voice of the wind
that howls among the high rocks:
nothing but air, but nevertheless very strong.
Andean music
is the flight of the condor
making a design against the sky:
it appears to be art, but gives sustenance.

Antikuna ñauraytaki (Quechuan version)

Antikuna ñauraytaki
Chay paqcha tarikun
juk sunqoyakusqa sacha sachapi:
puqllayqachaq ye atipaq chay kikinmantapacha.
Antikuna ñauraytaki
wairaqpa kunkanmi
pura sayaq qaqakunapi autiq:
wairallamanta paqarisqa zhaqa ancha kallpayuq.
Antikuna ñauraytaki
kunturpa phawayninmi
janaqpachapi qellqayta ruwan:
ricukun allin ruwasqa, zhaqa kausaytataq qon.

The roots of Ecuadorian music have been traced back to pre-Colombian times. The earliest music was said to have been influenced by the "whistling echo" or "singing" of water vapor from heated water, and by the sounds made by animals such as the toad and ape! The earliest musical instruments are believed to have been conches and flutes. Different types of flutes were commonly used, such as *quenas*, *sampoñas*, and *chirimías* (large, transverse flutes made of bamboo).

Indigenous music was traditionally played during religious rituals, courting activities, life cycle ceremonies, to alleviate the tedium of work, and for recreational purposes. A group of African people inhabit the Chota Valley of the northern plains. The combination of African, Andean, and European cultures produced a very particular kind of music, that has become popular even outside the region. It is called *bomba*, after the drum that creates the rhythmic base for this music and its dances.

The blacks living in the province of Esmeraldas, located on the northern coast of the Pacific Ocean, have retained much of their African cultural heritage. The *marimba*, also an essential part of the old traditions, was imported directly from Africa. Their vocal music includes a large repertory of music for funerals, which is sung with a heavy percussion accompaniment.

When the Spaniards arrived, the Catholic Church forbade the playing of native music and many of the traditional instruments were destroyed. The Church dominated the music scene during colonial times and ordained Spanish priests were appointed as choir directors. The harp was introduced.

However, by the end of the 16th century professional musicians began to take the place of priests. Many of these musicians were creoles or mestizos who introduced new traditions or fused old and new ones. The three most distinctive styles of music to develop in Ecuador are the *sanjuanito*, the *pasillo*, and the *pasacalle*. Catholic and indigenous religious traditions influenced the hypnotic, trancelike, and melancholic rhythms of the *sanjuanito*, played during the Festival of San Juan in the Otavalo region every June, to coincide with the summer solstice. The *pasillo* is slower in rhythm and originates from the classic Viennese waltz. It originates from folk culture and has a slow rhythm, poetic and sentimental texts, and melancholy melodies. The *pasacalle* has its roots from the Spanish *pasodoble* and is written in 2/4 time. Other popular rhythms in Ecuadorian music are the *albazos*, *tonadas*, *danzantes*, and *carnavales*. Many originate from the music of the indigenous population. Another popular Andean rhythm and dance is the *huayno*, which sounds very happy and originates from Andean rural villages. A sadder tune is the *yaraví*, which became popular during the 18th century and is accompanied by guitars.

Ecuador boasts thousands of professional musicians who are, sadly, unheard of outside the country. In the 1960s the wonderful musician Guido Garay brought the folk music of the *montubio* (slang for "ignorant farm worker") to the rest of the country. Mr Garay now

The talented but humble Guido Garay.

in his 80s, was a trained accountant but gave that up in 1940 to be an opera singer. In 1965 a friend of his found an old book written in 1929 about the folklore and music of the *montubios*. He was encouraged to put on a show although he thought that no one would like the music, especially the upper classes. Mr Garay was pleasantly surprised by the warm reception, and for 10 years performed more than 300 shows with his troupe all over Ecuador to standing-room-only crowds. But when one of the founding members died, Mr Garay stopped the shows. He sold his rights to the recording studios and now lives quietly in a second-floor apartment in Guayaquil with his wife, although he still sings everyday.

LAND OF LORE

What is a chapter on culture without a taste of the folklore of the land? Ecuador has thousands of myths and stories depicting numerous aspects of its intricate cultural influences from Spain, Arabia, and Africa. One way to understand a country better is to visit different regions and ask residents for interesting stories from their region. Here is a small sampling of local folk stories:

Beautiful Women of Chone

The most beautiful women in Ecuador are believed to come from a small town named Chone in the Manabí province. (Although most Ecuadorian men will say most women from the Costa are good-looking, with their big hips, small waists, nice legs, and pretty features.) Chone women are regarded as particularly feminine and sexy with their cinnamon-colored skin, curly hair, and brown eyes. After many years of visiting and living in Ecuador, I occasionally come across a woman from Chone. When I ask her if she is from Chone, she is usually flattered.

I have heard varying stories explaining why the women are so beautiful. Some say that it due to the intermarriage of the Spaniards and Indians from hundreds of years ago. Chone's own legend goes like this: When the Indians inhabited the area, there were no doctors to deliver babies. Witches, thus, stood in as midwives and instructed the mothers to drink a special elixir, called *filter of love*, at the time of birth. This elixir, made from special ingredients including roses, gave the little girl white skin and an unearthly beauty.

The Veiled Woman

In the city of Guayaquil there is an old tale about a mysterious woman dressed in black. She would walk the streets in the middle of the night and flirt with the men who approached her. No one could see her face because it was covered with a black veil. When men approached her, she disappeared into the shadows. One night, an admirer decided to follow her. He was later found unconscious. Many believe that when she removed her veil, he had seen that she had the face of a skeleton.

The Rich Man and the Poor Man

Many years ago, in the small village of Zaruma in the province of El Oro, there was a very rich man. One day he was walking and came across a poor man. The rich man acted as if the poor man was beneath him and told him he smelt bad.

Later, the rich man visited a witch on some business. To his horror, the witch foretold that he would lose all his fortune to the poor man. The rich man anxiously sold all his belongings and bought a large diamond, which he hid in a turban on his head. One day, when he was walking by the beach, a large wind suddenly whipped up, knocking the turban off his head and the diamond into the sea. He jumped into the sea after his diamond and dove again and again into the waters but couldn't find it.

The next day, the poor man was at the market and bought a fish for a few cents. When he got home, he sliced the belly of the fish open and was amazed to find a large diamond sparkling up at him. Overnight he had become the richest man in his village. The moral of this story is: don't feel hatred or disdain for the poor because one day you could be poor yourself.

PILGRIMAGES

For many Ecuadorians, Catholicism is part of their national identity. And for many Ecuadorian Catholics, religious festivals and pilgrimages are an intrinsic part of their faith. Each festival has a patron or *alcade* (mayor) who serves as the leader of the festival. He must organize and personally finance the festival. Refusal to do so is seen in resulting in bad luck for the town but adherence as bringing good luck and a position of leadership in the community.

Thousands of worshipers, seeking guidance and miracles, attend a number of pilgrimages throughout the country. Here is one occasion when the upper and lower classes mingle. These events have become increasingly popular in the late 1990s, as Ecuador reels with social and economic problems.

Here are some of the more popular pilgrimages:

• La Virgen de el Cisne (August 17 through to August 20) is one of the most popular in Ecuador where some people walk for as long as three days. Located outside of Loja in a beautiful cathedral in a sparsely populated area. A number of the visitors are from Peru. Visit the website: http://www.Lojanos.com/virgendelcisne.htm#lnicio.
• Virgen de Agua Santa de Baños, Tungurahua province, Easter week.
• Cristo del Consuelo Guayaquil, Guayas province, Easter week
• Jesús del Gran Poder, Quito, Easter week
• San Jacinto, Yaguachi, August 16.
• 8 Virgen de la Natividad de Huayco, Bolívar province, September 8.
• Virgen del Quinche, Pichincha, November 21.

116

Remember that hotel space in these areas can be booked months in advance and that facilities may be limited. Many of visitors will opt to camp. Transportation facilities are usually also stretched to the limit during these periods.

Chapter Six

LANGUAGE

"Class distinction pervades the language as well."
—Albert B. Franklin, *Ecuador: Portrait of a People*.

In Ecuador, there are about 12 million Spanish-speakers; about 3 million speakers of American Indian languages; 65,000 English-speakers; 32,000 German-speakers; 11,000 Bokmål- or Dano–Norwegian-speakers; 7,000 Chinese-speakers; and 1,800 Arabic-speakers. If you're going to live in or visit Ecuador, Spanish is the most useful language to master, although American Indian languages (especially Quichua) may be the first language of many indigenous people.

ECUADORIAN SPANISH

Spanish is the official language, spoken by about 90% of the population. If you're looking for a school to study Spanish, good news, Ecuador is one of the most popular destinations in Latin America for *estudiantes del idioma español* (students of the Spanish language).

The form of Spanish used here is more accurately referred to as Castilian (*castellano*), the basis of modern standard Spanish (*español*). Castilian was commonly spoken in northern and central Spain and became the official language in the 15th century. It came to be spoken in southern and western Spain but with a different accent. (The most obvious difference between northern and central Castilian and southern and western Castilian can be heard in the pronunication of the letter *c*. In the northern and central region, it is pronounced as an English **th**; and in the southern and western regions as an English **s**.) It was the southern and western form of *castellano* that became the standard in Latin American Spanish.

Accents

There are three distinct Spanish accents or intonations in Ecuador originating from the Costa, the Sierra, and the Oriente regions. After some time here, you will be able to distinguish which part of the country the speaker comes from. Look out also for the regional differences in pronunciation and words.

Along the coastal region you will find that most inhabitants will drop the s, y, and z off the end of a word. This can cause havoc for a nonnative speaker. For example, if one is to say *los libros*, *los pollos*, or *los zapatos* the listener will hear **lo libro**, **lo pollo**, and **lo zapato**. The nonnative speaker will wonder why the s has been dropped off plural nouns. An example of the z being dropped in coastal speech is

119

lápiz (pencil) and *maíz* (maize), pronounced as **lapi** and **mai**.

Many linguists believe that the Spanish spoken in Quito and Loja are the purest form of Spanish spoken in Ecuador. There is a slight difference in the cadence of Spanish spoken in the Sierra as opposed to in the Costa or Oriente. There is a small stress on the third syllable from the end of the word. It almost sounds like music when *serranos* speak. Some have compared their pronounciation to birds singing but many *serranos* find this comment derogatory. The *serranos* enjoy pronouncing their r's. So much so that the *costeños* like to do the same, calling them *serranos*! The *serrano* would pronounce *carro* (car) as **carro** whereas the *costeño* would say **caro**. The regional accents really come into play with words like *caballo* (horse), which sounds like **cabasho** in the Sierra but **cabayo** on the coast. Have fun learning to distinguish between the regional accents!

SLANG

Some of the Spanish spoken in Ecuador is slang. Using slang will help you break the ice more quickly with the locals.

I remember the first time I used the slang word *pana* ("good friend"), the local I was speaking to was pleasantly surprised. It is important, however, to remember that slang takes time, study, and experience to use properly. When I used the same word on a second occasion, the female Ecuadorian I was addressing was not impressed. She explained to me that she understood the term as being used with someone you wanted to smoke marijuana with. I quickly informed her that I had no intention of doing that, and learnt later that this term had different meanings when used with different classes.

Slang is also more commonly used by the lower classes. When I used the word *pluto* to announce that I was drunk, a local friend haughtily replied that she didn't belong to the lower classes and not to use that term around her. I have included some common lower-class slang words in the Glossary.

There are numerous slang words which are used by all strata of society, however. I have given several examples in the Glossary. I was once in a cab several years ago when it ran over a speed bump very roughly. The driver exclaimed: "*¡Odio el vigilante acostado!*" (Literally translated: "I hate the traffic officer that is lying down!") I turned around thinking he had run over a traffic cop until I realized that the speed bump here is referred to as a traffic officer lying down. (In the Sierra, the word for *vigilante* is *chapa*.)

NICETIES

Another aspect of Spanish in Ecuador are niceties. Ecuadorians are generally more courteous or formal in their language than in the United States. They try not to give commands but make requests to everyone from superiors to cabdrivers. This is especially true between employees and employers. For example, it is very rare for employees to call their bosses by their first names.

Diplomacy is a common characteristic in much of the language use. A person might say *"No, usted no me ha comprendido."* ("No, you don't understand me.") But the more appropriate and polite way to say this is: *"Me he explicado mal—voy a expresarme mejor."* ("I explained it poorly—I am going to express myself better.") Notice the attempt to avoid conflict. This is an important cultural custom in Ecuador.

Ecuadorian writer Rómulo Vinueza explains that one should speak with "elegance" and "sincerity." Another example of this are the various ways to express thanks. While saying *gracias* conveys thanks, the following phrases express the same emotion more genuinely and sincerely. In fact after receiving a compliment it is considered rude by some to answer with a mere *gracias*!

"¡Le quedo muy agradecido!"—"I am very grateful!"

"¡No sé como agradercerle!"—"I don't know how to thank you!"

"¡Muy agradecido!"—"I am very grateful!"

NAMES

Ecuadorians' first name is usually followed by their father's last name and the mother's maiden name. Juan García Lopez's father's last name is García and his mother's maiden name is Lopez. You would look up the Juan's name in the phonebook under "García Lopez, Juan." In most cases, you would use the first last name, except in formal occasions, in writing, or for legal purposes, i.e. Juan García Lopez would more often be referred to as "Juan García."

The use of the last name with a married woman can also be confusing for an English speaker. If Julia Batista Guzman marries Juan García Lopez she may be referred to in several ways. The one form she is never referred to is "Señora Juan García," thus using her husband's last name. In a formal situation, *de* (which means "of") is inflected after her husband's last name, i.e. Julia Batista de García). In many cases she will still be referred to as Julia Batista or Julia

Batista Guzman. When her husband introduces her he will introduce her as such: "May I introduce my wife, Julia Batista Lopez, to you". In referring to her you may say "La Señora Julia Batista," still using her father's last name. Addressing her directly you would say "Señora Batista (father's last name)" or "Señora García (husband's last name)."

Another confusion for foreigners is how to address a woman—Señorita (Miss) or Señora (Mrs)? There is no "Ms" title in Ecuador. The simple rule I use is if the woman is relatively young, address her as "Señorita." She will correct you if she is married and respond by saying "Señora." If she appears middle-aged or older it relatively safe to address her as "Señora."

TITLES

The most common professional titles in Ecuador are: Doctor/Doctora (male and female titles for Doctor), Ingeniero/Ingeniera (male and female titles for Engineer), and Licenciado/Licenciada (referring to a male or female who is a specialist or is qualified in a particular field, often a lawyer). The last name is usually used with the title, e.g. Licenciada Lopez or Ingeniero Guzman. It is just as common to address Ingeniero Guzman as Ingeniero, even in a room full of other Ingenieros!

Doctors are sometimes referred to as *medicos*. Even if the person does not actually hold such a title, titles are sometimes used in jest and as a form of endearment.

NICKNAMES

You will soon discover in Ecuador that most people have a nickname of sorts among good friends or family. Nicknames or *apodos* are a very strong part of Ecuadorian culture. You will most probably be given one too.

I know someone who was a little chubby when she was young and was nicknamed *Pocha* (meaning short and pudgy). Nearing 50, fit, and slim, she's still called *Pocha* by her family and friends. She even introduces herself as *Pocha*.

Many of the nicknames in the Sierra use Quichua combined with Spanish. There are literally hundreds of nicknames, such as Huevito (little egg), Carepavo (turkey face), and Pelusa (referring to someone with fine hair).

Nicknames are also used for people from different regions of Ecuador. Care should be used if you're going to use regional *apodos* as they are often perceived as derogatory. These should only be used if you're a close friend. Here are some examples: Guaitambos from Ambato, Morlacos from Cuenca, Morenos or Negros from Esmeraldas, Monos from Guayaquil, Puendos from Imbabura, Mashcas from

Latacunga/Cotopaxi, Pata Amarilla from Manabí, Cara de Papa (meaning potato face), Longo, and Pachuco from Quito.

FORMS OF ADDRESS

What is the correct way to address an individual? In English, there is only one word: *you*. Spanish has two forms: *tú* or *usted*. *Tú* is considered the familiar form and *usted* the formal.

Tú is primarily used with very close friends and family, although children may use *usted* with a parent. To be on the safe side, I always use *usted* if there is any ambiguity. This is the correct form with strangers or in business. If someone wishes you to refer to him or her with the *tú* form, they will let you know. *Tú* can also be used by someone wishing to put you down, indicating that the speaker is of a higher social standing.

INDIGENOUS LANGUAGES

It is believed that at the time of the Spanish conquest, some 30 indigenous languages were spoken in Ecuador. Today, only about 12 indigenous languages exist in the lowlands (of which nine are used in the Oriente: Siona; Secoya; Tetete; Cofán; Huaorani; the Jívaroan languages Shuaran and Achua; Quichua; and Zapora.). Only three indigenous languages (Colorado, Cayapa, and Coaiquer) are still spoken in the western coastal lowlands, with a total of about 48,000 speakers. The only indigenous language left in the Sierra is the northern dialect of the Quechuan language family(known as highland Quichua or *chinchay*), with about 3.5 million speakers.

The decline of many indigenous languages and the increasing bilingualism with Spanish is a product of the locals' increasing contact with whites and mestizos. The domination and exploitation of indigenous communities by whites and mestizos in the quest for "progress" has posed a threat to the land, and to the people and cultures who originally inhabited it.

Quichua

The Quechua refer to themselves as *runa* ("the people"). The Quechuan languages were the languages of the former Inca Empire (*Tawantinsuyu*). The version of Quechua (*qheshwa*) used in Ecuador is Quichua.

Some Quechuan words have entered the English language: cocoa (*cuca*), guano (*huanu*), guanaco (*huanaco*, *huanacu*), pampa (*pampa*), puma (*puma*), quipu (*quipu*), and quinoa (*kinua*, *kinoa*). The most difficult sound for English-speakers is the Quechuan **q**, which sounds like the German **ch** in *Bach*, except it is pronounced even further back in the throat. Quichua can be heard in Andean music, which is getting easier to find in the United States, either in its purer form, used by groups such as Markahuasi, Ayllu Sulca, and Ch'uwa Yacu, or it's more Westernized forms, used by the group Inti-Illimani. The Peruvian singer Yma Sumac has a Quechuan name: *ima sumaq*, which means "how beautiful!"

Quechua has been heavily influenced by Spanish. Some 30% of the lexicon, even in monolingual speakers, comes from Spanish. Examples include *riru* (from Spanish *dedo* meaning finger), *arwi* (from Spanish *adobe* meaning sun-dried brick or seasoned), *chufir* (from Spanish *chofer* meaning chauffer), and *sirbisa* (from Spanish *cerveza* meaning ale or beer). Some Quechuan words have also passed into Latin American Spanish, such as *papa* (potato), *choclo* (corncob), *chompa* (jacket), *cushma* (shirt), *china* (maid or worker), *cuy* (guinea pig), *pachamanca* (earth oven), *quena* (flute), *cachaco* (cop), and *chacra* (farm).

LEARNING SPANISH

Spanish schools are a very important source of income for Ecuador. Walking along Avenida Amazonas in Quito, you will find no shortage of choice. But you will also find varying degrees of quality. The competition is so keen that I have even seen offers of as little as three dollars per hour. Most schools offer live-in arrangements with Ecua-dorian families which will, no doubt, help you improve your Spanish.

Here are a list of a few things you should look for when choosing a school:

- How long has the school been in operation?
(Newer schools may not necessarily be better.)
- What types of programs do they offer?
- What is the teacher-student ratio?
- What is the educational level of the teacher?
- Will the school provide references?
- Will the school help you in the event of an emergency?

I believe that references are a very good indicator of what a good program is. Another option for finding a program is a broker or agent located in the United States representing the school. These are usually paid a commission and may represent several schools. Three such services based in the United States are: **Language Link** (http://www.langlink.com/), **Spanish Abroad** (http://www.Spanish abroad.com), and **AmeriSpan** (http://www.amerispan.com).

Here are a few more recommendations:

Academia De Español Quito
http://regio.com/ecuador/learnsp1.html

Academia De Español "Surpacifico"
http://www.surpacifico.k12.ec

Academia de la Lengua Española or **Mundilingua**
http://www.mundilingua.com

Academia Latínoamericana de Español
http://www.ecuador-Peru-bolivia.com

American Spanish School
http://schoolamerica.hispeed.com

Bipo and Toni's Academia de Español
http://homepage.iprolink.ch/~bipo

Centro de Español Vida Verde
http://www.vidaverde.com

Escuela de Español Simón Bolívar or **Simón Bolívar Spanish School**
http://www.simon-bolivar.com

Galápagos Spanish School
http://www.galapagos.edu.ec

Instituto de Español Indoamérica
http://www.indoamerica.edu.ec

Instituto Superior de Español
http://instituto-superior.com

Mitad Del Mundo
http://www.ecua.net.ec/mitadmundo

San Francisco Spanish Language Institute
http://ecuadorexplorer.com/sanfrancisco

Sí Centro de Español e Inglés or **Si Centro Spanish School**
http//www.ecuadorexplorer.com/sicentro/home

Chapter Seven

CUSTOMS AND ETIQUETTE

We look like you, sometimes we talk like you, but we do not think like you.—Colonel Borja from the book *Tumult at Dusk: Being an Account of Ecuador* by Walker Lowry.

Understanding Ecuadorian culture will require some adjustments and study. Those who think Ecuador is like all other Latin American countries are very mistaken. While there are resemblances, Ecuador has its unique cultural mores. You will no doubt make blunders in your communication no matter how good your intentions. This chapter will introduce you to some of the intricacies of Ecuadorian life, customs, and etiquette. I have had to make some generalizations and beg your forgiveness if some of my observations are not always accurate. I do hope, however, that they will lead you a short way into the maze of communicating in this country.

ASI ES LA VIDA

Ecuadorians are by nature optimistic and positive in many of their attitudes to life. There is a feeling within the Ecuadorian spirit that one should not fight one's fate but make the best of a bad situation. Common expressions may include "*Asi es la vida*" which translates to "Life is so" or, more literally, "What can I do? What happened, happened. So let's start all over again!" Another popular expression is "*Si Dios quiere*" which means "God desires it."

Many Americans, in contrast, believe that their destiny is in their own hands and that they can control the outcome. Ecuadorians concentrate more on being content with their station in life. But this doesn't mean that they are static or rest on their laurels. For example, millions of Ecuadorians left their country in the late 1990s to seek better financial opportunities abroad.

COURTESY IS THE BEST POLICY

Ecuadorians prefer to converse in an indirect way, as opposed to the American style of frankness and directness. Ecuadorians tend to be very good at paying compliments and showing respect to get what they want. They will often tell the listener what they want to hear and not necessarily what they intend to do. The language used is often courteous and diplomatic. Being straightforward is considered being rude in most situations. This also applies to telephone conversations.

One Ecuadorian who has lived many years in the United States provided the following example. A committee from the Ecuadorian Ministry of Health was trying to introduce sex education in schools. When they were making the "pitch" they stated: "Well, we have something that you will find fascinating, it won't cost you anything. You will find it so useful, especially for the beautiful young women in your school." My friend tried to get them to get to the point as she had to rush off for another appointment. The presenters then became offended and annoyed at her.

CRITICISM

A person's dignity is of utmost importance in this society, no matter what their social or economic status. Relationships are often based on a developing state of trust, which may develop over many years. You will find that many Ecuadorians will not be confrontational in their opinions and that to tell someone they're wrong may cause a very serious break in your relationships.

This is especially true in a public situation. I once criticized a new security agent at a check-in counter at the airport for discarding my tourist visa. It happened to be her first day on the job. When the agent didn't respond, I realized that I had made her lose face in front of her colleagues and superior. Her manager responded very delicately and acted as if was not important, in an effort to regain her dignity. One needs to be patient and to maintain your calm at all times. Yelling in public or raising your voice is also considered ill mannered and inappropriate.

GESTURES

There is a lot more handshaking going on in Ecuador than in the United States. But these are not as firm, almost expressionless, and last between two and three seconds. Almost always you would shake hands with someone when greeting them or parting with them. Also, the man will initiate the shaking of a woman's hand not vice versa. The handshake between a man and woman is less firm than that between two men.

Familiar Ecuadorian men will often hug each other and pat each other on the back, especially if they are good old friends. A familiar greeting between a man and a woman and a woman and woman is a light kiss on the cheek.

Pointing at someone or a group of people with a finger is almost always considered rude. Many Ecuadorians will sometimes make a pointing gesture by puckering their lips and will slightly raise their chin in the area they are making reference to. Pointing at objects is not offensive.

Another rude hand gesture is to give the height of someone with the palm down. This is only used when giving the height of an animal. If you were giving the height of a person or child, you would turn your palm sideways at about a 90° angle.

Waving or beckoning to someone to come over to you by using your forefinger or wrist with your palm up is not done. Instead, Ecuadorians make a motion of waving with the palm down, their fingers towards their body.

Whistling may also be used to get the attention of a person such as a waiter or porter. But, while this is practiced, it is considered poor manners.

Yawning in public is considered rude.

PERSONAL SPACE AND QUEUING

The personal space between Ecuadorians is much closer than what most North Americans are accustomed to.

Space within Ecuadorian homes is often cramped as large families are common. In many middle- and lower-class homes, extended female family members will often be entertained in the mother's room. My Ecuadorian wife, when visiting her mother, will often sleep with her in the same bed.

This different culture regarding personal space can become quite frustrating especially when standing in a line. I have to consciously control my discomfort. There also doesn't appear to be much respect for queues. Social status might indicate who can cut a queue. Often people who are white, considered to be of a higher social class, or those more senior in age may take a place in front of others or are given preferential treatment. In place of queuing, people tend to bunch up next to a counter, no one knowing who's next in place. Friends of the counter staff are often better taken care of. This happens quite often at airports as domestic flights are often very crowded.

Remaining calm and trying to move up is the best way to handle this situation. Yelling, making a commotion, getting irate, or complaining will work against you, especially if it is an elderly person that moves in front of you. Employees or counter staff might sometimes procrastinate in direct relation to how hard you push.

TIME

Time is seen as being quite open-ended in Ecuador. This is called *hora ecuatoiana* or the "Ecuadorian hour." There is a *mañana* (Spanish for "tomorrow") attitude, few people arriving on time for appointments and parties. Half an hour to one hour late is the norm.

When attending a party, if the appointment is 9:00 pm, you should not arrive at the person's home at 9:00 pm sharp. You will find your host still preparing and maybe not even dressed. It would be safer to arrive a half hour to forty minutes after the stated time. Going out for the evening usually gets started later in Ecuador. If you're going to dinner it would not be abnormal to eat at nine or later and stay out until two or three in the morning.

Ecuadorians are more punctual for work and business engagements. My experience, however, is that most appointments with businesspeople, especially if it is an owner of a small- or medium-sized company will not start before 10:00 am, and that the latest appointments will probably not exceed 6:00 pm. The provision of services is, also, not as prompt as what I am used to in the United States.

It is one thing for the Ecuadorian to be late but if the foreign business counterpart is late, it might be perceived by the Ecuadorian that you are not taking them seriously. I once had an appointment with a buyer in Quito who was already a customer for the company I represented. I wasn't too worried about being on time, and in fact missed the appointment by a day. I was embarrassed to find, when I met him, that he was far from amused with my untimely manner. My speculation is that the reason his *hora ecuatoiana* seemed different was because he was educated in Germany.

Working Hours

Generally speaking, in the Sierra, most offices will be open from 9 am–6 pm. Lunch is usually for two hours, starting at noon. Working hours are generally the same on the Costa but lunch may last for two to three hours, especially during the hot months of December through to April.

Banks are generally open from 9 am–1 pm. Many banks have longer hours than posted. Most banks have branches in the major malls that are usually open as long as the mall is and even on weekends. Most malls close by 8 pm.

ENTERTAINING

Dutch treat or *plan americano* is not often practiced in Ecuador. The general rule is that if you invite you pay. This is especially true if you're inviting a woman somewhere. If you're invited to a dinner or meal by someone, the custom is that you should invite and host that person in the future. Invitations are expected to be reciprocated.

GIFTS

This is an important part of Ecuadorian society both for social and business reasons. Here are some guidelines:

• Gifts when visiting a home may include chocolates and candies.

• Flowers such as roses or a small bouquet are always welcome. However, if they are for a business associate's wife, be sure not to pay her too much attention. Never give artificial flowers to anyone.

• If you know the gift-recipient well, something to decorate the home would be appreciated.

• Perfumes are always nice gifts especially if you know the person well. I always carry small bottles of perfume with me and present them to secretaries and staff. They will always remember you for that and it also becomes easier to work with them afterwards.

• Appropriate gifts for men include colognes, soaps, books, and liquor. I also purchase small bottles of Chivas Regal and other well-known liquors that only cost a few dollars. They don't take up much space and are always appreciated.

• CDs always make nice gifts, especially jazz ones.

• If you're going to a home with young people, I always bring pens, pencils, decals, or small rubber stamps.

• Post cards are appreciated as well, especially to show locals where you are from.

In business, women need to be very cautious about what they present as a gift to men. A book on a business subject is considered acceptable.

TABLE MANNERS

Good table manners involves keeping your hands above the table. This is difficult for many people from the United States since we have been taught to keep our hands below the table. Many locals will eat with their arms lightly resting on the table and use the right hand to eat. European norms apply here.

When eating, especially among the lower classes, you should leave a little left on your plate. If you finish everything, the host will assume you didn't have enough to eat and will offer you more. This is also true with drinking. I once visited a local's home and the hostess was serving beer in her finest glassware. It was a hot afternoon and I had no trouble drinking a full glass. I noticed as soon as it was emptied she would fill it back up, and I thought that as a good guest I should finish that as well. I soon found myself rather tipsy, and realized that it is good manners for locals to fill their guest's empty glass up. So, if you've quenched your thirst, leave some of the beverage in the glass or announce politely that you've had enough.

A drinking tradition among the lower classes is that at parties people will often break into small groups. There will usually be a bottle of beer or another beverage and one glass. People will take turns filling up that glass for each other. The person offered the glass will consume the whole glass. Not a very wise pastime during the flu season.

Another aspect of manners among the lower classes regarding food is when one of the family members goes out to eat. They will usually bring something back for the people in the house. This is a practice I still find hard to understand. If my Ecuadorian wife and I go out for a meal, she insists that we get something for the kids, even if they are out somewhere else, or have eaten at home. When I am in Ecuador and staying with my mother-in-law, I will bring something back, even if it isn't very much. I usually receive a nice smile, especially if it is pizza from an American fast-food restaurant, which she doesn't eat at very often.

VISITING

If a woman enters the room, men will stand and greet her after extending a handshake and a small brushing kiss on the cheek. When a man enters a room, women often remain seated.

You should also acknowledge each and every person with a hello and handshake in the room, especially if it is a small group. I have even been to large parties and functions where a new person entering the party will introduce himself to every person. If you enter a room and have been introduced, you shouldn't make a quick exit. It is considered courteous to stay and talk for at least a while.

SERVICE

For the most part, a high level of service does not appear to be the norm in most retail establishments here. Sales clerks are generally not well-

IFA LADY COMES IN REMEMBER TO STAND UP

paid and many establishments are family-owned.

Both clerks and merchants frown upon window-shopping. You may even be treated rudely if you say you are just looking. But this may not always be the case in more tourist-oriented establishments.

When paying for the item you have bought, many establishments require a clerk to write a ticket for the item. He will hold on to the item while you go to a window to pay for it. You will then pick the item up from another clerk or window before leaving. When entering some establishments, including grocery stores, your briefcase or other items will be checked as you enter. Your property will be placed in a cubicle and you will be given a claim ticket.

SOCIAL STATUS

One's educational accomplishments, family name, and titles count for a lot in Ecuador. People are treated differently depending on your gender, age, or social status. Titles are used even in conversation. Please refer to the titles section of the Language chapter.

PALANCA

The phrase "it's not what you know but who you know" is a predominant aspect of the Ecuadorian culture. While this is true of any place on Earth, it critical to operating in Ecuadorian society at all levels. Palanca, which means *lever* in Spanish, is the use of connections to obtain favors, employment, and business deals.

If you think having the lowest price and even a higher quality product is going to get the sale you may find yourself mistaken. I learned this the hard way. I represented a manufacture of universal joints that were new to the market and identified a distributor who could purchase a substantial quantity. My initial contact at the company identified himself as the general manager and buyer for the firm. He seemed quite interested in the product and liked the price. However, he said they had been happy with their supplier but would be interested in a lower price. After several visits he said if we would make a concession of 5% they would place a sample order. I left happy, thinking I would get an order and a commission check. After getting the ok for the discount he told me that they needed more of a discount to make a purchase.

I made a visit with the visiting sales manager from the United States. We made another price concession and the manager said to wait a few minutes. After a long wait, the manager returned and said that he was checking with his superior. I realized then that a sales manager is not always a decision-maker and that the real decision-maker usually has his own office. Upstairs, we met the owner of the business who was very polite and considerate but explained that they had a long relationship with their existing supplier who had agreed to meet our prices so they would not be changing suppliers. Having the best product and the price didn't help at all.

I strongly suggest that if you're new to Ecuador and trying to develop *palanca* that you join several organizations as soon as possible. One excellent group is the **Rotary**, which is quite prevalent throughout Ecuador and joined by numerous high-ranking business officials. Joining the Ecuadorian/U.S. Chamber of Commerce is another viable alternative. Relationships take a while in Ecuador to develop and they need to be cultivated. It is also a good idea to make as many friends from both the Sierra and the Costa.

BRIBES

Ecuador is often referred to by international organizations as being one of the most corrupt countries in the world. While most Ecuadorians denounce bribes, culturally speaking, this is a gray area and payoffs, especially for services at the lower levels of government and in business, is a part of daily life. The longer you are in Ecuador it will become evident that what many North Americans call bribes are seen by Ecuadorians as a means to smoothen situations to obtain what one needs. Many Ecuadorians will blame corrupt politicians for the cause of the country's ills and in the next breath conduct such a transaction.

I was once in a heated conversation with an Ecuadorian who was criticizing the politicos for having their hands in the till. When I then asked him if he would pay a traffic officer to get out of a ticket he smiled and said "Of course" with a large smile. I then asked him where the practice of paying bribes started. He responded frankly, "That is the problem."

The art of paying for services is deeply rooted in the Ecuadorian psyche and is well documented since the Spanish conquest. Politicians will often espouse their intent to eliminate graft but often find themselves participating in it. A case in point is ex-president Bucaram who appeased the poor with promises of improving their position but who was accused of stealing from the public coffers. One of his ministers was caught, after the fall of Bucaram's government, trying to leave for Colombia with suitcases filled with millions of dollars.

The government continues to try to tackle the problem having set up the Comisión Anticorrupción, or Comisión de Control Civico de la Corrupción (Commission of Civic Control of Corruption), which tries to make inroads. You can read about them and their efforts at: http://www.ecuanex.net.ec/anticorrupcion.

This author would never recommend that you do anything illegal. It is important, however, to understand that there is such a system. One of the ways to understand payoffs in Ecuador is that it is not always seen as dishonest behavior but a tip for a service. Bribes are also seen as a way for lowly paid government workers to keep bread on the table.

You should never allude to someone that a payment is a bribe. Any proposition for a payment would be dealt with in a very discreet and unobtrusive matter. I hope the examples below will demonstrate how such a system works.

The first time I encountered such a situation was when I was getting married. I needed a letter from the police department in Ecuador that I was offense-free. My fiancé and I approached an officer standing outside the station and asked him what to do. He took my information and said it would be ready tomorrow. However, if I wanted it in several hours I could. There was no specific verbal clue but my wife-to-be explained to me that I needed to ask how much the service would cost. He told me $10. I returned in several hours and I got my clearance. I wondered if they had even checked if I had a criminal record.

When I first moved to Ecuador I was in severe need of a post office box (*casilla*). I went down to the main post office and inquired about this. The clerk was very pleasant and said there were none available. He said to return next week. I returned next week anxious to get my box. However, he explained he was sorry but that there were none. This went on for about a month until a family member told me he could get me one within a day. I was upset that he hadn't told me this earlier. To my surprise I found out I could have it the next day but it would cost me $200. I thought he was kidding. He took me to an grungy old building where we walked up several flights of stairs and entered an office that looked like it was out of an old detective movie. There were several people typing away on old Royal typewriters. My relative introduced me to a gentleman who said that he would be happy to secure a box for me. I handed him $200 and of course I didn't ask for a receipt. He then told me to return to the post office the next day and a gentleman would be at the window to provide me a post office box. I returned the next day to be greeted by the same fellow who had told me there were none available, except this time he was smiling. He handed me a key and had me sign a few papers and I got my box! I have kept that box for the last 20 years even though I don't use it personally.

Traffic police, especially in Guayaquil, are notorious for graft when it comes to traffic violations. Several years ago during the Christmas season I was in a friend's car with two of my sons when we came across a roadblock set up by the police known as *vigilantes*. The officer came up to the window and instructed my friend to drive his vehicle just down the block. My kids were anxious to know what we had done wrong. We parked and my friend got out of the car and approached the officer. He returned to the car, took out some papers, and returned to the officer. Our friend's back was to us as he handed the officer the papers. When our friend returned he said his papers were in order and that he gave the officer something for Christmas. Traffic officers are respected, feared, and hated here.

My most revealing moment of understanding the payment system in Ecuador came many years ago. On that day I must admit I actually appreciated the "something-for-a-cola" system. In my early days in Ecuador, I would often ask others how bribes were conducted. I was always told that there would be no outright request for money but that the person asking for a payoff for a service would comment "How about something for a cola." I didn't believe this until one day I had the chance to buy some Ecuadorians a cola and was happy to do so.

Just a Little Something for a Cola

My family had suffered through the wet heat in Guayaquil for six months while I attempted to open a sales agency. I had imagined difficult times but had not anticipated some of the worst rains and floods in the history of Ecuador. It was the January of 1983. I had never imagined that we would be living in a mosquito net for eight to 10 hours a night. Even with the netting, my family would wake up with large quarter-sized bites, which made me fearful that they would catch dengue fever, or worse, malaria.

The climate was terrible but the economy was worse. I was a self-employed sales representative but could not make a sale. I could not believe that this was the same country where a year earlier I sold $50,000 of car parts in one week. Worse, I was broke and concerned about making my meager savings last.

Some months later, my wife and I decided to throw in the towel. If I was going to be poor, the United States was the place to be, not Ecuador. We were depressed as both of us wanted to remain there. My wife's dream was to be with her family in Ecuador. My dream was to go to some exotic land, build a fortune, wear Indiana Jones hats, and smoke Cuban cigars, while my employees worked my large banana plantation. I went to bed that night knowing tomorrow I would have to start making plans to get back to the U.S., broke. I thought, what a hero, my friends will call me Indiana Loser. I was hoping a large mosquito bite would wake me from the reality of this terrible nightmare.

The next day I went to see my Ecuadorian attorney about my visa. My tourist visa had expired and I was trying to obtain a permanent working visa. The permanent visa was as yet unavailable since my attorney had not paid off several bureaucrats to obtain it. She advised me that immigration would understand my predicament and I would have no problems at the airport. Boy, was she mistaken. I left her office shaking my head. I never understood this game of paying people off to get things, which should be available through regular channels to the masses. My wife had explained to me many times that this was the way of life in her country and public servants supplemented their meager salaries in this manner. It was viewed as a tip for faster service.

We decided to leave the following week. We arrived at the airport and waited through the long line of people making the trek to Miami. After saying our good-byes to friends and family we exited through the security gate to leave. My wife and son presented their documents and were signalled by the immigration officer to pass. I then presented my passport and began to walk through the second security clearance when the officer yelled, "*¡Alto!*" The officer had a grin on his face as though he had caught a thief. He explained to me that my tourist visa had expired and I could not leave the country. I was told I must report to the immigration office on Monday to clear up the matter. Of course it was Saturday and Immigration was closed. I pleaded with him to no avail.

At that moment I suggested to my wife that possibly this matter could be resolved with some type of payment. It's funny how one's perspective changes when you are in a serious predicament. We decided that she would conduct the negotiation since they might put me in jail if I was suspected of trying to bribe a public official.

My wife got the attention of the officer who seemed to sympathize with our plight. She offered him $60. He went to the sergeant and we watched as they discussed our fate. My heart dropped to my shoes when I saw him start shaking his head at the offer. At this point I thought I could hear the plane engines revving up to depart. I looked around a pillar and saw the door on the plane close. I told my wife to offer more money and to beg the junior officer. My wife handed her passport to him, who then handed it to the sergeant. The junior officer returned and gave my wife back her passport.

The sergeant then contacted airline officials and told them to open the plane for three more passengers. I couldn't believe it. We were running like crazy as security officials rushed us to the tarmac of the waiting plane. I could hear people laughing but did not know why until I realized my Sansabelt slacks were drooping toward my knees, exposing the rear portion of my anatomy. It was moon over the Guayaquil airport. At that point I didn't mind being the butt of laughter.

As we reached the plane, the junior officer had accompanied us. I began to shake his hand to thank him for his assistance. He then looked me in the eye and asked, "May I have a little something for a cola?" Clearly he was paying me a compliment by knowing that I understood his culture so well that I would not be offended. He explained that the cola money we previously supplied was only for the sergeant. I reached into my pocket and only had twenties. At that point only $20 separated me from home. This was no time to be budget conscious or to ask if he had change. I handed over a twenty and told him I hoped he enjoyed the cola and to drink one for me. I had a feeling it would be some wonderful Ecuadorian cold draft. He smiled as he shook my hand and felt the bill pass to his. He then said that he hoped I had a good trip and to return to his country.

As I buckled my seatbelt with the sweat pouring down my face, I took my wife's hand and yelled, "Yes!" My wife asked me what happened with the officer. I told her that I had just contributed to the officer's emergency fund. She smiled and congratulated me, saying that I was now officially Ecuadorian.

As I reran the recent events through my mind I could not believe the whole event took place. Was I wrong in paying or was I simply following the rule of a culture different from my own? I could even rationalize that I was being fined for my visa having expired. Whatever happened, I was glad I followed the cultural norms that day. I reclined in my seat and started to drift off to sleep when the stewardess came by and offered me a cola. Coca-Cola would never taste the same again.

MANAGING EMPLOYEES

Consensus management is not the norm in Ecuador. Management decisions often come down from high up in an organization, as previously mentioned in the *palanca* story above. While labor unions do have clout in Ecuador and it is hard to fire someone, most employees seem to fear their supervisors. Ecuadorians as employees will often tell supervisors or managers what they want to hear, trying to avoid conflict. Ecuadorians are generally viewed as hard workers who show up on time, but more out of fear than punctuality. A foreign manager from Denmark, interviewed for this book, feels that Ecuadorian employees need lots of direction and guidance even after having done a specific job for a length of time.

Managers will not generally socialize with subordinates, and if you're a male with a female secretary it will be assumed by many employees that she is also your mistress. Foreign women managers must set a serious tone, especially with male subordinates. You're already fighting a tough stereotype by Ecuadorian men that most foreign women (especially from the United States) are available for sexual liaisons. It is important to understand as a manager that joking or laughing at one's self should be minimized, as you will not, then, be respected. It is important to remember that yelling or criticizing employees in front of others will cause great embarrassment for the employee. Remaining calm and under control will yield better results with employees.

ECUADORIAN VIEWS OF EACH OTHER

Like people all around the world, Ecuadorians are just as fond of making broad generalizations of each other. Most commonly, stereotypes abound between people from the Sierra and Costa. These distinct regional groups do not have a lot of affection for each other. Here are some examples:

What people from the Costa say about people from the Sierra:
• They are tightwads.
• They are crybabies and are referred to as *chichihueros*.
• They are hypocrites.
• They think they are aristocrats and won't admit that they are mestizos.
• They always want more after an agreement has been made.

What people from the Sierra say about people from the Costa:
• They are monkeys
• They spend all the money they make and party all the time.
• They can't keep a secret.
• They don't do what they say they are going to do.

These divisional differences are important to keep in mind if you're assigning representatives in the country or hiring.

I know of an operation based out of Quito who hired an office manager from Guayaquil. After looking at the situation I understood why. Clearly the office staff didn't like the fact that she was from Guayaquil and not one of them. However, being from Guayaquil himself, the manager figured that her loyalty would probably be with him and that she wouldn't team up with the staff. She was also good looking, and that was good for business. Many *serrano* men find women from the coast particularly alluring.

If assigning an agent in Ecuador, one should try to have representatives both in the Costa as well as the Sierra. Many manufacturers will assign dual representation in Ecuador despite it being a relatively small market for most products.

NEGOTIATING

Here are some general guidelines that are important to successful negotiations while in Ecuador:

• You really should speak Spanish at an acceptable level. If you don't, you will need an interpreter or representative that speaks both languages. While using an interpreter you should meet with him beforehand and discuss his preferences while conducting a negotiation. Make sure you are speaking more slowly then normal and not to use slang. You may have to go over highly technical terms together before your negotiations. You should also keep comments brief by pausing to allow the interpreter to convey the message. Speak to the recipient of your message and not to the interpreter.

• You will be judged by your appearance. Be sure that your shoes are shined and your fingernails clean and manicured. You should dress appropriately, depending on the business you are visiting. Suits are the norm in Quito. You cannot go wrong with grays or navy blue. White shirts and rep ties make a good impression. If you have a limited wardrobe I suggest mixing several grays and tan pants with a navy blue sports jacket. White and light blue shirts should work well. It does not look good to show up in Quito dressed as if you're going to a beach resort. Guayaquil is a little less formal. However, businessmen, especially from financial institutions, do wear suits. Lighter material is preferred to help beat the heat. Women should also dress conservatively in business attire suitable for conducting business in places such as San Francisco or New York.

• Pleasantries and small talk are often good ways to start conversations. Avoid talking about Ecuador's problems with Peru or Colombia. I like to focus on positive things about the region that I am in. While in Quito, for example, you might talk about the beautiful architecture. In Guayaquil you can comment on the beautiful Malecón project along the Guayas River. Remember regionalism is a very serious issue. I suggest that during negotiations that you try to ascertain as quickly as possible where the other parties are from. That would help you make conversation.

• Politeness is a sign of breeding to most Ecuadorians and it is almost impossible to be too polite. However, remember that their politeness is no indication which way they are leaning in a negotiation.

• Negotiations take time and it may take you several trips to build up a relationship with a potential customer or partner. Once I used a representative that had been in Ecuador for over 30 years and was well trusted. Even then, the customers for our product started off by purchasing small amounts. Assure Ecuadorians that their market is important to your firm and don't group Ecuador with all the other Latin American countries.

• Remain patient throughout all negotiations. They will try to exploit any show of temper. Assure them that you're interested in both parties succeeding and that you are after long-term results.

• Talk to non-competitive companies doing business in Ecuador for advice on dealing with Ecuadorians.

• Don't underestimate the influence that secretaries and support staff can have. They can make things very difficult for you, for example by taking any opportunity to delay you. Being courteous and cheerful will reap rich dividends.

• Remember being direct or frank doesn't normally produce good results. Keep things open-ended. Don't show all your cards at once. Keep alternative plans that may be acceptable to both parties.

• Most Ecuadorians will never say "No" and will evade the final decision. They may also be trying to gain more in the negotiations by this method. Friderich Hassaurek commented in his book *Four Years Among the Ecuadorians* (a reprint of the 1867 book *Four Years Among the Spanish-Americans*) that they are very difficult to deal with in business. Often when agreements had been made, they would change things right at the end and demand more or change prices. I once contacted a Spanish school in Quito who was not really known on the Internet but had a website. I suggested that they place an advertisement. The lady proprietor stated how hard business was and that if a small discount could be offered that she would place an advertisement. I told her that I would have to think about it. I told her that I would be back in a week to ask her again. The next week I approached her and agreed to the discount and she replied that she would love to do it in the future, not actually saying "No." I was very polite and suggested that I would e-mail her in the future to see if she were ready. Ecuadorians love to haggle politely and never want to pay full price.

— Chapter Eight—

CUY, CALDOS & CHICHA

"I like hamburgers for a change. But to eat, to really eat, soup of cow's foot."—Maria Cristina Carrillo in *El Sabor de la Tradición* (1996).

While there are significant divisions in Ecuador's society, food is one thing Ecuadorians can agree on. Ecuadorian food is truly unique. Learning the cuisine and consuming the food of Ecuador will be one of your most interesting and enjoyable experiences in Ecuador. Many of the dishes are a result of the blending of indigenous and Spanish culture over the centuries, although ingredients and preparation methods have remained much the same over time. While numerous

North American fast-food franchises have moved into Ecuador (often a great relief to those who are suffering from culture shock), Ecuadorians take great pride in their local cuisine. It's a strong part of their national identity. I have often heard Ecuadorians conversing on the return flight home about how they can't wait to get back to eat.

BREAKFAST

A typical Ecuadorian breakfast may include small rolls (*pancitos*) with butter and jam along with coffee. Ecuadorian coffee is often very thick and not very good but is considered a delicacy because it is expensive. Most Ecuadorians drink instant coffee. Hot chocolate is often part of the breakfast along with various juices. Larger breakfasts are not the norm.

LUNCH

Throughout Ecuador most people will eat three meals a day. Ecuadorian dishes are often referred to as *platos tipicos* and can be generally described as hearty fare, substantial and very starchy. Lunch or *almuerzo* is the main meal of the day. This is probably one of the most enjoyable moments in the day for an Ecuadorian. It may last up to two hours and they often eat at a very slow and leisurely pace. Even when you see Ecuadorians eating in a fast-food restaurant, they may often stay for an hour or more, especially if they are enjoying the company of friends. However, modern living has shortened this tradition. Familiar fast-food friends can all be found here: Taco Bell, Pizza Hut, McDonalds, Baskin Robbins, and Burger King, but they are considered expensive by local standards.

Many restaurants offer an *almuerzo*, which is often a set meal at a fixed price. They are usually very inexpensive and a way of life for Ecuadorians. Usually the restaurant will have a signboard reading *Almuerzo* and listing the menu. You can be sure that an *almuerzo* will begin with soup. Soups are so popular in Ecuador you would think that someone named Campbell started a soup company there.

Generally there are two styles of soup in Ecuador, known as *locro* and *caldo*. *Locros* are usually a heavy type of soup, which will always contain potato and often pig skin. There is a children's riddle which goes, "How do you say soup of potato (*soupa de papas*) without pursing your lips?" The answer: "Just say *locro*!" *Caldos* are more like a broth. Soup of cow's foot is called *caldo de patas*. This broth contains chunks of cow's feet knuckles and ingredients such as corn (*mote*). This is really tasty and considered a delicacy by locals.

The main lunch dish is referred to as *seco*. In most cases this will include a portion of meat (beef, chicken, fish, or lamb) with potatoes or another vegetable. Rice is often the staple but if you are eating in the Sierra, you may find more potatoes on the plate than rice. Many working Ecuadorians buy their lunch from small stands and have them packed in small pastel-colored plastic containers.

DINNER

Dinner may also may be called *merienda* and is often a smaller version of *almuerzo*. For working-class families, leftovers from lunch are often used for dinner.

TYPES OF FOOD

This is a sampling of the food you will find during your stay in Ecuador:

Achiote—This is a seed also referred to *anato*. It provides much of the color and flavor in Ecuadorian food. The Colorado Indians use this for coloring their hair.

Ají sauce—There is not a table in a home or restaurant in Ecuador that doesn't have some type of *ají* sauce. This is made of red peppers and is not as hot as hot sauces from Mexico. *Ají* sauce from the Costa is usually made with onion, cilantro, and tomato. The *ají* sauce in the Sierra is usually thicker, with tomato as the primary ingredient. You may see *ají* sauce served either in a bottle or in a cup on the table in a home or restaurant. *Ají* sauce is available at grocery stores. The chilies on the coast of Ecuador are often pickled with carrots, onions, and cauliflower in a banana vinegar (*encurtido*). Chilies are also used in a sauce named *agrio* combined with local corn beer (*chicha*), cloves, spices, and chives to be served with roasted pig (*hornado*).

Avocado—Throughout history this has been heralded as an aphrodisiac. There are festivals that revolve around the avocado and the avocado tree is revered by many of the indigenous population. Avocado is often prepared in a blender and made into a fluffy sauce, served with boiled potatoes or on plantain chips. It is also often cut in half and peeled or scooped out of its shell and added to soup.

Beans—An integral part of Ecuador's cuisine. Corn and beans are often consumed together in the Andes. It is legendary for giving a satisfied feeling. You can still see many of these combinations in the Indian markets. Michelle O. Fried, a nutritionist in Ecuador, refers to some of these combinations as ancient fast food. Many beans are sold in huge baskets. They are often combined with scallions and cilantro and served on pieces of newspaper. Some combinations include corn on the cob with fava beans and corn nuts with lupini beans.

Bebidas gaseosas—These are soft drinks, often served without ice. International brands such as Coca-Cola, Sprite, and Fanta are available. Some Ecuadorians believe that you can catch a cold by drinking this with ice.

Ceviche—Another important national dish, this is usually raw or cooked fish (including shrimp, lobster, mussels, or oysters) served in a cold soup with small pieces of popcorn on top. It has been said to cure a hangover. Cilantro, lemon, and onions are often part of the recipe. Exercise caution, however, as improperly prepared *ceviche*, especially *de concha*, may become a primary vector for cholera and other nasty bacteria.

Another fresh fish-catch for the Chanduy markets.

Cuy for sale at an Indian market. It is both eaten and used for religious ceremonies.

Cuáker—This is a drink made with Quaker Oats and is fantastic for breakfast. To be served very cold.

Cuy—One of the most exotic foods of Ecuador, and deemed by some as one of the most disgusting foods in the world, is the legendary guinea pig (known as *cuy* in South America). The *cuy* is an important part of the Andean diet and culture. It was probably domesticated in about 5,000 B.C. and also plays a role in medicinal and religious practices. Two of a number of religious or festival purposes of the *cuy* include the *ashanga* and *castillo*. In Latacunga, there is a huge basket of food that is offered to the city. A roasted pig is placed into a basket

155

and roasted *cuy* tied to the pig. The basket is carried down the street as onlookers applaud. Roasted *cuy* is often sold on a stick by street hawkers.

Empanadas de Morocho—This is a white flour-fried tart filled with meat and rice.

Empanadas de Verde—These are plantains not yet ripe, stuffed with cheese and fried.

Vegetables for sale at the old railroad station in Ibarra.

Fritada—Fried pork. Typical rural dish cooked in a large brass pan.

Fruits—Ecuador is a paradise for fruit. You are in for a treat if you have only tasted papaya or mangos in the United States. When I first sampled these fruits in Ecuador I couldn't believe how large, sweet, and juicy they were. One my favorites is *mora* (blackberry), but you need to make sure it's well-boiled when prepared. Its also a great flavoring in some local ice cream. Other fruits include *babaco*, *maracuya* (passion fruit), *granadilla* (a local and sweeter type of passion fruit), *guanábana*, and *ovos*. You can also enjoy a large variety of delicious *jugos* (fruit juices), such as *naranjilla* (similar to a bitter-sweet orange), and *tamarillo* (tree tomato).

Guineo—Banana

Hornado—A mouth-watering rural dish, this is slow-roasted whole pig. Ecuador's main dish for festivities, it is usually served with a sour/vinegary sauce and a choice of garnishes.

Humitas—This is a wonderful combination of sweet corn off the husk, mixed with grated cheese, eggs, and butter. The grated cheese and corn are wrapped in a corn husk and then steamed.

Fanesca—This is a special soup which is made at Easter and is a combination of 12 different types of beans and cod. There always seem to be numerous articles published during Easter about the cost of *La Fanesca* and the role it plays in Ecuadorian culture.

Llapingachos—This is a very famous dish from the Sierra. It is a fried pancake made up mashed potato and cheese. It is sometimes served with a fried egg on top.

Locro—A chowder made with potatoes, fresh cheese, and avocado.

Chugchucaras—These are pastries, made of pork fat, potatoes, lettuce, tomatoes, and avocado. This dish is usually served with a fried egg and originates from Latacunga.

Meat and fowl—Meat was not a significant part of the indigenous diet before the arrival of the Spanish. Meat is often eaten on the weekends and is sold in open-air markets. Much of the beef in Ecuador is raised without hormones and is not aged. Hormones are used in the cultivation of chickens. Pork is the dominant meat used in the Sierra, which is also a corn-growing region. For large family-gatherings fattened pigs are sacrificed and most of the parts are consumed. Often a neighborhood party may share in a pig. While this may be traditionally done in the country I have also experienced these types of gatherings in the suburbs of Guayaquil. The pig is actually killed in front of onlookers and the party begins.

Morocho—This is made from cracked kernels of white corn cooked in water with cinnamon and milk. It is similar to a hot cereal and is delicious.

Patacones—This is plantain which has been cut up and fried in lard. It is then smashed and refried and is often served with *fritada*, looking like a pancake and cut in one-inch slices.

Plátanos—These are plantains and look like bananas. They may be fried or broiled. Wonderful, especially when served with cream on top. They play a big role in the culture along the coast and are seen by many as a staple.

Potatoes—Without a doubt, potatoes are a mainstay in the Ecuadorian diet. They are indigenous to the highlands and come in numerous sizes and colors. In the highlands, potatoes may be eaten several times a day and are a central source of vitamin C. Potatoes are boiled and served with a chili sauce, cheese, peanuts, or pumpkin seeds. (The pre-colonial inhabitants prepared potatoes in much the same way.)

You will find no end to the varieties of potatoes. *Molo* is a style of mashed potato that is served with ground peanuts. The *oca* potato has an unpleasant bitter taste. It becomes sweet after it has been exposed to the sun. The pale *oca*, which is similar to a bent icicle, is often used as a dessert, cooked with raw cane sugar. It is also used for making pastry and jelly. The stems are good fodder for cattle and horses. *Mellocos* or butter potatoes don't require sunning. They have a crisp texture and are often consumed after harvesting. *Camote* or sweet potatoes are harvested at lower altitudes. This is a true delicacy.

Onions—Red onions are the predominant onions in Ecuadorian fare. They may be prepared by soaking them in sugar water along with lemon and salt.

Quinua—This is a unique high-protein grain, indigenous to the Andes. Early indigenous groups found that the *quinua* whole grain could replace a lack of milk or meat in the diet. It has a sweet nutty taste and is high in fiber.

Refrito—This is a combination of ingredients placed into all soups and stews. It is often a mix of red onion, green pepper, tomato, achiote, and salt. Garlic may also be included. These items are often chopped up.

Sandwich (*Sanduche Mixto*)—When I feel like a fairly light lunch, I go for the *sanduche mixto* comprised of white cheese (melted) with ham on toasted bread.

Tamales—There are numerous types of tamales in Ecuador. They are often made of dough and wrapped in a leaf and then steamed. They are usually stuffed with beef, chicken, or pork.

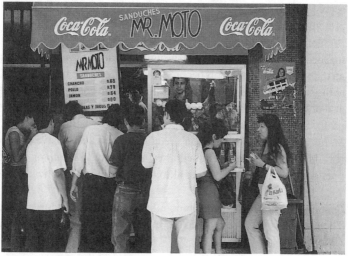

Sandwich stall on 9 de Octubre in Guayaquil.

FOOD PREPARATION WORDS

A la brasa: grilled
A la plancha: From the griddle with oil or butter
Al vapor: steamed
Apanado: batter-fried/breaded
Brosterizado: deep-fried
Encocado: stewed in coconut milk
Frito: pan-fried
Hornado: roasted
Reventado: deep fried

REGIONAL SPECIALTIES

Many of the regions of Ecuador are known for specific foods. An entire book could be written on the specialties of each province. The Manabí province is known by many Ecuadorians to have the best food. You will see numerous restaurants throughout Ecuador using the name *Manabí* in the hope of attracting customers. Not to steal the thunder from professional cookbooks on local cuisine, here a humble sampling of certain specialities along the coast near Guayaquil.

Pascuales

Many of the working-class inhabitants of Guayaquil would travel here on the weekends to eat and party. It is known for *fritada* and pig's intestines, beer, and dancing. (Saturdays and Sundays are often referred to *dias feriados* or "holiday days.")

Juan Gomez Rendon (Progreso)

This tiny village outside of Guayaquil is a famous stopover for tourists from Guayaquil on their way to or from Salinas and Playas, where there are famous beaches. Many of the people there make their living from the tourist trade. There are numerous stalls or vendors called *ambulantes* who specialize in meat served on a stick, corn-on-the-cob

161

with white cheese (wrapped in paper), and *rellenas* (small potato pies). *Fritadas* are also very popular along with *bebidas gaseosas*.

Zapotal

This is another small village on the way to Salinas which has a number of small restaurants along the highway that specialize in lamb or *seco de chivo*. My favorite place in Zapotal is the Chivo Erotico. *Chivo* means goat and I like to ask to meet the erotic goat and the waitress always just give me a dirty look.

WATER

For the well being of your intestines, drink only bottled or boiled water. These are easily available throughout the country, of good quality (tapped from Ecuadorian springs) and can come distilled or sparkling. Remember that tap water is used in ice, so request your beverages "*sin hielo*" ("without ice") in restaurants.

LIQUOR

Alcoholic beverages have a long history in Ecuador. I find Ecuadorian beer among the finest in the world. I was not a big fan of beer but this changed when I consumed my first Pilsener. It is excellent. Several years ago Budweiser made a campaign into Ecuador. But on my last trip I saw very little Budweiser being served, the Ecuadorian beers remaining more popular, the favorite brands being Club and Pilsener. There are a number of other of local beers but are not as widely consumed, such as Chop, Club Café, Club Verde, and Biela. (Biela is not popular because it is regarded by many as contributing to the downfall of a major bank in Ecuador, its owner accused of using funds from the bank to finance the beer manufacturing.)

Brandies in Ecuador are derived from fruit flavors and not grapes. They are about 30% in alcoholic content. Some combine them with fruit juices. One of the local brands is Brandy Naranja.

Chicha was the first alcoholic beverage in Ecuador and used by the Indians. It is made from fermented *yuca* (cassava) in the Oriente, maize in the Sierra, and sometimes rice in the Costa. A few tribes in the Oriente sometimes aid the fermentation process with human saliva, *chicha*-makers chewing the ingredients and spitting them back into the pot to brew. *Chicha* made this way may give you Hepatitis B! When sugar is introduced, *aguardiente* ("fire-water"), also known as *puro* or *caña*, is produced. This is quite potent, most Ecuadorian brands containing about 50% alcoholic content. There are number of Ecuadorian brands of *aguardiente* including Caña Manabita, Cristal, Frontera, Licor del Mono o Guagua Montado, and Zhumir.

Anisados are alcoholic beverages flavored with aniseed. Their alcoholic content is about 35% and it has a sweet flavor. It may not seem at first like a powerful drink but it sneaks up on you. National brands include Anisado Patito and Tropico.

Seco almost tastes like vodka. It is very inexpensive. The best known brands are Patito Seco and Seco Montero.

SUPERMARKETS AND SHOPPING

One area of retailing, which has greatly improved in the last several years, is shopping at supermarkets. There are basically two chains in Ecuador—Mi Comisariato and Supermaxi. They each have more than 20 outlets locally and own warehouses in Miami. The sale of U.S. products in these supermarkets, popular a few years ago, has diminished, due, in part, to Ecuador's financial difficulties in the late 1990s.

In my opinion, Supermaxi is as well-run and clean as any large food chain in the United States. The quality of many of the local products has also improved. Supermaxi offers a discount card, which is quite difficult to obtain. One area that I think needs to be improved are the bakeries where the bread sits out and gets hard very fast. Supermaxi is usually open until 8:00 p.m.

Much of the shopping in Ecuador is still conducted in open-air markets where many go daily to get the freshest food. However, more

163

Megamaxi is part of the Supermaxi chain, both owned by the Wright family.

and more shopping is done on a once-a-week basis. Two unique products are organic lettuce under the name **Andean Organics** and a purifier for fruits, vegetables, and lettuce called **Vitalin**. There are several other brands of purifiers but **Vitalin** doesn't leave an after-taste.

BAKERIES

Panaderias (bakeries) are great here! You can get hot, freshly baked rolls for 10–25 cents and a tasty *empanada* for $1. Bakeries often have fresh products. Many families will purchase their bread needs on a daily basis from a local bakery. A number of bakeries will be owned by or have employees from Ambato which is known to have the best bakers in the country.

STREET STANDS

The meat from street stands may not be thoroughly cooked, so be careful. Even if there is a respectable crowd around the stand, I have learnt from bitter experience that the food may still be contaminated.

FOOD ETIQUETTE

Here are a few tips:

• Smoking is allowed in most restaurants. Someone might ask before they light up but it would be rude to say "No" or to ask someone not to smoke. Some hotels have adopted a policy of non-smoking rooms.

• Ecuadorians dine out later than what is customary in the United States but earlier than other places in Latin America, such as Argentina. A dinner time of between 7 and 9 pm is quite common in most parts of Ecuador. Some complete a long evening out at a hotel coffee shop.

• In most cases there is a service charge on the bill. However, it is common to give a tip of between 5% and 10%, especially if the service was good.

• In Quito it is appropriate to be dressed up when dining in a "nice" restaurant.

• If you are driving to a restaurant you should park out in front so that someone can watch your vehicle. When you leave you should pay these "car guardians" a small amount (usually under a dollar). Valet parking is not common here.

HEALTH TIPS

• Allow yourself a bit of time to adjust to the local cuisine. It would be wise to consume small amounts of food in the beginning and make sure it is well cooked. Always be cautious with uncooked vegetables and lettuce.

• Do not assume that water is safe to consume unless it is bottled. Ask for bottled water (*agua pura* or *agua con gas*). Make sure you see the bottle opened in front of you if in a restaurant. Many Ecuadorians will often clean the top of the bottle with a napkin. Waters and colas are often consumed with straws. The safest way is to boil it yourself. Once the water cools, it can be recontaminated, so keep purified water in a covered container. Iodine tablets are an alternative when boiling is impractical.

• The classic food-poisoning culprits are some salads and fruit. Fruits that must be peeled before being eaten, such as bananas, pineapples, and oranges, are usually safer. Organic lettuce should still be purified and this is more popular now in many foreigner or gringo-orientated restaurants.

RESTAURANT GUIDE

Ecuador's restaurants range from the very basic to some of the most elegant in Latin America. In the province of Pichincha (where Quito is) there are more than 1,800 restaurants. Guayas province (where Guayaquil is) has more than 1,500. Here is a guide to some of my favorite restaurants in Ecuador, with an emphasis on Quito. One of my favorite delicatessens that can be found at several of the malls both in Guayaquil and Quito is **El Español**. One of the branches in Quito is in the tourist area at Juan León Mera 863. This is also one of the few restaurants in Ecuador where the employees wear gloves whilst handling the food.

Cuenca

La Herradura. Avenida Remigio Crespo in the Zona Rosa. This restaurant specializes in Argentinean dishes and sausages. A full dinner costs about $10 without alcohol. It is decorated in a traditional Argentinean motif.

Rancho Chileno is located at Avenida España near the airport. It has been operating for 30 years and specializes in unique dishes from Chile. Meals go for between $3–$5.

Guayaquil

Cielito Lindo. Jorge Pérez Concha 623 between Ficus and Monjas. Located in the Urdesa neighborhood. Excellent traditional Mexican dishes combined with a good family atmosphere.

Hotel Continental Coffee Shop. Chile y 10 de Agosto. This is a great place to eat at any hour of the day and is one of my favorites after a long night of dancing. It is still very popular and has been around for years.

La Fontenella. P. Icaza y Pedro Carbo. An excellent choice for lunch when downtown and not visited by many foreigners.

La Parrillada del Ñato. Avenida Victor Emilio Estrada 1219 y Laureles in Urdesa. This has been one of the best steak houses in Guayaquil for a number of years. The main dining rooms are not air-conditioned but there is always a breeze floating through this establishment.

Morocho. Portete y 39. This is a small stand in Guayaquil. When I used to live near Portete Street, I loved to go down on a Sunday night to get a small bowl of *morocho*. There are many such stands along Portete.

Quito

Ecuadorian

La Querencia. Eloy Alfaro 2530 y Catalina Aldaz

La Choza. Av. 12 de Octubre 24-551 y Cordero

Las Menestras. This restaurant had no address when I last ate there. It is about three doors down from the hotel Mansion de Angel, which is located at Wilson E5-29 y Juan León Mera. It serves excellent Ecuadorian cuisine and seats 25 people at the most. On paydays, which are the 1st and about the 15th of the month, this place is packed at lunch.

International
La Viña. Isabel La Catolica y Cordero
Avalon. Orellana 155 y 12 de Octubre. Expensive by Ecuadorian standards.
La Terraza del Tartaro. Veintimilla 1106 y Amazons. Great view with good quality meat and fish.
Pims. Isabel la Catolica y Cordero. Has a great atmosphere and is very popular.
Clancy's. Salazar y Valldolid. It has great food and is very cozy.
La Escondida. General Roca N33-29 y Bosmediano. It features Californian cusine.

Café
La Boca del Lobo. Calama 284 y Reina Victoria. It is very good but only open at night.
Le Grain Café. Baquedano y Juan León Mera. It is rated good and has a very inexpensive lunch.
El Cafecito. Cordero y Reina Victoria.

Italian
Il Risotto Pinto 209 y Diego de Almagro. It is closed on Mondays.
Pavorotii. Av 12 de Octubre 1955 y Cordero. This is a high-end restaurant.
El Arcate. Baquedano 358 y Juan León Mera. It serves excellent pizza and great pasta. It is closed on Mondays.
La Briciola. 1255 y Luis Cordero.

Sushi
Sake. Paul River N30-166. This is an upscale sushi establishment.

Mexican
Mero Mero. Suiza 343 y República de El Salvador. This is not Tex Mex or Sonoran-style.

French
El Rincon de Francia. Roca 779 y 9 de Octubre. This establishment was founded nearly 25 years ago and is still excellent. It has a very elegant setting but is not extravagant. It is clearly upscale as many businessmen and famous personalities dine here. The service is exceptional.

Fish and Seafood
Mare Nostrum. Foch y Tamayo.
Las Redes. Amazonas y Veintimilla.

Meat
San Telmo. Portugal 570 y 6 de Diciembre.

Chapter Nine

SETTLING IN

"Lodgings were scarcely to be had for money, and services were difficult to secure."—Edward Whymper when arriving in Ecuador in 1879.

Ecuador is still not an easy overseas assignment, although things have changed since 1879. Stresses are increased by language, cultural, societal, and geographical differences. Nothing happens in a hurry in Ecuador, except when you don't want it to. You will have to consciously adjust your patience level. The information provided in this chapter should significantly increase your learning curve and hopefully soften some of the shocks you might face. For the most part, many assignments will take place in Quito or Guayaquil. You will find that many of the same systems exist in much of the country. The Resource Guide chapter of this book will provide you much contact information for settling into and smoothening your transition into Ecuador.

ACCOMMODATION

Choosing where to live in Quito or Guayaquil is an important significant decision. Both cities are metropolises and are subject to the same problems any large city might have. Choosing the best neighborhood you can afford is important. Most of the better neighborhoods will have access to supermarkets and drug stores. Rents are typically less expensive in Quito, as compared to Guayaquil.

When selecting your residence it is best to live as close as possible to work and school. Distance is important, as driving in Quito and Guayaquil can be a horrendous experience. Try to cut down on commuting time. Before selecting a residence it may be wise to settle in an apart-hotel, which can accommodate you for a short- or long-term stay. Apart-hotels in Ecuador are typically a hotel-type operation with suites varying in size, usually including a kitchen and maybe a dining room. This will allow you the freedom to explore the different neighborhoods before signing a lease. Taking your time to locate the most appropriate housing for your needs is advisable. It is also possible to rent rooms and live with families where no lease is involved. Be prepared to take a month to several months before you find appropriate housing.

In Quito you will find a number of differing architectural styles to choose from, both colonial and modern. There is a fantastic use of wood, many of which are native to Ecuador. The city is divided into four sections: south, north, historical, and valley. The best neighborhoods in Quito for expatriates are Bellavista, El Batan, El Bosque, El Condado, Gonzalez Suarez, and Guapulo. The Gonzalez Suarez area

Apartment sprawl in Guayaquil.

close to the Hotel Quito is among the nicest in Quito. There are a number of nice apartment buildings in this area. Some expatriates have found a number of suburban areas attractive. Valle de los Chillos and Valle de Tumbaco have numerous housing options and services available. They are both about 15–20 minutes outside of Quito. Do remember that as areas grow, commuting time will increase to and from Quito. Just a few steps down in quality are the neighborhoods of El Inca, Granda Centeno, Jipijapa, La Floresta, and La Granja.

While Guayaquil has similar rental and buying systems for real estate, there are not as many options as in Quito. Rents in Guayaquil are also generally more expensive than in Quito. There also appears to be little negotiating when it comes to price. The best areas for expatriates are Los Ceibos, Puerto Azul, Santa Cecilia, and Los Parques. Urdesa may still offer options, although it has become rather commercial and less residential of late. My favorite is El Barrio Centenario. It is located in the south of the city and for years was the most posh neighborhood of Guayaquil. Its residents are rather well-to-do and the area is kept immaculate. The biggest drawback is commuting time into Guayaquil or the northern part of the city. There are also a number of apartments in this area.

There are several ways to locate your residence. The major newspapers run advertisements in the classified section. The best day for this is Wednesday. In Quito there will be numerous places that may display rentals or have access to individuals who know of rentals. The major schools that cater to expatriates would be a good option. A number of Spanish schools also have apartment listings, as does the South American Explorer's Club. Another source would be your country's embassy or consulate. Using a rental agency is another way to obtain your housing requirement. However, as they usually receive one month's rent from the landlord as their commission. Some may be rather pushy and few seem to speak English.

The rental contracts are quite standard in their wordings, covering duration, monthly rent amount, deposits (guarantees), any annual increase as a cost of inflation, the condition the residence should be in prior to departure, responsibility in the event of damage, prohibitive activities of the tenant, and reasons for early termination of the contract. Most rental agreements will require a one- or two-year lease. You are normally required to pay for all the utilities.

A landlord may terminate a contract if you fail to pay the rent for two months, use the premises for illegal purposes, use the residence for other purposes other then what is in the contract, and subletting without the approval of the owner. The owner must notify you three months in advance if he intends not to renew the contract for some legal reason. A rebuttal to this would have to be handled in a tenancy court by your attorney. However, this happens very seldom.

Deposits range from one to three months. If you're renting a furnished residence, make sure there is a list of all items and the condition they are in. Have both parties sign this and attach it to the contract. The chances of receiving your deposit back are very slim unless you return the flat in an immaculate condition. In Guayaquil the expression: *lagarto que traga, no vomita* ("the alligator that swallows doesn't vomit") can be accurately used here.

Electricity

Ecuador uses 110 volts, 60 AC, compatible with North America but incompatible with Britain and Australia. Plugs have two flat prongs, as in North America. Be prepared for numerous blackouts in Ecuador. Many businesses and residences use generators as backup. Also, it is a good idea to have surge protection equipment for your computers. Electric bills are delivered to each home. You can pay the bill at any of the offices printed on the back of the bill. Some banks offer debit services to pay electricity bills.

Garbage

The municipality takes care of garbage collection. Pack your garbage in plastic bags and it will usually be picked up outside the front of the house (there are no back alleys here). In Quito there are receptacles outside some homes where you can place these plastic bags. Trash disposal is billed yearly on the property tax bill. Depending on where you're staying in Quito, trash collection will usually take place three days a week, i.e. every other day except Sundays.

Sewage

The sewage system in Ecuador is poor and the pressure is too low to accommodate toilet paper. To avoid clogging bowls and to prevent overflows, no matter how unpleasant this sounds, please remember to place toilet paper or tampons in the receptacle next to the toilet. There are a few major hotels, which don't request that you do this. Most do, however, and this should be adhered to. Clean public bathrooms are almost non-existent. Once I arrive in any area of Ecuador where I am to stay for a while, I always scope the area out for hotels with lobbies or restaurants, such as Burger King, in case I need a toilet.

Temporary Digs

Making the transition to a new residence can be very stressful. It is therefore important to have a short-term place to stay whilst locating your permanent housing or are getting it set up. I have found the **Latin America Reservation Center** (LARC) a good reservations site. The booking office can be contacted at 1-800-361-7003 or http://www.larc1.com. LARC staff members can attend to residential needs in Latin America, Australia, and New Zealand.

In Quito, I recommend **La Colina Suites** as an excellent housing alternative for either short- or long- term stays. It is a small establishment with 22 suites of which all are quite modern and very elegant. Popular with embassy personnel, it is dedicated to a high level of service and can assist you in almost any of your needs in Quito. The suites all have a dining room and kitchen and sufficient space for families. It is also the only hotel in Quito that will accommodate pets. They are also one of the only hotels in Quito that carries an insurance policy and that provides treatment if you require emergency care at the hotel in the event of an accident or illness. In the event that you need more serious treatment they will make sure you get safely to a doctor or hospital. Prices are even negotiable for longer stays. The hotel is located at La Colina N26-119 y Av. Orellana, http://www.lacolinasuites.com, tel 593 2 234 678.

Another option for a short- or long-term stay is the **Apart-Hotel Antinéa** located near Avenida Amazonas. They have a number of "French-style" hotel rooms and suites, and have eight apartments. Details: Juan Rodriquez 175 y Diego de Almagro, Quito, Ecuador; http://www.hotelantinea.com; tel 593 2 506 838 or 593 2 506-839.

Please refer to a list of hotels in the Enjoying Ecuador chapter.

Domestic Help

Another key to comfortable living in Ecuador is domestic help. As with housing you should take your time in selecting suitable domestic staff. Many household employees are from very humble origins and are often from the countryside. Many may have as little as a third-grade education and speak only Spanish. It is wise to obtain recommendations from your embassy or consulate staff. Part of the selection procedure is to conduct an interview and secure letters of recommendation from former employers, not just friends or family. The same methods mentioned under finding a residence will also suffice. There are also employment agencies that specialize in domestics. Many domestics prefer to work for expatriates as they are thought to pay and treat household help better than Ecuadorian nationals.

Live-in maids are still a common practice in Ecuador. Many residences have maid's quarters. This will include a furnished room with a bathroom. The employer may also furnish uniforms and personal items. Uniforms in Quito may be purchased at El Uniform in the mall Quicentro and their main store at 6 de Diciembre in the Plaza Argentina (tel 239-616). In 2000 the average complete uniform (two sets) including shoes cost about $40. Make sure that your agreement covers salary (current salary is about $50 per month in 2000) and days off. (Sundays are normally the day off for domestics.) Standard duties include cleaning the entire residence. Live-in maids will also prepare and serve most meals and should eat as well as your family.

There are a number of labor laws protecting domestic workers that are important to keep in mind. There is a minimum wage. (On top of this, experience and special skills such as cooking may demand a higher price.) If the employer wants to dismiss the employee there should be a 30–day notice given to the employee. She must also be given at least two hours a week off to find another position. If your maid becomes ill she can ask you to provide an illness document, which would entitle her medical care at an Ecuadorian Social Security facility. Ecuadorian law also requires employers to pay additional bonuses. Payable in December, this is called the 13th salary since it is an additional one-month salary. The 14th salary consists of two minimum wages, paid between September 1 and 15. There is a 15th salary payable in April. A 16th salary is payable every month and is one-eighth of the paid salary.

Depending on the size of your home and number of children, it may be appropriate to have a nanny as well. This can be an excellent experience for your family and children. Ecuadorians dote on their children and this will probably be true with your nanny. The children will grow close with her and learn Spanish from her.

Some general tips to relating with your maid are as follows:

• Respect the privacy of a maid's quarters and try to communicate with her when in the common work area.

• Address maids with the polite form of you—"*usted.*" Some North Americans falsely believe they should be addressed with the "*tú*" form. Only if a maid is very young is "*tú*" an appropriate form of address.

• Maids should be kept at a proper social distance but be treated in a polite matter. Saying "thank you" and "please" are common courtesies.

• Maids don't eat with the family.

• Don't set the table, clean dishes, or sweep. This may often be perceived as a way of telling them they don't know how to do their job.

• If you're a guest in a home, it's inappropriate to be too sociable with their maid.

• In most cases don't pay too much attention to the maid's children.

• In most instances don't introduce your maid to your guests.

Lawn Man

While yards such as those in the United States are not the norm in Ecuador, you may have a small area of garden or yard that needs maintaining. You can request for a lawn man to tend to the plants and upkeep the house. They will probably have other customers and will come to the house only on an agreed schedule or on a need-to basis.

EDUCATION

If you have children, I think you will be happy with the various school options here. The schools are often close-knit groups where your children will get the chance to mix with both local and foreign students. The private schools tend to attract children of diplomats, executive expatriates, missionaries, and wealthy Ecuadorians. The environment in the schools, whilst more demanding, seems to be generally more wholesome or innocent than schools in the United States. Discipline problems and drug use don't appear to be as much of a threat here as in U.S. schools. Many of the children speak two or more languages and this is an environment that fosters cross-cultural learning and interaction.

The Ecuadorian Ministry of Education must approve the schools' curricula. School curricula vary and have different operating permits.

The private schools, which cater to international students, operate on the U.S. school calendar. Ecuadorian public and some private schools run on the Ecuadorian school calendar. Schools in Quito run from October to the end of July. Schools in Guayaquil operate from May to January. The cost of private schooling here is comparable to the United States. Many of the schools are computer-equipped. In fact, the Inter-American Academy in Guayaquil was using computers and web pages before many schools in the United States. There are several school options listed in the Resource Guide. Please contact these schools as far in advance as possible, and be equipped with references and academic records.

SAFETY

Ecuador has become a much more dangerous place to live for nationals and expatriates over the last few decades. Petty crimes, such as pickpockets, have always been a problem in the larger cities and along the coastal areas. The last several years have seen a dramatic increase in the number of violent crimes against individuals and businesses. Kidnapping has become a cottage industry. Security should be considered in your travels through Ecuador.

There are a number of security companies operating in Ecuador. Please do check that they are qualified and that the company's documentation is in order. They should have permission from the Minister of Police and with the Ministry of Defense. A security company needs to have authorization to operate from the Commander of the Armed Forces and the Superintendent of Companies. If you are really keen about security, you can expect to pay about $350–$400 dollars a month for protection. I would advise checking the company out with your embassy and recommend companies that have contracts with large organizations such as airlines.

One of the most frequent comments among travelers to Ecuador regards safety. I often overhear them advising each other to stay away from dangerous places, not to act foolishly, and to use common sense. This may be naive, however, as something that makes common sense in your homeland may not make common sense in a foreign land.

I have found the following tool, used by the police, very reliable in increasing your chances of not being victimized while traveling in Ecuador. Being aware of your environment is critical to your safety. But what level of awareness is necessary? Let's think of different levels of awareness in terms of colors. **White** constitutes you not being aware of your surroundings due to distractions, being tired, or assuming there is no risk of danger. A **yellow** state of alertness has you in a relaxed state but observing what is going on around you. You are not be expecting a physical attack but will be aware that it may happen. An **orange** level of alert is when you are aware of an impending problem that may escalate. This is a very volatile situation but you have a plan of defense. You may not need to physically protect yourself but should have a plan how to get away from the threat. The most intense state of alert is **red**. This is a situation where there is trouble and you need to take immediate action and your whole sense of purpose is to protect yourself by all reasonable means.

There will be times when you shift between all four color levels.

While it would be nice to live at the **white** level all the time, you will be asking for trouble if you do. Examples of different scenarios with different levels of alert may include the following:

White—Bars on the windows, full-time security guards, and alarms may provide such an environment. Choosing a nondescript home may also provide you some protection. In certain malls in both Guayaquil and Quito you may feel quite safe, as there is substantial security for customers. However, even in such an environment, you may find yourself going into **yellow** mode especially when leaving a mall.

Yellow—When you are in public you should be at least in yellow mode. Walking down the Malecón in Guayaquil or Avenida Amazonas in Quito you should always be aware of what is going on around you. This may be include walking closer to the buildings, making yourself less of a target by holding your knapsack, briefcase, or purse on the side closest to the building. You might wish to shift your gaze from left to right and occasionally glance behind you. As of late 2000, Avenida Amazonas has become significantly more dangerous at night. A source indicated to me that it is actually off-limits to U.S. military personnel in the evening.

Orange—Walking along Avenida Amazonas you are in the yellow height of awareness when a small group of children run up to you and start holding their hands out to ask for money. This is a perfect time to shift into orange alert. While the children may be harmless you must prepare for trouble from any angle. It is here that you may have a plan in place such as making sure your briefcase or bag is closer to you. You could also look for a business establishment to enter. A woman once approached me as if she was going to ask me a question. It is very uncommon for a woman here to approach a strange man in public. I immediately went into an **orange** mode of alert and then to a **red** by shouting at the woman, delaying her approach and attracting the attention of passersby. I then dashed into a store. This allowed me to disarm a situation that was most probably a setup for theft.

Orange status should always be your modus operandi when entering or leaving banks or using ATM machines. I advise using ATM machines in major malls. Many criminals have become more sophisticated and are better dressed. One scam along Avenida Amazonas is that an attractive and well-dressed woman will drop something in front of you. When you bend over to help her, her accomplices will come up from behind and rob you.

Red—In this mode, your safety is at risk and you must react immediately. Your adrenaline is running at 100% and you must take control of the situation. While I have never found myself in a true state of **red** in Ecuador, I have had a number of situations where I was on the highest level of **orange** about to go to **red**. The first situation was walking at night along Avenida Amazonas. At night, this area becomes another world with numerous small groups of young people out looking for trouble. You should be on constant alert and probably not be in this area at all at night. The second situation was when I entered a very rough neighborhood filled with prostitutes in Guayaquil. My camera attracted so much attention that there were as many as 50 people following me thinking I was from a newspaper. Luckily, I had a good friend with me. I adopted a confident stride and a non-confrontational manner to those on the street and didn't stand in one place for any more than a few minutes.

Types of Crimes

Here is a small summary of some types of crimes that take place in Ecuador and some places to be cautious of.

Car theft is a very significant problem in Ecuador. It is highly organized with well-equipped gangs. Many gang members are armed and have false identification papers. They are very good at obtaining false papers for the cars that they have stolen.

Buses traveling through Ecuador are at a high risk of being assaulted. Bus companies take no responsibility for protecting their passengers from assault. This is actually stated on the back of most

181

tickets. The owner of a bus company mentioned that in July 2000 five of his buses were assaulted.

The most dangerous routes are in the northern part of the country, sharing a border with Colombia and certain sections of Guayas province. The route north from Guayaquil through Daule and on to Velasco Ibarra (El Empalme) is the most at risk. Also included in Guayas are the routes from Nobol to Pedro Carbo and south from Guayaquil to La Troncal and the alternate route between Boliche and Puerto Inca.

Many of the assaults are from passengers. You are not required to provide a photo I.D. when purchasing tickets. Often the aggressors purchase three to five tickets and will use an attractive female as a decoy. Guns and knives will be smuggled onto the bus underneath one's pants or inside a basket or a fruit such as a watermelon. The highest number of assaults in the Guayas province occur between 6:00 am and 9:00 am. This is true for buses in Guayaquil and for buses traveling between different cantons of Guayas. Some of the other dangerous routes in the country are the ones from Guayaquil to Riobamba and from Guayaquil via Durán to de Milagro, Jujan, and Tres Cerritos.

The border with Colombia is considered quite dangerous. Guerillas from Colombian groups such as FARC and the ELN have made significant inroads into northern Ecuador, especially in the Sucumbios province. The selling of exotic animals is illegal. It is also illegal to purchase or export the hides of various animals, i.e. turtles.

Crimes of violence are an increasing problem among young people in Ecuador. Gangs are called *pandillas*. In Guayaquil alone there are at least 300 gang members. Gangs in Guayaquil go by names such as Los KK de Perro, Los X-15, and La Muerte. They are often dressed in a similar fashion as gang members in the United States. Extra long pants that hang very low on the waist. All black or red are common gang colors. They are usually armed with knives and revolvers. A unique gun made locally is a tube which uses a 22-caliber ammunition. It is called a *rambo*.

The local newspaper, *El Universo,* reported in a special report in 2000 that 50% of gang members are from homes which suffer from domestic violence. Seventy percent are from lower-middle-class homes, 28% from middle-class homes, and 2% from upper-class families. Between January and June of 2000 there were 728 crimes committed by minors in the province of Pichincha, which includes Quito. This included 458 robberies along with 213 assaults. The province of Guayas, including Guayaquil, reported 700 crimes by juveniles with 266 robberies and 149 assaults. Guayaquil placed a plan, called More Security, into effect in August 2000 to address increasing crime rates.

There are times in Ecuador when civil rights are suspended so that security can be increased. During 1999 this happened as the banks failed and the economic crisis deepened. Fifteen agencies and groups were involved with the common objective of keeping an eye on crime and acting against it and corruption.

Ecuadorian Police

There are numerous police organizations in Ecuador. You will see many types of uniforms and colors. Here is a listing of some of the police units in Quito, their assigned duties, and the color of their uniforms.

• National Civil Police—They are charged with public safety and order. Their uniform includes olive-green trousers, olive shirt, olive jacket, and white helmets.

• Regimiento Quito Número 1—They are riot police with similar uniforms: olive-green trousers, shirt, and jacket.

• National Transit Directorte—In charge of traffic and signals. They wear blue pants and light blue shirts.

There are a number of other police units in Quito. Although officers are armed in Ecuador, there was an increase in police deaths in 2000.

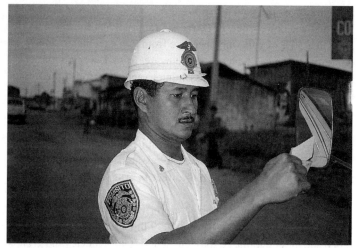

Ecuadorian policeman at a road block in rural Ecuador inspecting a driver's papers.

FINANCIAL MATTERS

September 13, 2000 was "D Day" in Ecuador and the United States invaded. That is, the U.S. dollar invaded. This date marked the official replacement of Ecuadorian sucres by the U.S. dollar as the official form of currency. Since then, the sucre is no longer used and has no official monetary value.

It was not until late 2000 that the new coins started circulating. U.S. coins, minted in the United States, are also in circulation and accepted. The new Ecuadorian 1-, 5-, 10-, 25-, and 50-cent coins resemble the U.S. currency but are not the same. They bear images of famous Ecuadorian rather than famous American figures. You can't take a new Ecuadorian coin and spend it in the United States but you can the Ecuadorian paper currency.

Be careful not to confuse the old 50-sucre coin with a U.S. 50-cent piece. Individuals may try to pass the old coin off as a new Ecuadorian 50-cent piece to an unsuspecting person. Fifty-cent pieces seem to be more common in Ecuador than they are in the United States.

Most vendors also examine bills for counterfeits. At first this may offend you but counterfeit money is a chronic problem in Ecuador. Employees are held responsible if they accept a counterfeit bill. Between October 1996 and September 1997 it was estimated that 34 million counterfeit U.S. bills were in circulation. Ones, fives, and tens are the most common counterfeit bills. One hundred dollar counterfeit bills are also present.

Government authorities believe that many of the illegal bills are produced in clandestine facilities in Colombia. There are several clues to spotting legitimate bills. First, feel the bill for a change in surface especially in the area where the person is on the bill and their clothing. You will feel a small rising on the surface. Second, on hundred dollar bills you will observe watermarks on the bill by holding it up to the light. Third, all 20-, 50-, and 100-dollar bills since 1996 have a security thread which can be seen by holding the bill up to the light. I carry with me a pen, which can be purchased in most stationery stores, which helps to detect if a bill is counterfeit.

Many people are still adjusting to the dollar conversion. If you visit markets in rural areas you will probably find more people offering you a price in sucres. The last official sucre rate for the U.S. dollar was 25,000 sucres to one U.S. dollar.

Having many smaller denominations is still recommended for paying for inexpensive items. Dollar notes in twenties, fifties, or hundreds could prove difficult when trying to negotiate for change. The smaller denominations you have the fewer hassles you will have. One of the most frustrating aspects of conducting transactions is the lack of change from many stores, individuals, and vendors. This had been a problem in Ecuador even with the sucre. It is not uncommon to purchase an item to find that the cashier does not have enough change, conveniently keeping the balance. It is a common phrase that "a man in Ecuador with hundred dollar bills is like a man with no money" referring to the change and counterfeit problem. Many individuals, and even banks, will not even accept hundred dollar bills because of the risk of counterfeiting.

Banks

Banks in the late 20th and early 21st centuries are seen by many as the culprits of Ecuador's financial woes. Numerous banks failed and many of the county's residents lost their money when the banks were unable to meet withdrawal demand. Banks are creeping back into operation and locals are beginning to use them, but only sparingly.

Many of the better-known banks have branches in the major malls. This may prove convenient in that they have weekend hours. Banks are generally open from 9 am to 1:30 pm on weekdays. In some cities, banks may be open on Saturdays, especially if it happens to be market day. Currency exchange bureaux (*casas de cambio*) are usually open from 9 am to 6 pm weekdays and until noon on Saturday. In Quito and Guayaquil, the international airport and major hotels have exchange facilities that stay open for longer.

Most banks have ATM machines. Most of them demonstrate the logos of banks, such as Cirrus or Star, that they have affiliations with. If you are using a card from an unaffiliated institution there may be an additional service charge. There is no notification of service charges at ATM machines, as is required in the United States. I have noticed I am often charged two dollars per transaction for withdrawing funds from my U.S. account. Wiring money from abroad to Ecuador sometimes involves a small fee paid in Ecuador and in the country from which the money was sent. (Western Union is the bank I use for this.) Ecuadorian ATMs accept foreign credit cards, such as Visa and MasterCard. (Only MasterCard is accepted in the Galápagos Islands, however.) This will be indicated by the logos on the ATMs. For foreign credit cards, you might have to pay high interest rates on cash withdrawals. To get around this, obtain a debit card in the form of a credit card from your bank. All the major towns have ATMs that accept Cirrus (MasterCard) or Plus (VISA) cards.

Most banks have a hundred-dollar withdrawal limit per day. You also can take out as little as one dollar at some institutions. It is not permitted to use your cellular phone while inside a bank. This is to deter bank robberies and crimes against patrons. I know of one scam several years ago when a bank employee, after helping a customer make a withdrawal, got on his cellular phone and called an accomplice outside who robbed the customer after leaving the bank.

When opening bank accounts, you will usually be required to provide your passport, identification, and letters of reference. People, generally, still do not trust banks with large amounts. Many in Ecuador practice a form of banking called *colchon bank,* which means hiding your money in your mattress.

I advise to place as little of your personal money in banks as possible, at the time this book was written. A number of the banks were not solvent and were experiencing problems. Another concern includes ATM machines that have been known to make duplicate withdrawals on an account. In 2001 a number of consumers had complained that there were double or ghost withdrawals from their accounts via ATMs. Customers had reported that they would make one withdrawal and then find the same amount debited twice from their accounts. It has also been reported that a customer would fail to withdraw money at an ATM but later find on their bank statement that their account had been debited for that amount. It is highly recommended that you keep all receipts for your ATM transactions and that you check your statements.

Edward Whymper, the great mountaineer, commented about the banks in Ecuador in his book *Travels Amongst the Great Andes of the Equator,* first published in 1892. He was referring to the problem he experienced with changing his money if it was not in perfect condition. He noticed on how the arithmetic the banks used "differed from that in common use when transacting business." Referring to how the banks would not accept the notes they issued after they became worn, he explains that this was a handsome way for the banks to earn money and that seemed to "be accepted by the people with perfect resignation...." He continues with great insight that this practice contributed heavily to "the universal mistrust of each other and of everybody that is exhibited throughout the country." How little things have changed since then.

CLOTHING

Ecuadorians judge others by their clothing and are class-conscious about the way they dress. For example, you will not find many upper-class Ecuadorians wearing Panama hats. Like people everywhere, Ecuadorians are also quite brand-conscious. Polo and Tommy Hilfiger are popular here.

A general rule is that people in Quito dress more conservatively then people from Guayaquil. This is in part due to climate. Quito is colder and requires heavier clothing. Dark colors are advised, such as blues and grays. Wool is often used. Many businessmen also wear suits in Guayaquil. There are a number of options available. Ralph Lauren, for example, has stores here.

The problem for the expatriate is if you have a large build. It is difficult to find trouser sizes of 38 or larger and shirt sizes of 17 and above. Ecuadorians have smaller physiques than many expatriates. This is also true with shoes. Finding a size 11 or 12 is difficult. As a solution, you may choose to make clothes and shoes locally. The tailors and shoemakers are good here, especially in Quito.

Shoes should always be well polished but this shouldn't pose a problem with the army of shoeshine boys vying for business through-out Ecuador. Women's sizes don't appear to be as difficult to find except for the very tall women with large-sized feet. In business, women, especially, should dress conservatively.

Shorts for both men and women in the highlands is not the norm. Shorts are more prevalent in Guayaquil but should be used with discretion. Shorts and next-to-nothing bikinis are the norm, however, at the beaches. Men should avoid T-shirts but wear polo shirts or long-sleeved sport shirts instead. Fanny packs should also not be worn as they make you stand out as a tourist and an easy target for thieves.

Traditional dry cleaners abound in the larger cities and prices are largely comparable with the United States. **One Hour Martinizing** is one of the more popular establishments in most major cities.

COMMUNICATIONS

Ecuador possesses most of the communication facilities available in most developed countries but reliability seems to be an issue, especially when it comes to telephones.

Telephones

Obtaining a telephone is a very expensive and onerous task. Remember, when renting or buying, to make sure the phone is included in the purchase or rental. **Andinatel** (mainly in the highlands and Oriente) and **Pacifictel** (mainly in the coastal lowlands) are the main telephone service providers in Ecuador.

Cellular or mobile phones have invaded the country and people of all classes use them. Private companies in Ecuador provide mobile telecommunication services such as cellular telephones, paging and message services, conventional radio communications, trunking services, teleport, and satellite communications. Today, Ecuador has two main cellular service providers, **Bell South** and **Porta**. The telecommunications sector is still underdeveloped and has a huge potential to grow. As a result, prices have dropped substantially since the early 1990s. Cellular phones are a status symbol in Ecuador. Both **Bell South** and **Porta** have prepaid cards which are available in grocery stores, pharmacies, and small markets. Some hotels also rent out cell phones to tourists.

Phone cards are available in several denominations and usually start at three dollars. When purchasing a card you need to let the clerk know if you want a card for your cellular phone or a phone booth (which is called *cabina*). The cards for **Bell South** can only be used in their booths and the same for **Porta**. **Porta** and **Bell South** booths don't accept coins. These cards are especially good if you are traveling within Ecuador and need to make local or international calls. (**AT&T**, **MCI**, and **Sprint** provide international calling services from the U.S. via satellite links.) *Cabinas* are available throughout much of the country and the reception is very good.

Another favorite option for local calls is using private phones for a small fee, which are available in many commercial centers. Some can even arrange for you to make international calls. You will see many such phones available on the sidewalk with a person attending the phone. Simply dial the local number. Some phones are blocked from calling cellular numbers. The drawback of these phones are a lack of privacy and the inability to hear if you're in a noisy area.

Calling Codes

The country code for Ecuador when calling from abroad is 593. Local numbers have six digits and area codes have two digits. If you're in Ecuador and calling a cellular phone locally you will dial 09 and then the number. There is a charge both from the dialing phone and the receiving cell phone. Many local phones are blocked from calling cellular numbers. Be aware that hotels charge anything from 20 to 50 cents a minute for local calls.

Use the following area codes only when calling from outside these provinces:

Azuay (incl. Cuenca)	07
Bolívar	03
Cañar	07
Carchi	06
Chimborazo (incl. Riobamba)	03
Cotopaxi	03
El Oro	07
Esmeraldas	06
Galápagos	05
Guayas (incl. Guayaquil)	04
Imbabura	06
Loja	07
Los Ríos (incl. Babahoyo and Quevedo)	05
Manabí (incl. Manta and Portoviejo)	05
Morona-Santiago (except Palora 03)	07
Napo	06
Orellana	06
Pastaza (incl. Puyo)	03
Pichincha (incl. Quito)	02
Sucumbíos	06

| Tungurahua (incl. Ambato) | 03 |
| Zamora-Chinchipe | 07 |

Because of the saturation of telephones, both land lines and wireless, the phone numbers in Ecuador have recently changed. At the time of publishing this book in October 2001, these changes only affect the provinces of Pichincha and Guayas. Other provinces will be changed soon, however. Numbers will now have seven digits instead of six. Cellular phones nationwide will also have seven digits. The emergency and service numbers 911 (police), 101 (police), 102 (fire departments in Quito, Guayaquil, and Cuenca), 105 (national operator), 116 (international operator), and 104 (information) will not be affected. For the time being if a caller uses the old system, an operator will come on and inform them of the error at no cost.

For calls within Pichincha or Guayas, place a 2 in front of the six-digit number:

Pichincha: **2** 567 007
Guayas: **2** 567 007

To call cell phone numbers in a local area, place a 9 before the six digit number.

Before: (09) 201 740
Now: (09) **9** 201 740

To call a land line in provinces outside Pichincha and Guayas you now place a 2 in front of the six-digit number:

Other provinces to Pichincha:
Before: (02) 566 566
Now: (02) **2** 566 566

Other provinces to Guayas:
Before: (04) 566 566
Now: (04) **2** 566 566

Other provinces to any cell phone:
Before: (09) 566 566
Now: (09) **9** 566 566

From international destinations please drop the zeros:

Pichincha (Quito)
Before: 593 (2) 566 566
Now: 593 (2) **2** 566 566

Guayas (Guayaquil)
Before 593 (4) 566
Now 593 (4) **2** 566 566

Calling a cell phone from an international location:
Before: 593 (9) 566 566
Now: 593 (9) **9** 566 566

All the major carriers in the U.S. provide their own phone card service to call the U.S. or other countries. If you are using **Andinatel**, dial: 999 119 (**AT&T**); 999 171 (**Sprint**); 999 170 (**MCI WorldCom**). Dial 1 800 999 170 if you're using **Pacifictel** lines. It is not possible to use a card from these companies from public phones.

TELEVISION SERVICES

There are two major companies that provide cable and satellite TV services—Direct TV and TV Cable. Direct TV is a franchise of Galaxie, an American satellite company, while TV Cable is an Ecuadorian company that provides cable TV services and is part of a consortium of companies that includes **Satnet** and **Americatel**.

Direct TV is available in most of the country. They can be reached at 1 800 888 999 in Ecuador. There is an installation fee and a monthly charge depending on what program is ordered.

Cable TV is widely used throughout Ecuador. The major supplier is **TV Cable** (http://www3.tvcable.com.ec). Contact numbers: Guayaquil tel 884 114, 884 744. Quito tel 413 500, 413 501.

MAIL

The national mail service is a continual problem in Ecuador. Many companies use private mail courier services for mail between their Ecuador office and corporate offices back home. **DHL**, **UPS**, and **Federal Express** are quite commonly used but not cheap. A normal letter costs about US$21 for a two-day delivery to the United States with these services.

There is no regular door-to-door mail delivery. Obtaining a post-office box (*casilla*) is necessary if you're planning on receiving mail from outside the country. If you go to the post office there probably will be none available. It usually takes special connections with the post office staff to secure a post-office box. (See the Social and Business Etiquette chapter for my story on opening a *casilla*.)

INTERNET

The Internet has taken Ecuador by storm and is becoming more popular everyday. There are literally hundreds of Internet cafés throughout the country, especially in Quito. In March 2000 it was not uncommon to be charged about $5 per hour of use. In November 2000 most Internet cafés appeared to be charging about $1 per hour. Most of these cafés permit smoking, which can be annoying for non-smokers. Also, bandwidth is in shortage in Ecuador and most comput-ers run much slower than what you may accustomed to in the United States. Most Internet cafés have Net-to-phone available and will usually be charged about 25 cents a minute for calls to the United

States. Be prepared, however, that almost everyone in the café will be able to hear you.

PASSPORTS AND VISAS

You will need a passport which does not expire within six months of your stay. Bring this everywhere with you as you might be asked to produce it, your visa or tourist card.

If you are from the United States and visiting Ecuador for fewer than 90 days, you don't need a visa. If you are a tourist and a national of any of the following countries you do need a visa: Algeria, Bangladesh, Costa Rica, Cuba, El Salvador, Guatemala, India, Indonesia, Iran, Iraq, Jordan, Lebanon, Libya, Nicaragua, Nigeria, North Korea, Pakistan, Palestine Authority, Panama, People's Republic of China, Sri Lanka, Syria, Tunisia, and Vietnam. These regulations are subject to change and you should obtain the most current information from your local Ecuadorian embassy or consulate.

If you are a foreign national planning to stay in Ecuador for more than 90 days, you will need to apply for a visa and must present the following documents. When applying for this type of visa in the United States you must also present a valid U.S. visa/green card:

• Valid passport for more than 6 months
• Police certificate with criminal record, if applicable, from the state where you reside
• Medical certificate
• Return ticket (for air, land or sea travel)
• Two photographs
• Application form
• Proof of economic means to support yourself while staying in Ecuador. (In more than 20 years of travel here, I have never been asked this question but it's good to be prepared.)

When dealing with the embassy or consulate staff, always remember to be very polite whether in person or via the telephone. Always ask for the name of the person you're speaking with as this may help in future correspondence. If sending documents to the consulate, remember to include a return envelope with paid postage. I also strongly recommended that you send your documents or return envelope as registered mail.

The airplane crew will distribute Visa 12-X forms before arrival. It is short and straightforward and is both in English and Spanish. When you arrive, present it and your passport to immigration. Many of the officials don't speak English. They will ask you how long you plan on staying in Ecuador and what address you will be staying at. I usually request a week or two more then I anticipate staying, in the event that my plans change. If I don't know exactly where I will be staying, I will usually name a well-known hotel.

The most important thing about this tourist visa is not to loose it. I staple it or secure it into my passport. It is very small and can be overlooked until you try to leave and can't find it. If you misplace it, you will be required to go back to the airline check-in area and request a new one from the airline. It is up to the discretion of the immigration officer to let you go without the tourist visa form. It is also important to remember that you cannot change your tourist status in Ecuador nor take up employment. A number of years ago I had applied for a visa to reside in Ecuador. While under the tourist visa I was informed that I would have to return to Miami to pick up my resident visa. The official stated that he could send a fax stating that I was ill and could not return to Miami at the moment and the resident visa could be secured. Off the record, I do not think that this is not something a bribe or "cola" could not get you. (See the Social and Business Etiquette chapter for a story on "colas.")

Other than the tourist visa there are other non-immigrant-type visas. Student visas are a type 12-V and required by all educational institutions in Ecuador. You will also be required to demonstrate financial worthiness to cover your expenses while in Ecuador. It is usually sufficient to provide a letter from your bank or a letter from a relative guaranteeing that your expenses will be taken care of.

If you're required to work in Ecuador or are a government representative, your employer or government agency must also show that you will be financially supported. Also mandated is a labor contract, legalized by an Ecuadorian labor court. Highly technical or specialized employees will need to obtain a work permit from the Ministry of Labor. Managers, officers of a company, or a legal representative will need to obtain a certificate from the Superintendency of Companies. The duration of this visa will be set according to your personal requirements.

Religious visas have several unique requirements. The religious organization where the visa applicant is to work must supply a letter explaining why he/she is needed and what he/she will be doing. The organization must also provide a letter from the government of Ecuador permitting the organization to operate in Ecuador. Also required is a copy of the organization's rules and a statement identifying the legal representative of the organization in Ecuador. This visa is usually valid for only two years.

Cultural exchange visas are for teachers or students involved in exchange programs here. An application from the Ecuadorian authority that is sponsoring the visitor is required. This application must include a statement that the visitor will not receive any Ecuadorian funds for the work done.

If you are going to Ecuador for tourism or business, you can receive a visa for more than 90 days and up to 180 days. The main requirement here is that your consulate is to receive a document verifying that you have sufficient funds. This may include a statement or letter from your bank.

If you are planning on immigrating to Ecuador there are six types of immigrant visas. They are:

• Annuitant (10-I) is an immigrant who will live on income from abroad. Usually this is a person who is retired and can demonstrate an income of at least US$8,000 a year.

• Real Estate (10-II) is an immigrant who will invest capital in purchasing real estate or securities. In most cases the amount must be equivalent to 350 minimum Ecuadorian monthly salaries. Plus 100 minimum salaries per dependent which may be specified by the consular officer in the United States. It is usually a minimum of $15,000.

• Industrial (10-III) immigrant will invest capital in agriculture, export trade, industry, or livestock. The sum of capital must be equivalent to 600 minimum monthly Ecuadorian salaries or what the consulate office in the United States specifies. Normal minimum amount is $25,000.

• Administrative or technical immigrant is considered a general agent status (10-IV) and is usually someone who has been requested to work for an Ecuadorian company. This also applies to foreign local agents of companies who possess unlimited power of attorney to represent the company in Ecuador, provided that 80% of the company's local personnel is Ecuadorian.

• A professional immigrant (10-V) is designated for those with university degrees who desire to practice their profession in Ecuador. Should the applicant's profession not exist in Ecuador, the degree must be locally certified. The applicant must also fulfill the requirements for such practice, e.g. the bar for lawyers.

• A dependent immigrant (10-VI) is a spouse or blood relative who will receive their support from another person.

If you have been granted a visa it is necessary to present your documents to the General Directorate of Alien Affairs to register. This is normally done within 30 days of registration. Remember that you are only allowed to stay as long as your visa states. It is possible to change the status of a visa by applying no later then 30 days before it expires.

If you have emigrated to Ecuador, you must renew your census card annually in the immigration office. As an immigrant you are required, when leaving the country, to obtain a departure permit from the immigration office. You must present your passport with the visa, your Ecuadorian identification card, payment of a departure tax, and military permit (for men aged 18–55). This departure permit is valid for a year. Minors under the age of 18 and going to live with one parent are also required to have an authorization from the juvenile court. The exit permit can sometimes be obtained from the travel agent you purchased your airline ticket from. Some travel agents will also handle a minor's permit, if he/she is traveling with only one parent. In the event of a divorce, both parents may need to present themselves to the juvenile court for authorization. There is usually an additional fee for this service.

TRANSPORTATION

Getting to or around in Ecuador is fairly straightforward except during festival and holiday periods.

Air Travel

From the United States, the major carriers to Ecuador are American Airlines and Continental from Houston, Miami, and Newark. Most flights arrive late at night. Other carriers from the United States are Avianca and Copa from Los Angeles. KLM and Iberia have flights to and from Europe. The main domestic carrier is TAME (an airline run by the Ecuadorian Armed Forces). Prices are comparable, so choose the one whose schedule best matches your own.

Airports are quite dated and lack sufficient facilities. There are airports in Quito, Guayaquil, Machala, Manta, Loja, Cuenca, Macas, Pastaza, Portoviejo, Esmeraldas, Tulcán, Lago Agrio, and Coca. The airports in Quito and Guayaquil are circa early 1960s. Passengers are required to walk to their plane on the tarmac or a bus will transport them to the ramp to enter the plane. Disabled passengers are always given special consideration and are usually assisted by airline personnel.

Internal flights are comparatively cheap and there is a two-tier pricing system on some flights, foreigners paying more than Ecuadorians. A foreigner would pay about US$53 for a one-way flight to or from Quito and an Oriente town (e.g. Macas, Lago Agrio, and Coca). Locals would be charged about half that amount. A roundtrip from Guayaquil/Quito to the Galápagos Islands would cost between US$330–80 for foreigners, depending on the season. This is double the rate for Ecuadorians and four times that for islanders. Flights between Guayaquil and Quito cost around US$50 one-way if bought in Ecuador. Getting to Manta and Esmeraldas in the Costa takes approximately 20 minutes and to Lago Agrio in El Oriente approximately 30 minutes from Quito.

If you're going to visit Ecuadorian cities, it is best to purchase your tickets while in Ecuador. There is no reserved seating for the flights between Quito and Guayaquil. Flights run on the hour between about 6:30 in the morning until early in the evening. The flight time is about 30 minutes.

You can reserve seats for the other destinations in Ecuador. It is advisable to purchase your ticket direct from the TAME counter or their local offices. It has been my experience that tickets sold by travel agents are sometimes not confirmed. This airline offers discounts to the Galápagos Islands for Ecuadorian citizens and residents. You must provide documentation in order to purchase a discounted ticket.

Coming from abroad, after the plane lands, you will enter the terminal and get in line for the immigration. In the last two years this process has been computerized and your passport will be imprinted via an electronic printer. You will then dash to the baggage area and pray that your luggage has arrived. (Airports here are known to have problems with the theft of luggage.) If you require a baggage cart they are at a dollar. There is a clerk who will take the dollar and give you a small receipt.

When you exit the airport there will usually be a swarm of people trying to assist you with your bags. It is a good idea to try to have someone meet you at the airport to help negotiate the crowds. This is especially true in Guayaquil. There have been cases where gangs will await visitors, watch you leave the airport, and rob you a short time later.

If you have an international flight I think it's best to be there at least three hours in advance. There have been efforts in the last year, however, to improve the check-in process at the airport. Both in Guayaquil and Quito, only passengers are allowed to enter the ticketing areas. This has helped smoothen the check-in procedure. Bags are no longer x-rayed in the counter area. A contract employee views them in a separate area. If he sees something that looks fishy, Interpol is called in. An agent of the airline then will go into the boarding lounge and ask you to go with him to the luggage loading area. They have drug-sniffing dogs. If you don't know what is happening it can be pretty scary. The agent or Interpol officer may ask you a few questions and have you open up the luggage. Your carry-on bags are checked twice before boarding: when you pass through immigration and as you enter the boarding lounge. Before boarding or walking to your plane on the tarmac, passengers may sometimes be asked to line up with their hand-held bags on the ground in front of them as police make one final sweep with their dogs.

One last piece of advice. If you have an onward ticket when arriving in Ecuador, you should confirm your seat on the flight with the airline at least 72 hours in advance. I have always had trouble getting through the telephone numbers provided. Therefore, I visit the airline's office at least half a day or several hours in advance to reconfirm my seat. Going in person means that the staff are forced to look at your ticket and verify that you have a seat and you can actually see the clerks keying this information into the computer. That makes me feel more confident that there will be a seat waiting for me.

Airport Tidbits
• If you're landing in Quito on an international flight, be prepared for

a hard landing. A pilot told me that they have been instructed, when making their approach, to get the plane down fast because of the short runway and the high altitude.

• If you have forgotten to purchase gifts, both Quito and Guayaquil airports have a number of nice stores once you have passed Customs.

• The airport in Guayaquil will almost always smell of insecticide due to spraying for mosquitoes.

• Both Quito and Guayaquil have planned to have new airports for years. The airport in Quito is considered somewhat dangerous, being blocked in by suburbs.

• Some veteran travelers will often not get up right away when arriving in Quito to adjust to the high altitude. It can take your breath away when walking to the terminal from the plane.

• Try to get through immigration as soon as possible to get your baggage in an attempt to prevent losing your luggage to thieves.

Driving

Ecuadorians are generally not considered good drivers. You should always be at least on **orange** alert. The less you drive in Ecuador, the better. Traffic accidents are among the top killers in Ecuador every year.

Ecuadorians, for the most part, don't heed traffic rules or courtesies. In 2000 the government made it a law for drivers to wear seat belts. The police strictly enforced this law, especially with taxicab drivers. However, most backseats in cabs still lack seat belts.

You will notice a lack of road signs or markings, especially with curves in the various highways. Drivers seldom heed blind curves. Assume that drivers will pass you no matter what and that drivers from the opposite direction also overtake on blind curves. Stop signs and stoplights are not followed, especially at night. This is partly in an attempt to avoid robberies.

There was an accident in March 2000 when a utility vehicle was speeding over the bridge that connects Guayaquil and Duran. The vehicle crashed over the wall of the bridge and landed in the Guayas River. Investigators surmised that the driver was speeding to avoid thieves as the vehicle was carrying some supplies for a company outside of Guayaquil.

Many of the streets in Quito and Guayaquil are one-way. Several years ago one of my sons, with limited Spanish skills, asked me why all the streets in Guayaquil had the same name. He was referring to the signs and markings on the walls of the street indicating one-way traffic—*una via*.

Here are some basic guidelines when driving in Ecuador:

• Few roads have shoulders or safety lanes.

• Many towns that have a highway going through it will have speed bumps. These are often very high and can cause severe vehicle damage if taken at high speed. Be sure to slow down when entering towns or small villages.

• Drive only in the daytime. You will increase substantially your risk of injury or death by driving or busing at night. More crimes take place at night and many drivers drive without lights. This is supposedly to prevent the battery from wearing down.

• When driving in the country be sure never to leave your vehicle.

• Depending on which neighborhood you live in, you may spot a section of a residential block where numerous cars are parked at night. In many middle- and lower-class neighborhoods, car-owners will park their car with others and pay someone to guard their vehicles.

• When driving, be sure not to have your arms or hands hanging outside the windows or to have the windows wound all the way down. Thieves can steal watches and rings this way.

• Make sure doors are locked and that purses or briefcases are laid down on the floor, hidden from the view of thieves who may attack while you are at a traffic stop.

• Few Ecuadorians use turn signals.

• Ecuadorians are loud drivers. They honk at almost anything.

• If taking a day trip or longer, make sure your vehicle is properly equipped with safety equipment and supplies. Also, make sure you take toilet paper with you, as you will find gas stations sadly lacking in this. Public bathrooms are not usually well-maintained.

• Parking lots are hard to find in both Guayaquil and Quito. You might notice that in front of many establishments there will be someone who appears to be guarding cars. He may wave you into a space. You can ask him to watch your car and pay a small tip for his services upon your departure. There are also those who wave cars in and want the fee up-front. Be careful of them as they have been known to wave you into a no parking zone and by the time you return, your car might have been towed away.

• There are tollbooths on the outskirts of Quito. If you're driving a car, enter the lane with the sign that says *Livianos*.

• I advise you to drive 5–10 miles below the speed limit, especially when on highways. The roads are not well kept as maintenance is erratic so there are many potholes, especially during the rainy season. There are also numerous animals crossing highways.

• Many highways have a gutter running along the road for water runoff. Be alert to these as it is very easy to get stuck in one, causing severe vehicle damage.

• There are few, if any, safety lanes and having to stop along a road for an emergency is very dangerous. If you don't have flares, place debris or tree limbs several yards behind your vehicle to alert drivers of a stranded vehicle.

Fuel

Gas is sold in gallons and is sold at gas stations. **Texaco** is a popular brand. Many gas stations were constructed in the late 1990s. Gas is much cheaper here than in the United States, as a result of subsidization by the government. In November 2000 **Gasoline Super** was $1.04 a gallon, **Extra** 69 cents, and **Diesel** 52 cents.

The attendant will always pump the gas. **Extra** is equivalent to regular leaded. **Super** is the highest octane available and is also leaded. Diesel is widely available and the cheapest fuel available. You will see credit card emblems displayed, if they are accepted. But not all stations accept credit cards, especially if the credit cards are not local.

Automobile Club de Ecuador

If you're going to be in Ecuador long term it may be advisable to join an organization such as Automóvil Club del Ecuador (ANETA). ANETA is similar to **Triple A** in the United States and offers a variety of services such as towing in all parts of Ecuador. It claims to be available 24 hours a day and 365 days a year. ANETA has an office located in Quito at Avenida Eloy Alfaro 218 y Berlín, tel 02 504 961/ 229 020, http://www.aneta.org.ec.

Accidents

Accidents can be a very traumatic experience in Ecuador. To add to an already stressful situation, the rules in Ecuador are prohibitive.

Pedestrians are at the mercy of drivers. You must be on your guard as a pedestrian. Vehicles will seldom stop for you, even if you have the right of way. However, once a pedestrian is hit, you suddenly have all the rights in the world. It becomes the immediate assumption of the authorities that the driver is at fault. The driver is obliged to obtain and pay for the victim's medical attention. Expect to go to jail for a while if you hit and kill a pedestrian or a passenger in your car. Your vehicle will also be moved to the transit division.

In the United States, more often than not, people will react unemotionally when involved in an accident, as the less said the better legally. However, if you hurt someone or run them over in Ecuador, it is important to show your concern and compunction for the injured party/parties. Not doing so might result in more strident claims from the victim or their family.

In all automobile accidents, you should contact the authorities immediately. Be sure not to move your vehicle until they arrive. A police report is mandatory if you expect your insurance company to make any payment. Make sure that you obtain names, addresses, and license plate numbers of all vehicles involved. Also request for the names of their insurance companies.

However, many Ecuadorians don't have insurance and it can get difficult to get insurance companies to pay. Be careful not to take blame for the accident unless interrogated by a police officer. Don't sign any documents unless they are from your insurance provider. Go over the police report and verify the facts. You will also want to get the policeman's name and identification number and make sure he obtains all the names of the witnesses.

Many people do a hit-and-run in Ecuador to avoid being jailed or the financial responsibility. I have heard of a situation several years ago when a drunk walked in front of a U.S. citizen's car. Before he knew it, several people had surrounded him and someone even drew out a gun. The streetwise U.S. citizen got the drunk to the hospital, took care of the bills, and contacted an attorney. No police report was made. He then left the country and worked through his attorneys until the drunk was compensated adequately.

Another possible scenario in Ecuador is the development of a mob mentality when a car hits a pedestrian. The angry crowd may actually set the car on fire. I have witnessed a crowd chasing a vehicle to set it on fire after it hit someone. Driving in Ecuador is serious business, so beware!

If you're a tourist in Ecuador you are permitted to use the driver's license from your own country. An international driver's license may also be used. If you're going to stay long-term in Ecuador, you will need to obtain an Ecuadorian license. In Quito this may be secured at the transit authority at José Herboso Calle y Avenida Occidental. The required paperwork includes blood type, two passport-sized photographs, passport, eye exam (taken at the transit authority listed above), and your driver's license. You are originally granted a 30-day permit, which is extended for a total of 90 days before your permanent license is issued. If you don't have a license you will need to take a course which is available from the ANETA.

Cabs

Cabs are an integral part of Ecuadorian transportation for the masses. During 1999 taxicab drivers were among the hardest hit by the severe recession. With the change in dollar exchange, few drivers were able to maintain their vehicles, let alone support a family. This caused a very severe situation when there were massive strikes in Ecuador in 1999 by all transport workers.

Meters are used during daylight hours by many of the taxicabs in Quito. Rates are reasonable, thanks to the government's gas subsidy. In Quito, however, drivers don't use meters at night and during holiday periods and I have never seen meters used in Guayaquil. It is always advisable to negotiate the price before using a cab.

If you're on a strict budget and you don't have a lot of luggage, you might try walking across the street from the airport in Quito to take a cab. It's a very short distance and you're likely to get a better price. The rate from the airport to most parts of Quito or Guayaquil should be in the $5–$10 range.

In Quito if you have a question about rates you might ask for the list of tariffs, which all drivers belonging to taxicab organizations should have. I once had a driver tried to charge me four times the going rate for an excursion in Quito. When I told him that the tariff list stated that the going rate was three dollars an hour, he immediately asked me what I wanted to pay. I ended up paying $10–$15 for several hours of sightseeing.

For the most part, cab drivers are reliable and honest when it comes to charging. It is important to get into a marked cab, usually yellow or yellow and black. If the driver doesn't seem to understand where it is you want to go, I would be hesitant to take the cab, especially if your Spanish is not very fluent. It is unusual for a cab driver not to know a location. The exception to this would be in Quito, where the city tried to change the address system being used and most drivers still use the old system.

One rule when it comes to using a cab is to never slam the door. Even if you think you're not slamming the door, you might be by Ecuadorian standards. Please refer to the Resource Guide for more information.

Buses

When I first moved to Ecuador in the early 1980s, buses for travel throughout the country and within the cities was a substantial part of the transportation system. This is still the case in the early 21st century. However, being older and a bit wiser, I avoid them when possible nowadays, although they can be a wonderful way to see Ecuador. This is because bus travel in Ecuador can be very dangerous, especially at night. Buses can get extremely crowded during holidays and the security risk on highways multiplies. (Please refer to other bus safety information in the Safety section of this chapter).

Buses have become increasingly popular with middle- to lower-middle-class Ecuadorians as air travel is not the bargain it once was. There is virtually no city or hamlet that is not connected by bus and fares are relatively inexpensive. There are different levels of service from chicken-carrying buses to ultramodern sleek buses with movies and hostesses on board. Buses come in two types: city buses that offer transport within a city area and inter-provincial buses which offer services to various destinations within a province or another province.

Most cities have a least one bus hub for inter-provincial destinations, usually referred to as *terminal terrestre*. Quito and Guayaquil have large terminals where you can catch a bus to virtually any destination in Ecuador. The Quito terminal is located near the Old Town at Cumandá Square (tel 593-2-2570-529). I have called that number on several occasions and there is usually someone on duty that can give you information about bus arrivals and departures. One of the better-known bus lines is **Panamericana** which serves long-distance routes especially to Guayaquil. (As of October 1, 2001 a one way ticket to Guayaquil from Quito was $9.) **Panamericana** has locations at the main *terminal terestre* and another one about 15 minutes away at Colón 852 y Reina Victoria. This facility may be considered a little safer than the *terminal terrestre*. Their telephone number is: 593-2-2570425. They use large comfortable buses which they call *ejecutivos*.

There are also a number of buses available for intra-provincial travel in Pichincha at the Plaza La Marin which is located near Pichincha and Chile. In Guayaquil the main bus station is located just outside the airport (cab is recommended to reach this). It is a huge facility that reminded me at first of a sports complex. It is also reminiscent of large bus stations in the United States from the 1950s or even an airport. There are literally hundreds and sometimes thousands of people at the facility in Guayaquil. There are all types of stores and buses depart from the second level. When using buses I will usually go to the terminal a day or two in advance and look at all of the different companies and check prices and availability. It is usually wise to purchase your ticket for such a trip at least a day before. If you're in a small town the bus hubs are not difficult to find and seldom have any offices. You simply look for a bus which has the names of the towns and cities on its route painted on its side.

A number of companies advertise bus services to international destinations such as Colombia and Peru. I think it wiser to take a bus to the border, then to cross the border at immigration, then to purchase an onward ticket to either Colombia or Peru.

Quito and Guayaquil have substantial intra-city routes which are usually called *collectivos*. In my early days in Ecuador I used them but have found them dangerous. Cabs are usually a better bet if you don't have your own vehicle.

Electric Trolley

In Quito another form of transportation is the electric trolley, known also as *el trole*. This is an amazing piece of transportation specially designed for the inhabitants of Quito. You will have to try it for yourself to find out why!

It runs north to south of Quito and has two main terminals. In 2000 the charge was 15 cents. Millions of passengers have used the electric trolley and there are facilities for handicapped riders. While it is a viable transportation mode, there are problems with theft as with any public mode of transportation. Many people use the trolley to connect to buses that run to destinations beyond its reach, further north or south.

Trains

Trains, for the most part, are now non-existent in Ecuador, a stark contrast to the early 1980s. It is a real shame that there is no more need for railways now that highways have basically connected the entire country.

I was very lucky in 1981 to get to ride the train from Guayaquil to Riobamba, which is one of the most beautiful yet hair-raising train rides in the world. However, there is now no more need for this line and the authorities have not maintained it, which could have been a tremendous tourist attraction. Two years ago it was still operating on a limited schedule. I made my early morning jaunt over to Duran after the manager of the station promised me the train would be running. However, when I arrived at 6:00 am he said he was sorry but there was no fuel. When the El Niño rains hit, that pretty much put the lines in disrepair.

There is a limited service train on weekends that leaves in the morning from Quito to Cotopaxi, which is a very fun trip. Another line that I missed before it closed two years ago was the line from Ibarra to San Lorenzo. This was another hair-raiser from over 8,000 feet in the Andes to the small town of San Lorenzo on the Pacific coast. The line shut down when a new highway was constructed. Previously San Lorenzo was accessible either via the train or by sea. Some tourist companies claim to have tours from Quito to Riobamba on that train. However, the service is so irregular that it would be best to inquire at some of the larger agencies, such as **Metropolitan Tours**, about its service times before making any plans.

It is a shame that Ecuador has not maintained its train lines, unique engineering marvels that they are. If you are a railroad buff, it is worth while visiting the old station in Duran (Guayaquil) where you will see nearly a hundred old cars, dating as far back as the 1930s, rusting away. This is also a great opportunity for photographers.

BUDGET GUIDELINES

Ecuador is often listed as one of the least expensive places in the world. However, with the economic collapse of the late 1990s inflation was nearly 100% in the year 2000. Therefore, it is important that you have a real sense of what is needed to live in Ecuador and the costs involved. **Academia Cotopaxi** in Quito provides a cost of living survey at their website (http://www.Cotopaxi.k12.ec) for prospective teachers to plan their budgeting in Ecuador.

I have made some estimates of my own, and after numerous interviews, to help you work out your costs. The following prices are on a per month basis.

Singles

Rent	$200–$400
Groceries	$75–$300
Electricity	$10–$30
Telephone	$10–$50

(Includes cell phone and a few long distance calls. I advise using the dialpad at internet cafés for non-confidential calls.)

Transportation	$100–$150

Dining Out	$50–$175
Entertainment	$50–$150
Maid	$40–$50
Cable	$30–$40
Internet	$30–$45

Family with Two Children

Rent	$400–$650
Rent deposit	$300–$1250
Groceries	$375–$500
Electricity	$20–$45
Telephone	$10–$50
Transportation	$25–$130
Dining Out	$70–$175
Entertainment	$50–$175
Maid	$50–$125
(May include a nanny and a garderner)	
Cable	$30–$40
Internet	$30–$45
Private school (per year per child)	$3500–$5500
Refrigerator	$250–$700
Stove	$200–$600
Basic furniture	$1000–$3500
Washer and dryer	$1000–$2200
Automobile (used)	$5000–$10000
Automobile (new)	$15000–$40000

LEGAL ISSUES

As with any place in the world, there are legal issues to deal with. In Ecuador's paternalistic and bureaucratic society, this is especially so. There are just so many forms to be filled in, and when you think you have done them all, you find that you've missing one that some clerk hadn't even noticed before.

One thing is clear, drugs are illegal in Ecuador and the legal system is lethargic and slow. You are assumed guilty and must prove your innocence. I visited a women's prison in Quito several years ago. There were approximately seven women from the United States in custody awaiting deportation. Some of them had been there for several years and were all there thanks to drugs. Several indicated that some man they fell in love with used them and planted the drugs on them. I have received reports that drug use is on the rise, especially amongst the young. Don't feel secure about drug use just because you are around friends from Ecuador who are using illegal drugs. Your embassy has very limited means to help you in this case.

If you spend any time in Ecuador you may find yourself in need of a notary. This is a very high-level position in Ecuador. Basically, any legal document filed or signed in Ecuador involves a notary. There are very few in Ecuador and usually only law firms use their services.

Chapter Ten

SOME SERIOUS MEDICAL STUFF

"After the arrival of the Spaniards, the scanty coastal population along the coast was decimated by the spread of diseases, such as malaria, yaws, intestinal ills, tuberculosis, smallpox, and measles."—John Leddy Phelan, author of *The Kingdom of Quito* (1967).

Ecuador is generally safe but it is wise to be on your guard against any potential health risks you might face. A number of medical issues have increased here, largely due to disorganization in the public sector and lack of funds to fight off certain diseases. For example, in the late

1990s, malaria became a severe threat due to decreased spraying because of financial constraints on local governments. Poor sanitation and food handling has also contributed to significant health risks in the country. Nearly all children in Ecuador, for example, carry worms of parasites in their bodies.

CHAGAS' DISEASE

Chagas' disease is named after the Brazilian physician Dr Carlos Chagas who first described it in 1909. It has also been called a poor man's disease. This is because the bloodsucking bugs (part of the assassin bug family) which carry the disease (the flagellate protozoan *Trypanosoma cruzi*) make their homes in the crevices of walls and roofs of poor houses. The victim is infected through the feces of the bug, which defecates into the wound whilst sucking the victim's blood. This disease can also be transmitted through infected blood transfusions.

This bug (*Triatoma megista*) is called *chinchorro* in Ecuador. It is oval in shape, brown, and is about two centimeters long. It was first found in Ecuador in 1923. It usually attacks the face at night while the victim is sleeping and feeds for about 20 minutes. Many victims will rub the wound, which pushes the parasite's feces into the blood system. The feces may also enter via the mucous areas of the mouth and nostrils.

Children usually manifest the most obvious symptoms, developing fever, inflammation around the bite, swelling of the lymph glands, or an enlarged liver and spleen. With children, it can result in rapid death.

In two-thirds of cases, there are no symptoms, and the victim appears healthy. For the unlucky rest, if an acute infection occurs, the patient may develop heart disease 10 to 30 years later. This, sadly, usually leads to death. There is currently no effective treatment available. A serological test is required to determine infection.

Dr Angel Gustavo Guevara, a leading authority on Chagas'

215

disease in Ecuador, usually takes three tests before giving a diagnosis. While there is no known cure, he will treat it with antiparasitic drugs such as Benznidazole. The provinces most affected are El Oro, Guayas, Manabí, Morona–Santiago, Loja, Orellana, Zamora–Chinchipe, and Sucumbios.

Poor housing and a lack of insecticide are primary reasons for the spread of this disease. While rural areas are at a higher risk, the movement of large population groups to urban areas have had an impact on the spread of this disease. There is currently no preventive drug. There are some precautions one can take, however:

• Try not to sleep in huts. *Chinchorros* reside in palm-frond roofs and in the cracks of walls.

• If you are staying in older or budget hotels, be sure to check for hidden insects in mattresses, drawers, and dark areas such as closets. Insect repellent may help. Spray under your bed and in cracks.

• If handling insects, be sure to use gloves.

• Bed nets may be helpful.

• Blood banks in both Quito and Guayaquil screen for the parasite. (However, outside of those two metropolitan areas it is doubtful that screening takes place.)

DENGUE FEVER

In the coastal and tropical areas of Ecuador you will notice that the newspapers are full of articles about dengue fever. It affects thousands of people and can be fatal. A viral infection, dengue is transmitted by mosquito bites. It is endemic in rural and urban areas of Ecuador.

You will normally notice symptoms between 5–8 days of infection. The victim will experience sudden high fever, severe headaches, joint and muscle pain, nausea/vomiting, or rash. One may be ill for about a week. However, lasting affects of depression and fatigue may persist for weeks or longer. The *Aedes* female mosquito is the culprit. This malaria-carrying mosquito usually feeds at night whereas the dengue-carrying mosquito usually attacks during daylight, especially during the early morning and late afternoon.

I remember one day in 1999, during the height of El Niño in Duran (a suburb of Guayaquil), coming across swarms of mosquitoes around a large stagnant pool of water. You will notice, especially in the coastal areas, water that just sits for days and days. Many people store water in large trash-can-sized receptacles for their personal use. Most of the sitting water, however, is due to environmental conditions and poor drainage.

The dengue fever infection can be diagnosed by a blood test. It is treated with bed rest, lots of fluids, and medications to reduce fever. There is no vaccine available. Avoid mosquito bites by remaining in well-screened or air-conditioned areas. Apply mosquito repellents to clothing and dress protectively to cover as much skin as possible.

MALARIA

The female *Anopheline* mosquito carries a disease of a different sort—malaria. Malaria is a significant problem most especially in the coastal and tropical areas of Ecuador. It is referred to here as *paludismo* and affects thousands of people each year, especially during the rainy season of November through May. Poor and rural communities are the most badly hit.

In 1999 the government reported that the numbers of malaria cases had nearly doubled, from 40,000 in 1998 to 80,000 cases in 1999. The destruction of sanitary infrastructure in much of the rural areas during the 1998 El Niño contributed heavily to the surge in cases. Combined with the lack of funds for cleaning areas where water collects and the lack of spraying contributed to as many as 3,500 new cases of malaria a week.

The goal of the female *Anopheline* mosquito, like the rest of her kind, is to feed on your blood. Blood provides her the protein that she needs for her eggs. The malaria-carrying mosquito does not hum or linger like an uninfected mosquito. You will not feel it when she bites you. This femme fatale usually attacks during the evening hours and

217

especially between midnight and dawn. She uses a stylet, which contains a duct connected to the salivary glands. Before the feeding she injects her saliva which works like an anaesthetic so you don't feel the bite.

The symptoms of malaria usually develops about 8 days or up to several months after infection. Early diagnosis is paramount to successful treatment. Delay may lead to coma, fluids in the lungs, kidney failure, or death. Symptoms are flu-like and include pain in the joints, fever, chills, cough, diarrhea, nausea, profuse sweating and shivering, and even convulsions and coma. If you have any of these problems after being in an infected area you should consult a physician. Be sure you tell him/her the areas you have visited. A serological test should be conducted to rule out the presence of malaria. Assuming it is only flu may prove dangerous.

The provinces of Esmeraldas, Manabí, Guayas, and Los Ríos are the most susceptible to malaria. Most cities in the Sierra including Cuenca, Quito, and most of the highlands are risk-free. However, there are sections of provinces in the Sierra just below 5,000 feet where malaria exists. This group includes Cotopaxi, El Oro, Manabí, Morona–Santiago, Napo (now Orellana), Pastaza, Pichincha, and Zamora. The Galápagos Islands are risk-free. How to prevent malaria:

• Discuss with your medical professional or local health officials for an appropriate antimalarial regimen. Make sure you do this at least six weeks before your planned departure.

• Window and door screens are mandatory. Make sure they are as tight-fitting as possible and that the mesh is as small as possible. Air-conditioning will minimize the threat of mosquitoes.

• Bed nets should be used. Twenty-six holes per square inch are recommended. However, the tighter the mesh the hotter you will be. You might also wish to treat the mesh and your clothes with permethrin insecticide. Permethrin is often sold as Duranon and Permanone.

• Wear long-sleeved shirts and long trousers once the sun goes down. Avoid using colognes or perfumes.

• Repellent is mandatory and OFF is a good brand to use. Apply repellent to exposed areas of the skin as well as thin clothes. Avoid the eyes and mouth. DEET, the active ingredient, keeps the mosquitoes away but doesn't kill them. Repellents may damage plastic items such as sunglasses so use them sparingly.

• It is probably wise not to use repellents with greater then 30% DEET on the skin. This is especially true with children and for pregnant women or nursing mothers.

• The brand **Raid** (with pyrethrin) will kill mosquitoes by attacking their nervous center. You can spray nets, baseboards, walls, corners, furniture, behind pictures, and inside closets. Spraying under sinks is also a good idea.

Most local health agencies can advise what medications to take. Malaria is chloroquine-resistant in Ecuador. Larium is often recommended by health professionals. Larium in many cases is well endured without major side effects. However, this author highly recommends that you discuss the possible side affects of Larium or any other anti-malarial drug. It is recommended that individuals should not take Larium if they suffer from heart disease, epilepsy, liver, kidney, or psychiatric disorders. Children under 30 pounds, pregnant women, and pilots are also advised to refrain from using Larium.

Several years ago during El Niño I began a regimen of medication with Larium. The side effects were horrendous and took a substantial time to diminish. The drug cannot be taken long-term. Be sure to discuss the other medical options with your health care professional.

In October 2000 the Center for Disease Control reported that Malarone had been approved in the United States as an antimalarial drug. It has also received good results as a preventive drug.

HIGH ALTITUDE SICKNESS

If you choose to live or travel in the Andes area of Ecuador the high altitude may affect you. Between 8,000 feet and 14,000 feet (2,438 meters to 4,267 meters) is considered high altitude. Above 14,000 feet to 18,000 feet (4,267 meters to 5,486 meters) is considered very high altitude. Anything above this is called "extreme altitude."

Local slang for high altitude sickness is *soroche*. Caused by the lack of oxygen, some simple planning may help you deal with the change of altitude. I remember my first trip to Quito after living at sea level for most of my life. It took me some time to make the adjustment. I had a splitting headache in the temple region and felt fatigued. Insomnia, vomiting, rapid breathing and increased urination may also be occur.

It is hard to anticipate who will adjust well to high altitude. The afflicted may be disoriented especially if fatigued, and may need help to descend. Those who appear quite healthy may react poorly. Children seem to adapt easier to high altitudes. The solution is the same for all: descend, descend, descend! Other cures include rest, deep breathing, adequate fluid intake, and mild painkillers such as aspirin or Tylenol to alleviate headaches. There has been at least one study, which shows Ginko biloba, a plant native to China, may lessen the symptoms of high altitude sickness.

The worst form of high altitude sickness is high altitude cerebral edema (HACE). Symptoms include blurred vision, disorientation, dizziness, even changes in levels consciousness, seizures, and paralysis. Loosen any restrictive clothing and the afflicted person might have to be carried down. Medical attention may be necessary and give oxygen if available.

Ecuadorians use a phrase *chupa el caramello* (which means "suck on candy") to treat *soroche*. Many believe that a small amount of sugar via a piece of candy helps alleviate high-altitude sickness. Some Ecuadorians also believe that a part of sugar cane, called *panela,* does help. Several doctors have told me that this does assist the sufferer. *Panela* is very sweet and you only need to put a small piece in your mouth.

Precautionary measures include gradual ascent, avoiding high fat and high protein diets, and drinking lots of water. An excellent online resource is http://www.high-altitude-medicine.com.

CHOLERA

This can be a real problem in Ecuador. It is a very strong intestinal bacterial infection common in areas where sanitation is not very good. Symptoms can be mild but one in 20 people have it bad: profuse watery diarrhea, vomiting, and leg cramps. Rapid loss of fluids leads to dehydration and shock and can result in death within hours.

Infection is usually acquired by consuming contaminated food or water which contains the vomit or feces of infected individuals. Some of the lettuce and other food products in Ecuador are fertilized with human feces. Raw or uncooked shellfish are also potentially danger-ous.

The illness may be treated with antibiotics and lots of fluids. The vaccine that was available in the United States (Wyeth-Ayerst) is no longer being sold. Cholera can treated by replacing fluids and salts lost through diarrhea. Patients can be treated with oral rehydration solution, a prepackaged mixture of sugar and salts, mixed with water and drunk in large amounts. Severe cases require intravenous fluid replacement. With prompt rehydration, fewer than 1% of cholera patients die. Antibiotics shorten the course and diminish the severity of the illness, but they are not as important as rehydration.

To prevent contracting cholera:

• Drink only water that you have boiled or treated with chlorine or iodine. Other safe beverages include tea and coffee made with boiled water and carbonated, bottled beverages with no ice.

• Eat only foods that have been thoroughly cooked and are still hot, or fruit that you have peeled yourself.

• Be careful when eating undercooked or raw fish or shellfish, such as *ceviche*.

• Make sure all vegetables are cooked and avoid salads.

• Avoid food and beverages from street vendors.

• Do not bring perishable seafood back home.

WATER CONDITIONS

Water in Ecuador should be considered contaminated. Tap water is called *agua potable*. Bottled water is a big business in Ecuador and there are numerous brands available in markets. Bottled water is delivered to homes and businesses. You should also be cautious about ice, which can be contaminated. There are establishments that provide ice which has been made out of purified water. It is better to be cautious and not use ice in most cases. You also need to be careful about the water you use to brush your teeth. I always use bottled water plus a peroxide mixture. I also use mouthwash with alcohol. Be careful not to lay your toothbrush down on the sink without it being protected by a plastic cap.

INTESTINAL PROBLEMS

It is very likely that you will suffer some type of intestinal ills while in Ecuador. Expect that you are going to have a change in your bowel movements, which may be caused by dietary change. I have learned, after some 20 years here, that simple precautions in what you eat and drink may save you several days of discomfort and make all the difference to your visit.

Here are some things to avoid:

• Food from street vendors

• Nonpasteurized milk. There are numerous brands of powdered milk available.

• Fruit you haven't peeled or washed yourself

• Raw fish

• Raw vegetables

• Salad: most salads in restaurants have not be cleaned properly.

Imodium A-D anti-diarrheal caplets may be beneficial if your stools get loose. Pepto-Bismol caplets has been shown to help protect one from getting traveler's diarrhea by taking two tablets a day. Some side effects are black stools and constipation. It is also related to aspirin, which can cause problems if you're allergic to aspirin or taking anti-coagulants. Drinking plenty of fluids is also important to help prevent dehydration.

If you have a sudden burst of watery diarrhea you may have contracted a form of bacterial diarrhea. Other indicators may be a combination of nausea, cramps, fevers, and blood in the stools. Three drugs often used to treat bacterial diarrhea are Ciprofloxacin, Norfloxacin, and Ofloxacin. Remember these are antibiotics and have side effects, some quite serious. You should always consult a physician before using them.

ONCHOCERCIASIS

Onchocerciasis is also known as *river blindness*. Originally found in Africa, it was brought to South and Central America through the slave trade. It is debilitating but not fatal. It is transmitted by the bite of the female black fly, which is found near rapidly flowing rivers and streams. Found especially in the province of Esmeraldas, it is referred to in Ecuador as *onco*.

Juan Carlos Vieira from the Hospital Vozandes has been involved in a program to eliminate this illness. There is still a small area in the Cayapas River region where *onco* exists. He only knows of one case where a foreigner has contracted this illness. Short-term visitors are usually at low risk. However, no vaccine is available. Avoid black fly habitats and protect yourself against insect bites.

YELLOW FEVER

Yet another mosquito-transmitted disease, yellow fever is a viral disease transmitted between humans. Vaccinations are given by most government agencies and are usually good for 10 years or more.

Protective measures, as mentioned above with malaria, should also work here. Symptoms of yellow fever infection may be confused with malaria, typhoid, or leptospirosis. There are two phases of the disease. The first phase is characterized by fever, muscle pain, headache, shivering, nausea/vomiting, and sometimes a slow pulse. After three or four days, patients appear to recover. Fifteen percent enter a "toxic phase" within 24 hours. Fever is followed by jaundice, abdominal pain, and vomiting. The mouth, nose, eyes and/or stomach may bleed, and blood may then appear in the vomit and feces. The kidneys deteriorate and these patients die within 10–14 days. It is believed by some sources that the death rate may be as high as 60% for those not vaccinated. So please get vaccinated!

LEISHMANIASIS

This is a parasitic illness that threatens hundreds of million of people in 88 countries around the world. Luckily, only 10% of the world's cases occur in the Americas, Asia, the Middle East, and Africa. It is transmitted by bites from sandflies in the tropical and subtropical areas of Ecuador and was first reported in 1920. It is referred to as *sarna brava* or *charra brava* and can manifest in a cutaneous skin form (97% of cases in Ecuador) or visceral or internal form (3% of cases in Ecuador) which can damage internal organs.

The symptoms of cutaneous infection may appear several weeks to several months after infection. The exposed areas of the body are the most susceptible. The visceral form normally develops after several months but may lay dormant for years after infection.

The markers for cutaneous leishmaniasis are sores, which may be open or closed and sometimes scab over. These sores may sometimes be painful. Visceral leishmaniasis will give rise to fever and loss of weight. The spleen and liver may also be enlarged and blood counts low. If not treated, death may result.

Cultures and blood tests are usually taken to determine if leishmaniasis has been contracted. In Ecuador, Glucantine is usually administered in over 21 injections. This is one of the drugs in Ecuador where there may be counterfeit brands. The illness can cause severe disfiguring and may return after many years, even after the patient thinks it has gone. If you return to your home country and notice some symptoms, consult a doctor and inform him where you have been.

Most cases transpire in rural areas and can be found in the following provinces: Azuay, Bolívar, Cañar, Chimborazo, Zamora–Chinchipe, Cotopaxi, El Oro, Guayas, Esmeraldas, Imbabura, Loja, Manabí, Morona–Santiago, Orellana, Pastaza, and Zamora. Humid forests are a favorite habitat for sand flies, which can be found on trunks of trees and are usually not active during the day. However, they can bite during the day even though the most dangerous time is from dusk until dawn. It only takes one fly to infect you and they are very small and quiet.

LEPTOSPIROSIS

The number of cases of leptospirosis, a bacterial disease, increased significantly during the El Niño rains in 1998. Humans and animals become infected after being exposed to water, which contains urine from animals carrying the bacteria. Food or soil containing urine of infected animals may also transmit this disease.

The illness sets in between two days and four weeks. The victim will normally have a sudden onset of fever with flu-like symptoms. Some people recover for a time but become ill again later with even more severe symptoms, including liver and kidney failure or meningitis. There is no indication that it travels from human to human. It can be treated with antibiotics such as doxycycline or penicillin, which should be taken early on. To keep from acquiring this illness, stay away from bodies of water or soil which may have been contaminated. Even swimming or wading in such water puts you at risk.

RABIES

In many parts of Ecuador, dogs are often left unsecured and may bite humans. This is especially true in rural areas where dogs are also used to guard homes and shrimp farms. Bats and other wild animals may present a risk of rabies. Vaccination prior to your visit to Ecuador is advisable. There is often a shortage of rabies medication throughout the country.

SUNBURN

The sun is quite strong in Ecuador. Sunburn and damage to the skin is a strong possibility. Whether in the highlands or the coastal areas it is important to protect yourself with sunscreen and appropriate clothing. Sunscreen with a SPF of 30 or higher should provide adequate protection.

TYPHOID

Typhoid fever is an infection, which infects the victim with the bacteria—*Salmonella typhi*. It can be deadly. Contaminated food or water usually transmits this illness. Symptoms may reveal themselves between 10 and 14 days after exposure. These include a sustained fever as high as 103°F to 104°F (39°C to 40°C), flu-like body aches, loss of appetite, weakness in the body, a persistent dull headache, and a rash of flat, rose-colored spots. There may also be a fever as well as a rash with pink spots on the chest and abdomen.

Typhoid is treatable with antibiotics such as ampicillin, trimethoprim-sulfamethoxazole, and ciprofloxacin. If left untreated, 20% of people die from resulting complications.

There are oral and injectable vaccines available, which last about five and three years, respectively. The vaccines have shown to be effective in 50% to 80% of recipients. It may be better for pregnant women to refrain from taking the vaccination as well as people with HIV.

TUBERCULOSIS

This is an increasing problem in the last few years. A number of drugs to combat tuberculosis (TB) have proven to have a high rate of resistance in Ecuador. The World Health Organization reports there are over 100 cases for every 100,000 people in Ecuador and place the country in the highest risk category.

TB is spread by germs in the air which can be spread to others by sneezing, shouting, laughing, or coughing. If you are near an infected person you can breathe the germs into your lungs. Hopefully your immune system will fight off the bacteria and keep you from getting sick. Those most at risk are those with weak immune systems, such as babies and young children. If they spread, the germs attack usually the lungs, but can also spread to your brain, kidneys, and spine. A TB skin test will show if you have been exposed to the bacteria.

SEXUALLY TRANSMITTED DISEASES

Sexually transmitted diseases (STD) are a real part of Ecuadorian society, as in many countries. Many myths still abound as to who may have a sexual transmitted disease. For example many Ecuadorians still believe that HIV is a disease of someone who is gay or that someone from an upper-class position in society could not be infected. Condom-use is more prevalent than in years past but social values still disdain their use for the most part. Reasons for lack of use may in part be due to the country being largely Roman Catholic. However, there are other social implications. Women still feel that the use of a condom implies that they are a prostitute or that as a male you are questioning their morals, implying that they may be promiscuous. Male and female prostitutes are quite active in the major cities and the incidence of STDs, including AIDS, is increasing among them.

Condoms are not manufactured in Ecuador but are available in pharmacies. They may be of a poor quality, however, and you might consider bringing your own. The use of condoms minimizes but does not eliminate the chance of contracting an STD.

HEPATITIS A

It is strongly advised to obtain a vaccination for Hepatitis A. This is transmitted through contaminated food and water. The risk is higher in rural areas as well as restaurants with poor sanitation. A suggested counter measure is an immune globulin injection.

PHARMACIES

Pharmacies may dispense medications in Ecuador without written prescriptions from physicians. While this may sound advantageous it may be dangerous to your health. It is recommended that you see a doctor if ill in order to get a correct diagnosis and appropriate drug therapy. Many of the persons working in smaller or rural pharmacies may not have been professionally trained. Also, there may be a stronger possibility of picking up counterfeit drugs in smaller or lesser known pharmacies. This has been a problem in Ecuador, especially with the rarer prescription drugs. Also, there are many drugs available in Ecuador, which have not been approved by other government authorities. Of the non-aspirin pain relievers Advil seems to be the most popular. In large cities, pharmacies often have a rotating schedule to remain open for 24 hours and this is announced in most newspapers. However, a number of pharmacies are open 24 hours all year round. FYBECA is the largest chain in the country and appears to be operated professionally. They offer a discount card for a small charge. (Please refer to the Resource Guide for more information.)

MEDICAL SERVICES

Finding medical providers in Ecuador can be a challenge, especially if you don't speak Spanish. I have provided the names of some doctors who speak English or who have had some training in the United States in the Resource Guide. I have also included the names of the better reputed and more modern hospitals. One doctor advised me that anyone traveling to Ecuador should obtain insurance covering transportation costs home in the event of a medical emergency.

Also, one needs to check if your insurance will cover medical or emergency services while in Ecuador. For extra of security, I advise you to obtain a policy that will cover traveling to or residing in Ecuador. If you're working for a foreign company or government, such a service may already be covered. Medical expenses in Ecuador are, for the most part, much cheaper than in developed countries.

In 1998 my son received a pretty severe insect bite on a weekend. I took him to the emergency room at Clinica Kennedy in Guayaquil. There was no formal procedure in place. The woman at the check-in counter said that they wouldn't look at my insurance card unless the bill was over $100, which was my deductible. We walked into the emergency room and were quickly attended to. Luckily it was not severe but required the doctor to drain the bite. We were there for about two hours and the total bill came up to $30. The hospitals in the Resource Guide accept major credit cards and local checks.

MEDICAL KIT

It is advisable, if living or traveling in Ecuador, to maintain your own medical supplies as a kit. Here is a list to start you off:

Antibiotic ointment
Anti-diarrhea tablets
Anti-fungal cream
Antihistamine
Antiseptic
Aspirin or paracetamol
Band-Aids (wide assortment of sizes)
Calamine lotion or aloe vera
Cold and flu tablets, throat lozenges, and nasal decongestant
Gauze pads
Hand sanitizer

Insect repellent
Lip balm
Medications which might not be readily available in Ecuador
Mosquito net
Scissors
Syringe kit
Snake bite kit
Sterile kit
Sunscreen
Thermometer
Tweezers
Water purification tablets or iodine

You might also consider bringing a copy of your medical record, especially if you have some serious conditions. I would also recommend having that translated into Spanish.

IMMUNIZATION

While no shots are required for travel to Ecuador, you should consult your physician four to six weeks before your trip to discuss health precautions you may wish to take, such as:
• Booster doses for tetanus-diphtheria and measles
• Hepatitis A or immune globulin
• Malaria tablets, if you will be traveling to the jungle or the mainland coast
• Rabies vaccinations, if you are traveling to farms in the Andean highlands
• Typhoid, particularly if you are visiting developing areas in this region
• Yellow fever vaccination, if you will be traveling to the jungle

For more specific information, a good website to visit is the Center of Disease Control at http://www.cdc.gov/travel/.

FINAL NOTES

If you are currently taking prescription medication, make sure you bring enough to last during your trip, all medication must be clearly labeled, and bring along a copy of the prescription for the medicine. Medicine should be divided into two different pieces of luggage so that if one piece is lost or stolen your medicine is still available.

If you are carrying syringes for medical reasons, a medical certificate of explanation should also be carried.

Due to the high elevations if you are flying in or out of Quito, if you have high blood pressure or a heart condition, you should check with your doctor about any medical precautions before flying. You might prefer to fly in and out of the port city of Guayaquil rather than Quito.

Please take out a medical-insurance policy, no matter how healthy you are. This is good for an accident even if you don't fall sick.

Chapter Eleven

ENJOYING ECUADOR

"No one with the spirit of roaming within him can live long in Ecuador without cherishing a growing desire to explore its unknown parts."—Alfred Simson in *Travels in the Wilds of Ecuador.*

You will never lack for entertainment while in Ecuador. From ancient Indian markets to amazing national parks, Ecuador offers a diverse number of attractions for the visitor or resident. Ecuador is still surprisingly untouched by tourism and that adds to its charm.

This brief chapter will introduce you to three of Ecuador's cities (Quito, Guayaquil, and Cuenca), Ecuador's Indian markets, national parks, and a few other things to do in this land of unsurpassed beauty.

QUITO

"Every street of Quito has its story; every stone its history."—Victor Wolfgang von Hagen.

The cultural center of Spanish America, Quito was declared a World Heritage Site by UNESCO in 1978. It is also the world's second highest capital city after Bolivia's La Paz and the main gateway for most foreigners to Ecuador. Many flights land in Quito at night. If you have an opportunity, choose a daytime flight not to miss out on the spectacular view.

Quito sits at over 9,000 feet, nestled in the Andean mountains. The city expands through a narrow valley and is shaped like a forefinger. It rests on a ledge of a canyon with the volcano Pichincha to the west. The city grew most considerably in the 1960s and 1970s when oil exports took off. It now has about 1.6 million inhabitants. The weather is spring-like year round, with temperatures ranging from 72°F (22°C) to 45°F (8°C). Its rainy season is from October to May.

Quito is a fascinating blend of the ancient and the modern. The Old Town area is very well preserved and maintains much of its colonial charm. I have never tired, in 20 years of visiting Quito, of walking its narrow cobblestone streets and smelling *fritada* and *choclo* on the breeze. There is so much history in Quito that the ghosts almost reach out and touch you. Probably the best preserved historic center in Latin America, the Monastery of San Francisco, the Church of Santo Domingo, and Jesuit Church of La Compañia are all well worth a visit. Their rich interior decorations are pure examples of the Baroque School of Quito: a fusion of Spanish, Italian, Moorish, Flemish, and indigenous art. Quito's museums are filled with pre-Colombian art and the city full of ornate churches built during the times of the Spanish conquest. The Indians were largely responsible for constructing much of the architecture of this enchanting city.

Quito is also a delightful place to watch the world go by. My favorite spots are in the popular parks and along the Avenida Amazonas.

Quito's picturesque colonial streets.

Getting around Quito is fairly easy. Despite a new address system, most residents still use the old method of locating addresses. Cabs are a common mode of transportation and are discussed in the Settling In chapter. One of the newest transportation developments has been the electric trolley. It is inexpensive and traverses the north and south of Quito. It follows Avenida 10 de Agosto to the mall Recreo on Avenida Maldonado in the old city. Pickpockets do a brisk business, especially during rush hours, so do be careful.

Sightseeing

I highly recommend the book *Walks Through Colonial Quito* by Oscar Valenzuela-Morales. He is a transplant from Chile and has lived in Quito for 20 years. Some of his walks can be accessed on http://www.quitoforum.com/paseo/eng/historia.htm. This book offers, both in Spanish and English, seven different walks which give a good grounding on the history of Quito. It is available at most bookstores in Quito. Quito does not seem to have changed much from the 1860s when Friedrich Hassurek described it as a "spellbound town from Arabian Nights."

Interesting Sites
Palacio de Gobierno
Garcia Moreno y Chile

This Neoclassic Presidential Palace of pink quarry is open Tuesdays through Thursdays from 9:30 am until 12:30 pm. Admission is free. It was on these steps that Gabriel García Moreno was shot and then hacked to death in 1875. Check out: http://www.jalisco.gob.mx/cultudep/palacio to find out more.

Plaza de Santo Domingo
Bolivar y Guayaquil

This is the site of a popular artists' market on weekends. The Church of Santo Domingo is found here.

The Church of Santo Domingo
This church and convent date from the 17th century. Its façade is Neoclassical, its decorations Moorish, and its altar Baroque.

Church of La Merced
Cuenca y Chile

Began in 1700 and completed in 1742, this cloister contains much fine art, including works by Francisco Albán. It also has the tallest church tower and largest bell in Quito.

Plaza de la Independencia
Venezuela y Espejo

At the center of the Old Town, the city was basically planned from this site. The Cathedral is a stone's throw away, and this church contains the tomb of the independence hero General Antonio José de Sucre. Visiting hours are 8–10 am and 2–4 pm daily, except Sunday. Admission is free.

Church of La Compañia de Jesús
García Moreno y Sucre

The Company of Jesus Church is one of the most ornate buildings in all of Latin America. Built in the Baroque style by the Jesuits between 1605 and 1763, it is adorned with more than seven tons of gold in its gilded walls, balconies, and its elaborate, ten-sided altar.

Monastery of San Francisco
Mideros y Imbabura

Believed to be the first religious building constructed by the Spanish in South America, work on this Early Renaissance-styled church began in 1534, just weeks after Quito was founded. It boasts a gold altar, ornate woodcarvings, and intricate designs. San Francisco comprises an area of some 30,000 square meters, including a plaza, the Iglesia Mayor, the chapels of Cantuna and Villacis, and a large convent with magnificent cloisters. It is open from 9 am–12 pm and 3 pm–6 pm.

Museo del Banco Central
6 de Diciembre y Patria Avenues

The Central Bank Museum contains one of the finest archaeological and gold collections in the Americas. Some of its 1,800 items date as

237

far back as 1,200 years and include pre-colonial, colonial, and contemporary works. It is open everyday except Monday.

Museo Guayasamín
Bellavista
The Guayasamín Museum houses the beautiful personal collection and workshop of Oswaldo Guayasamín, Ecuador's world-famous artist. Admission is free. Opening hours: Monday to Friday 9:30 am– 1 pm and 3–6:30 pm, Saturday 9:30 am–1 pm.

Casa Museo María Augusta Urrutía
García Moreno 760 y Sucre
María Augusta Urrutía was a philanthropist and this was her home, left much as it was in the late 19th century, and complete with period furnishings. Opening hours: Tuesdays to Saturdays 9–5 pm.

Biblioteca Ecuatorina Aurelio Espinosa Pólit
Jose Nogales N69-22 y Francisco Arcos
Located in the Cotocallao area on the outskirts of Quito, this is the largest library in Ecuador, with more than 300,000 volumes. Closed Mondays only. Alas, books here are not allowed to be checked out. There is also a very interesting museum connected with the library, containing the clothes García Moreno was wearing when he was assassinated.

Train to Cotopaxi
On the weekends, a train runs from Quito to Cotopaxi Volcano Park. It usually leaves Quito at 8:00 am and Cotopaxi at 2:30 pm, returning to Quito by 5:30 pm. It is a three-hour trip each way. The train station is located at 315 Maldonado Street, tel 582921. Be sure to get your tickets the day before departure. The price for foreigners is $25.

Shopping

Quito abounds with numerous stores for both the tourist and locals. Here are some of my favorites in Quito:

Gift Shops
Ahuacuna: Avenida Amazonas 1036 y Pinto, Galeria Latina, J.L. Mera N23–69. tel 221098.

Mundo Arte: Avenida Amazonas 2019 y 18 de Septiembre.
Just across from the Hilton this is an established store with numerous high quality gifts from all over Ecuador.

Shopping Centers
Quito has a number of upscale malls where Ecuadorians love to congregate. The food courts have a number of Ecuadorian-style restaurants as well as North American franchise units. Most malls close at 8:00 pm. Here are a few:
• Centro Comercial Iñaquito, better known as C.C.I. On Amazonas y Naciones Unidas
• Centro Comercial El Jardín on República esquina Amazonas
• Quicentro on Naciones Unidas y Av 6 de Diciembre. This is my favorite mall in Quito with almost everything you need.

Traditional Markets

Many Ecuadorians use the traditional markets in Quito. These offer a real look into their culture. But be sure to watch out for pickpockets. There is a fuller write-up on markets toward the end of this chapter. No matter which market you decide to go to, you are guaranteed to be awed by the life that fills the air there and by the things you'll see.

One of the most famous markets is a couple of hours north of Quito called Otavalo (open everyday except Mondays and Fridays). This market is best known for clothing and gifts, such as ponchos, pipes, and many other bags and clothes that are beautifully colored and traditionally made by the same the hands that sell them. When you go to an open-air market you'll get your chance to try out your bargaining skills. Here are some rough estimates of some prices in U.S. dollars:

Hammock	$12
Knit Hat	$3
Pants/trousers	$7
Pipes	$2–$30
Ponchos	$16–$20
Shirts	$6
Shoulder Bag	$2–$6
Sweater	$10
Tapestries	$5–$25

Here are some of my favorite markets inside Quito, some of which you won't find in many tourist guides: Mercado Central, Pichincha y Esmeraldas, Mercado Santa Clara, Versalles y Marchena, and Mercado Ipiales. If you don't mind stolen or counterfeit goods, you will be able to find almost anything under the sun at Mercado Ipiales.

Nightlife

Quito has a very enticing nightlife. It is not as large as other South American cities but you will definitely feel at home here if you're a nocturnal animal. Quito's nightlife ranges from salsa to raves, from English-style pubs to karaoke beer lounges. The bars generally close at 2 or 3 am. Discos are another story. There are several discotheques (*discotecas*) that stay open until dawn.

Cover charges usually range from US$1 to US$3.50 and they're on the rise. The entrance fee system in Ecuador works like this:
- Cover charge: You pay a certain amount to get in the door but that won't cover your drinks; or

- *Consumo minimo*: there is no cover charge, but you have to spend a minimum amount or you pay the difference when you leave; or
- *Entrada con derecho*: by far the most popular in Quito. You pay a cover charge and they give you a ticket or token for a free drink.

Here are a few of my personal favorites:

Arribar
Juan León Mera 1238 y Lizardo Garcia
Techno music. This bar is apparently being sold for US$50,000 so, if you always wanted to own a bar and dance club that is mentioned in almost every guidebook and comes with an established clientele of eight years, this is your big chance! Check out: http://www.qni.com/~mj/arribar.

Ñucanchi Peña
Avenida Universitaria 496 y Armero
Peñas are folklore clubs or bars that have traditional music performances that are often quite expensive. This club is fairly inexpensive (about US$4 cover) and presents some of the best talent there is in Ecuador. I highly recommend it! The crowd is largely Ecuadorian.

Seseribó
Veintimilla y 12 de Octubre
Salsa music is the speciality here, and this is, allegedly, the best place for salsa in the whole of Ecuador.

Veradero
Reina Victoria 17-51 y La Pinta
Good Cuban music and food.

Hotels

There are literally hundreds of hotel options in Quito. Here are some of my favorites. Don't be afraid to ask for discounted rates especially if you're going to stay for a number of days. The longer you stay, the more discount you should receive. This is even possible at the larger "luxury" hotels. Some major hotels also offer special prices for Ecuadorian citizens and residents.

La Mansión de Angel Hotel

Wilson E5–29 y Juan León Mera

http://www.larc1.com/ecuador/angel/angel.html

The U.S. representative is LARC (http://www.larc1.com, tel 1 800 327 3573 for calls from U.S. and Canada)

This is a charming boutique hotel with beautifully decorated rooms. Located in the Mariscal Sucre neighborhood, called the cultural and gastronomical center of Quito, it is a 20-minute drive away from the international airport in the north of the city.

Hotel Sierra Madre

Veintimilla 464 y Luis Tamayo

http://www.hotelsierramadre.com

The U.S. representative is LARC (http://www.larc1.com, tel 1 800 327 3573 for calls from U.S. and Canada)

This is an excellent mid-priced hotel, styled after a Spanish villa. Karen Rasmussen from Denmark is the manager and has done an excellent job at making it a popular place for foreigners. The rooms are clean and the staff helpful.

Hotel Majestic

Mercadillo 366 y Versalles

http://www.majesticquito.com

Very well-run hotel in the budget category.

Hotel Santa Maria
Inglaterra 933 y Mariana de Jesus
http://interhotel.com/ecuador/en/hoteles/32200.html
A good value hotel with a great restaurant serving traditional Ecuadorian cuisine.

Cotacachi

La Mirage Garden Hotel and Spa
http://www.larc1.com/ecuador/lamirage/lamirage.html
This is one of the finest and most expensive hotels in Cotacachi. Spread over 13 acres in this lovely village, its owners have constructed a remarkable oasis of a hotel/spa. This can compete with the best spas in San Francisco or Paris. The service is among the best that I have ever experienced anywhere on earth. The employees should be very proud of their accomplishments in a country where good service is not the norm. The food is excellent and formally presented. The hotel's spa is excellent and offers a variety of services. I would highly

The lobby of La Mirage Garden Hotel and Spa, heaven on Earth in Cotacachi.

recommend it for a romantic honeymoon, seeing that it even has a wedding chapel! Otavalo is only 15 minutes away.

CUENCA

"Two things impressed Alsedo: the ordered loveliness of Cuenca and its magnificence."—Albert B. Franklin

Cuenca is well worth a visit. Cut off from the rest of Ecuador for hundreds of years because of its rugged topography and its undeveloped communications and road systems, this city has remained resolutely colonial in character. Cuenca rests at 8,517 feet (2,596 meters) in the southern Sierra. Despite being the third largest city in Ecuador and a major producer of Panama hats, jewelry, textiles, lace, and leather goods, Cuenca has managed to retain a provincial air. Its whitewashed buildings, interior patios, ironwork balconies, and flowery public plazas give it an Old World charm.

Sightseeing

El Sagrario Church (Old Cathedral)
Mariscal Sucre y Luis Cordero
This was constructed in 1557 at the time Cuenca was founded. Some of its foundations were stones from the old Inca city of Tomebamba, present-day Cuenca (which means *basin* in Spanish). It was the Inca Túpac Yupanqui who founded Tomebamba, giving it the name which means "space like the sky."

Todos Los Santos Church
Calle Larga y Bajada de Todo Los Santos
The first Catholic mass held in Cuenca was held on the site of this church. A newer church replaced it during the 19th century.

Museo del Banco Central
Avenida Huayna Capac in front of Calle Larga

Ingapirca is the largest surviving Incan structure in Ecuador.

Cuenca's best museum, the Central Bank Museum contains a major display of Inca and Cañari archaeological items and religious art. There are also ever-changing art exhibitions and a permanent collection of old black-and-white photographs of Cuenca. This museum also owns an Incan archaeological site, the Archaeological Park of Pumapungo, which contains tens of thousands of important archaeological objects.

Museo de Arte Moderno
Marisal Sucre y Talbot
The Modern Art Museum has both permanent and changing collections that show off the wide diversity of Ecuadorian art.

Ingapirca
Ingapirca (which means Wall of the Inca) is located just two hours or 43 miles (70 kilometers) north of Cuenca. It is the largest and best example of Incan architecture in Ecuador. There is a small museum

245

at the site, which includes a fascinating temple of intricate stonework. This thought to have been a Cañari observatory which was later converted into an Incan temple to the sun god. The long axis of its elliptical shape lies precisely along the east-west line, and its structure is said to look like a puma, a sacred animal to the Inca, from the sky.

Chordeleg
A very short drive from Cuenca, this small village features a weekly market which sells numerous arts and crafts including unique ceramics, jewelry, and embroidery work on shawls.

Gualaceo
Another short drive from Cuenca, this town is full of artisans. It has a very good traditional market on Sundays. Twenty-six kilometers south of Gualaceo is another good local Sunday market at Sigsig.

Hotels
Hotel Crespo
Calle Larga 793
http://interhotel.com/ecuador/es/hoteles/32175.html

Hotel El Dorado
Gran Colombia 7–87 y Luis Cordero
http://www.hoteldorado.com/index.htm

Hosteria Uzhupud
Via Paute Km 32, Chican-paute
http://interhotel.com/ecuador/en/hoteles/68838.html
Located a half-hour from Cuenca in Paute, this is in an absolutely gorgeous location. A very peaceful environment full of flowers and birds.

GUAYAQUIL

"Guayaquil is like a threshold between the world of today and the world of pre-history."—Albert B. Franklin.

Guayaquil is a tropical paradise that few foreigners like at first glance. There is no middle ground with Guayaquil. You will either love it or hate it. As for me, it captivated me on my first visit, some 20 years ago. Ecuador's main port town, a sensual place where fortunes are made and lost, resembles a Middle Eastern city with large cement buildings and crowded streets filled with people of all social classes. I think Guayaquil would make the perfect set for a Clark Gable, Humphrey Bogart, or Indiana Jones movie.

On the other hand, many travelers have commented that Guayaquil is the armpit of Ecuador. It doesn't offer the visitor or resident the colonial environment the Sierra does and the weather can be quite daunting between January and May. But, Guayaquil has a certain magic that bites like a mosquito, leaving you with a fever for living. I think Guayaquil offers all that is good and bad about Ecuador, its slums, muggers, and beggars, and squashed rats the perfect foil to its posh suburbs and malls, riverfront walks, and frolicking iguanas.

Weather-wise, June and December is quite pleasant and can get cool in the evenings, requiring a light jacket.

Prior to the Spanish settling in Guayaquil in 1537 it was populated by Indians. The natural port was developed into one of the largest on the Pacific coast and it became a large shipbuilder because of the tremendous amount of timber in the area.

Interesting Sites
La Catedral or The Cathedral
Chimborazo y Clemente Ballén
This double-belfried cathedral sits smack in the middle of Guayaquil. It has been destroyed by fire several times, the latest in 1902.

247

Botanical Garden

This is located in the Las Orquideas neighborhood and is open almost everyday. It has over 320 plant species, 70 species of birds, and 60 species of butterflies. If you love orchids you will find one of the best exhibitions in the country here, with more then 50 specimens on show. There is an admission fee of $5. Be sure to take a taxi and have it wait for you. Otherwise you will have to walk a long way through unsafe neighborhoods to flag one.

9 de Octubre

This is the large avenue that runs down the middle of Guayaquil. Start your walk from the Malecón Simón Bolívar straight down 9 de Octubre to the U.S. Consulate. This is a marvelous street that people from Guayaquil love. It is bustling with life with banks, large stores, restaurants, beggars, and street vendors.

Malecón 2000

The Malecón 2000 is a reconstruction project along the riverfront

A navy band performing at the Malecón.

walkway and street facing the Río Guayas (Guayas River). Its objective is to transform the pier into one of the most important civic-tourist-commercial sites from South America. You can trace its progress on http://www.malecon2000.com. This was where most of the early trade in Guayaquil took place. Nowadays, it is the site of numerous fiestas.

Museo Antropológico del Banco Central del Ecuador
Antepara y 9 de Octubre
The Anthropology Museum of the Central Bank of Ecuador has a fine collection of pieces ranging from anthropology to modern art.

Cerro Blanco
This is an ecological reserve located just outside of Guayaquil at Kilometer 16.5 Via a la Costa. It is a protected coastal tropical forest with an estimated 600 plant species, 33 mammal species (including monkeys, white-tailed deer, jaguar, and puma), and 211 bird species (eight of which are endangered). The Fundacion Pro-Bosque (Pro-Forest Foundation) protects this 5,000-hectare forest. Tourists can visit the nature trails and organic farms here, but reservations are required except on Sundays. This can be obtained from the office at Edificio Promocentro, tel 416975, vanhorst@ecua.net.ec.

Monument to Simón Bolívar
Chimborazo y Ballén
Simón Bolívar was the force behind the fight for Latin America's liberation from Spain. This monument to him stands in the middle of a small park called Parque Bolívar, which is famous for its friendly resident iguanas. The park is very well maintained and offers substantial shade from the strong sun.

Las Peñas
This small neighborhood was part of the original city that dates back

to the 16th century. Colonial architecture, art galleries, and the oldest church in Guayaquil (the Church of Santo Domingo) can be found here. It is probably a good idea to take a cab here, as the bordering neighborhoods can be dangerous.

Nobol
This is a small village just 30 minutes outside of Guayaquil and is rarely visited by foreigners. The body of the patron saint Narcisa de Jesús Martillo Morán lies here in a transparent casket. Many of the food vendors here dress in white.

Puerto Hondo Mangrove Ecotourism Project
Just outside Guayaquil, near Cerro Blanco, one km along the Via a la Costa is the Puerto Hondo Mangrove Ecotourism Project. You can take canoe rides through the mangroves. More than 40 bird species call this home, including the white ibis, yellow-crowned night heron, and rufous-necked wood rail. Contact Eric Horstman, Fundacion Pro-Bosque, Casilla 09 01 04243, Km.16 Via a la Costa, Guayaquil. tel 04 872236/871 900 ext. 32280; vanhorst@ecua.net.ec.

Shopping Centers
I recommend the following shopping centers:
• Mall de Sol: new, big, and near the airport. Relatively expensive with American fast-food restaurants, and a comfortable movie theater.
• Policentro: nice and more affordable with restful water fountains.
• Entre-Rios
• Riocentro
• Plaza Quil
• Albán Borja
• Unicentro: downtown by Parque Bolívar.

Markets
La Bahía
This is an open-air market located just outside downtown on Carbo and Villamil between Olmedo and Colón that looks like a bazaar. There is a lot of activity with people looking for bargains. I used to come here in the early 1980s to buy such things as peanut butter and other items from the United States. This market has developed into a place for selling surplus goods from ships visiting the port. Watch out for pickpockets.

El Mercado de Artesanía
Loja y Córdova, edge of Las Peñas
The Artisans' Market is held inside a huge warehouse-type structure that spans a whole block. Many handicrafts and jewelry are sold from small stands. Lots of bargains. You can easily spend several hours here. It is just as popular with Ecuadorians.

Nightlife
The residents from Guayaquil love to party. There is no shortage of nightlife from discos to gambling halls on 9 de Octubre. In fact, Guayaquil is notorious for providing its visitors with more action after dark than during the day. The scene varies from discos that rock until dawn to beer-guzzling pubs, but they all have an exotic tropical vibe.

Alto Nivel Discoteca
Av. Jun Tanca Marengo
The cover charge is between $2–$4. Thursday nights is Ladies Night and it's free for females. There are three bars featuring a discotheque, salsa room, and peña.

ApúMache
Centor Comercial Albán Borja
Rock and roll joint.

Equs Bar
V. And Estrada 819 and Fig Trees, tel 382261/889807.
Good live bands jam here.

Café del Sol
Vitor Emilio Estrada e llanes in Urdesa
This is both a bar and restaurant.

El Jardín de Salsa
Located near the airport, this is the biggest salsa dance floor in
Ecuador. It can hold several thousand dancers and is covered by a
large tent-like structure open on the sides. Don't forget the insect
repellent.

La Créme
Just across the Albán Borja shopping center.

Hotels
Hotel Continental
Chile y 10 de Agosto on Parque Bolívar
http://www.hotelbook.com/static/welcome_12600.html
One of the classiest hotels in the city. Its restaurants have won various
international gastronomy awards.

Hotel Oro Verde
9 de Octubre y García Moreno
http://www.ecuadordiscover.com/hotels/oroverde_Guayaquil.htm
Best downtown venue.

Hotel Plaza
Chile 414 y C. Ballén
A mid-priced downtown hotel.

Hotel Rizzo
Ballén 319
http://interhotel.com/ecuador/es/hoteles/64971.html
Downtown location with a good Ecuadorian restaurant.

Hotel Ritz
9 de Octubre 709
tel 530120/324134; fax 332151

INDIGENOUS MARKETS

One of the most unique features of Ecuador is its tradition of markets, where people gather to buy and sell animals, food, and other items. Indian markets can be traced as far back as 4,000 years ago. Many of the markets exist, as they have for centuries for the purpose of trade, not tourism. However, there are a number of markets that have become more touristy of late, such as the famous Otavalo market.

I've given you my market schedule. Please remember that there are seldom facilities, and that thieves and pickpockets are shopping whilst you are. Do also exercise caution when consuming any food. I promise a real look into indigenous society when you visit these markets.

I find it amusing to watch business being conducted in dollars but prices quoted in sucres. Bargaining is a very real part of these markets. One clue to successful bargaining is to go early. I often ask for a discount because I am the first customer of the day. You will likely receive one as a good luck measure by the vendor for the rest of the day. Another key to bargaining is to remain emotionless and detached, not showing how much you admire the item you wish to purchase. Also, most vendors will offer discounts for purchases of larger quantities. Most animal trading takes place early in the day.

Market Schedule
Monday

Ambato
This is a wholesale market for regional products. Traditional items are also on sale. It opens at about 8:00 am and starts to winds down about 3:00 pm. There are numerous markets throughout Ambato but the principal one is at the Mercado Central which is on the outskirts of Parque 12 de Noviembre. The markets here also sell some of the most beautiful flowers on Earth. The time to come for fruits and flowers is February, during the *Carnaval* festivities.

Tuesday
Latacunga
This traditional market starts at 8:00 am and finishes about 1:00 pm. There are lots of exotic fruits at this market. It is also open on Saturday.

Different types of grain for sale at a market at Saquisilí.

Wednesday
Pujilí
Some 56 miles (90 kilometers) south of Quito, this market is dedicated to trading within the indigenous community, i.e. this is the real thing. Open from 8:00 am until 1:00 pm, there are very few foreigners here. You will see llamas loaded with colorful fruits and vegetables and people from some of the smallest hamlets. It also operates on Sundays.

Thursday
Plaza Rotary
In Cuenca, this is a small-sized market selling numerous handicrafts.

Saquisilí

Open from 8:00 am until 1:00 pm, this is one of the most traditional and exciting markets in Ecuador. There are five main markets which seem to specialize in a one type of merchandise, such as food, tools, or weavings. The animal market is amazing and starts fairly early at about 8:00 am. You will see buses coming in with animals on the roof and people with wads of cash bargaining. The bargaining doesn't seem to get too loud or exaggerated. It is a very dusty extravaganza. More and more tourists attend nowadays. In November 2000 I

Tailors hard at work at Saquisilí market.

observed about 40–60 tourists going picture-crazy seeing guinea pigs and other exotic animals being sold.

Tulcán
Near the Colombian border, this market begins at about 8:00 am and ends at 3:00 pm.

Friday
Cotocachi
North on the Pan-American Highway, this is a meeting place for producers, buyers, and friends. Open from 8 am to 2 pm.

Saturday
Otavalo
Otavalos Indians are the most prosperous craftsmen in Ecuador. It is not surprising, then, that this market is the largest market in Ecuador. Prices, while still negotiable, are generally higher than most other markets. As an indication of how touristy it has become and the predominance of white foreigners, locals refer to Otavalo as *Ottawa*! Many tour companies leave Quito early in the morning or some visitors even spend Friday night in Otavalo. While Saturday is the big market day Otavalo has turned into a daily market, except for Mondays and Fridays. You can buy almost anything here from ponchos to wooden goods to Indian jewelry.

Zumbahua
Drive south on the Pan-American Highway through the Avenue of the Volcanoes to this trading place of llamas, riding horses, and Tigua art.

Sunday
Santo Domingo de Los Colorados
Beginning at 8:00 am, this market lasts until the late in the afternoon. This is a unique market as Santo Domingo is at the crossroads of the

Sierra and the Costa. The locals here will represent distinct areas of Ecuador. In the city center, this market is usually jam-packed with people.

NATIONAL PARKS

Ecuador is a very small country and much of the land has been exploited for commercial use. In the 1970s the government started to set land aside for preservation to protect Ecuador's diverse but fragile ecology. There are more than 20 national parks or protected areas, which includes about 17% of Ecuador's terrain. The national parks:

Andes: Cajas National Recreation Area, Chimborazo Reserve, Cotacachi-Cayapas Ecological Reserve, Cotopaxi National Park, El Angel Ecological Reserve, Ilinizas Reserve, Pululahua Geobotanical Reserve, Podocarpus National Park.

Amazon: Cuyabeno Reserve, Limoncocha Biological Reserve, Yasuní National Park.

Andes-Amazon: Antisana Ecological Reserve, Cayambe-Coca Ecological Reserve, Llangantes National Park, Sangay National Park, Sumaco-Galeras National Park.

Coast & Galápagos Islands: Bosque Protector Cerro Blanco, Machalilla National Park, Mataje-Cayapas Mangrove Reserve, Manglares Churute Mangrove Reserve, Galápagos Islands National Park.

Cajas National Park

This is a beautiful park located just 18 miles (29 kilometers) west of Cuenca with more than 270 Andean lakes. Its high-altitude grasslands are home to lovely birds such as hummingbirds, gray-breasted toucans, and giant conebills. You can take a bus from Cuenca to the park information center where there is a basic refuge with beds and a kitchen. A fee is charged for foreigners.

Cotacachi–Cayapas Ecological Reserve

Along the western cordillera of the Andes, this reserve straddles both Imbabura and Esmeraldas provinces. It covers an impressive range of ecosystems, from coastal tropical forest to pre-montane and montane cloud forest to paramo, ranging from 0.12 to 3 miles (200 to 4,939 meters) above sea level.

Its fascinating wildlife includes spectacled bears, anteaters, jaguars, tapirs, monkeys, caiman, bats, and more. The tropical forest section of this reserve is part of an ecosystem that has almost entirely disappeared in other coastal areas of South America. More than 20,000 species of plants have been recorded along with 500 bird types, making it one of the most biologically diverse regions on Earth.

The spectacular area around Cuicocha Lake is wonderful hiking terrain. This collapsed volcanic crater has a lake that is 0.12 miles (200 meters) deep and 1.9 miles (3 kilometers) in diameter. You can take a boat ride on the lake. You can get there by driving north from Quito towards Otavalo and continuing on to the town of Cotacachi. The more adventurous can enter the reserve from the lowlands by canoe via the San Miguel entrance.

Cotopaxi National Park

The most popular national park in Ecuador, the snowcapped Cotopaxi Volcano is Cotopaxi National Park's main attraction. The park covers 82,514 acres (33,393 hectares) that are primarily paramo (high altitude grassland), offering excellent hiking, climbing, and mountain biking opportunities at temperatures varying from between 32–59°F (0–15°C). I recommend the guidebook *Climbing and Hiking in Ecuador* (4th edition, published by Bradt Travel Guides) by Rob Rachowiecki, Mark Thurber, and Betsy Wagenhauser for some good hikes.

You can also visit the park's museum to view llama herds and Incan ruins. Conveniently located one and a half hours south of Quito

259

in the Pichincha, Cotopaxi, and Napo provinces, the park is accessible by car or on foot, but there is no public transportation within the park. There are two entrances, one south of Machachi and another north of Latacunga on the Panamerican Highway.

There are numerous tour companies, which can offer you guided tours of the Cotopaxi area. But there is an excellent guide that you will not find in the phonebooks or mainstream guidebooks. Sitting in his ten-seater four-wheel-drive truck on the road to Cotopaxi Volcano is Luis Medardo Topanta Q. He is waiting to share with you all he knows about this magnificent region. But he can only speak Spanish. I spent a wonderful day with him visiting several markets in the Latacunga area. His prices are negotiable and he can arrange most any type of excursion. He even took me to see a shaman which is not any part of any type of tour. He is very well known in the markets and in the area and can provide a tremendous amount of insight into Ecuadorian culture. He lives in Parroquia Guaytacama, about 5 miles (8 kilometers) from Saquisilí, but can be found most mornings at the main entrance to the Cotopaxi National Park. Tel 593 3 721 024, cell phone 09 98 826 74.

Cayambe–Coca

This protected area covers extensive Amazon forests, cloud forests, and paramo ecosystems in the eastern cordillera. There are several volcanoes in the reserve, including the Cayambe (18,996 feet or 5,790 meters), Cerro Puntas (14,602 feet or 4,451 meters), Saraurco (15,402 feet or 4,695 meters), and the Reventador (11,434 feet or 3,485 meters). There are 81 lagoons in the reserve, including the San Marcos and Puruanta, and the Papallacta lagoons. Besides the snowcapped volcanoes, one of the most spectacular places in the reserve is the San Rafael waterfall (426 feet or 130 meters high) along the Coca River, the highest in Ecuador. The Cayambe Volcano is one of the hardest climbs in Ecuador. And look out for the young and active Reventador

Volcano! The main access is from Olmedo to San Marcos lagoon, where there is a visitor's center. Another access is trekking from the Papallacta Pass from Quito to Baeza.

Chimborazo Reserve

Chimborazo is the highest summit in Ecuador, standing at 20,702 feet (6,310 meters). The Chimborazo and Carihuairazo (16,732 feet or 5,100 meters) volcanoes are hot favorites with mountain-climbers, backpackers, and trekkers. With a terrain ranging from 12,467 to 20,702 feet (3,800–6,310 meters), be prepared for cold emperatures and bring your own sleeping bags as the refuges here are very basic, although fireplaces and cooking facilities are provided. There is a Vicuñas Reserve here (with a government-donated stock of some 600 wild vicuñas, graceful wild llamas native to the Andes Highlands) on the northeast side of Chimborazo Volcano. This reserve is accessible by road from either Riobamba or Mocha.

OTHER STUFF TO DO

My best source for unique and fun things to do in Ecuador have been the local papers. Many of the news services do a good job. Many of the articles run in the papers, however, require you to read Spanish.

There are some good books listed in the resource section which will give you an insight to tourist sites. David Pearson has written two fine volumes on visiting Ecuador from an ecotourism point of view (they are *The New Key to Ecuador and the Galápagos* by David Pearson and David Middleton published by Ulysses Press in 1999; and *Ecuador and the Galápagos Islands: the Ecotravellers' Wildlife Guide* by David L. Pearson, Les Beletsky, Wildlife Conservation Society, John Myers (illustrator), and John O'Neill (illustrator), published by Academic Press in 1999). *The Ecuador Handbook* by Julian Smith, Moon Publications (First Edition, 1998) contains reliable information about tourism in Ecuador. Here is a small sampling of some little known things I have found to do in Ecuador which are not widely publicized.

Parasailing

There is a beautiful beach for parasailing on the coast in a little hamlet called Crucita in the province of Manabí, about one and a half hours from Manta. You can also do some hang gliding here. A scenic spot is a hill called Balsamaragua which is about 100 meters above sea level. And while you are there, visit the far end of the beach outside of Crucita, called La Boca, where the Portoviejo River empties into the sea. Here can be found, in about 20 acres, eight species of birds and the blue crab. A number of small restaurants are also located in La Boca, which serve, amongst other seafood delicacies, fresh sardines—a favorite with Ecuadorians.

Bike Riding

Thanks to the Inca's extensive network of road and bridges and its mountainous terrain, Ecuador is gorgeous biking country! Some world-class descents include the slopes of Cotopaxi Volcano, the Pichincha Volcano, and trips that take riders from the heights of the Andes to the Amazon Basin. Another magnificent route is a 37-mile (60-kilometer) stretch referred to as *La Ruta de las Cascadas* near the Tungurahua Volcano about two hours south of Quito. The route starts at El Pailón de Deablo and runs for about 12 miles (20 kilometers) where buses can be taken back to Baños. For hard-core bikers, the most rigorous part of the course continues on to Puyo.

Bikers will be pleased to know that there are biker-friendly buses and pickup truck taxis, and readily available lodging and food in most rural areas. But bike defensively on public road, as Ecuadorian drivers are not used to seeing bicycles on the road. Quito, I've heard, is one of the worst places to bike. Maps of varying scales can be found at the **Instituto Geografico Militar** behind the Casa de la Cultura. Don't bet your life on directions given by locals, as they'll send you off on a wild goose-chase rather than admit that they don't know which way to go. Here are a few websites to check out: http://www.eco adventour.com/mountainbike.htm, http://www.bikingdutch man.com, and http://www.ecuadorexplorer.com/html/biking _tours.html.

Isla Puná

Isla Puná is a little visited island near Guayaquil which is just opening up to tourists. Isla Puná or Puná Island, boasts the endangered saffron siskin (a small, brown-streaked, yellow-marked bird), priceless Incan relics, and much pirate history.

To get there, you can take a boat on the Guayas River on the first Sunday of each month. The boat leaves Guayaquil at Cuenca y la Ría at 8:00 am and arrives back at Guayaquil at 6:00 pm. On other days, there is a transport boat leaving from the same pier. This returns the following day, meaning that you will have to spend the night on the island. I recommend the **Hotel Miramar**, which can be located via phone at: 742034. On September 24, the island has a celebration of the Virgen de las Mercedes (Our Lady of Mercy). It is best to get up-to-date information from naval offices by calling 446248 or 297535.

Thermal Baths

One of the most enjoyable experiences I have had in Ecuador was at a little known thermal bath named Baños de San Vicente, located off the highway past Progreso on the way to Salinas. You take a dirt road from the sign at the highway nearly 10 miles (16 kilometers) through the desert and you arrive at a unique oasis that is enjoyed by very few tourists.

Operated by a private concession, it is owned by the government. Years ago the baths were basically just an ancient mud hole. Now, food is provided and the baths are housed inside a unique-looking structure. The buildings are set in an oasis in the desert, making you feel like you are on another planet! You are given a mud-massage then moved outside to bake in the sun. Do be careful not to stay outside too long. Ten to 15 minutes is about enough, any longer and you will probably burn. There is a small hotel outside the complex. It is very tranquil here and a wonderful way to de-stress. Admission is just a few dollars and the service is reasonable. Tel 282195. It is open daily.

The most famous Ecuadorian town for hot baths is Baños (*baños* means bath in Spanish). The thermal baths here are heated by the active Tungurahua Volcano (Tungurahua means *little hell* in Quichua) just 6 miles (10 kilometers) away. The best known bath here is La Piscina de La Virgen which has hot showers and concrete pools, some directly under a waterfall. The etiquette here is not to bathe nude but in a swimming costume. Do avoid drinking the water as it usually has a strong mineral content. The thermal waters can get as hot as 122°F (50°C). Other favorite locations in Ecuador for thermal baths are Oyacachi and Papallacta.

South American Explorers

This is a nonprofit entity that is dedicated to the spreading of information about Latin America. The South American Explorers have a clubhouse in Quito where there is at least one expatriate with an intimate knowledge of Ecuador. Their other clubhouses are in Lima and Cuzco in Peru and their U.S. headquarters is in Ithaca, New York. An annual membership entitles you to receive their magazine, free trip reports, and assistance in trip planning. I highly recommend this club if you're just visiting or going to stay in Ecuador for a length of time. It is an excellent place to find information on rentals and information about Quito and Ecuador in general. The privileges of membership includes discounts with a number of establishments in Ecuador. You can contact them at explorer@saexplorers.org or find out more at http://www.saexplorers.org.

*One of my favorite haunts—Biblioteca Ecua-
toriana Aurelio Espinosa Pólit.*

Libraries

Biblioteca Ecuatoriana Aurelio Espinosa Pólit

José Nogales N69-22 y Francisco Arcos Cotocollao, Quito.
tel 491 156.
This is an excellent for its research on Ecuador.

Bookstores

Abya Yala

Avenida 12 de Octubre 1430 y Wilson, Casilla 17-12-719, Quito.
editorial@abyayala.org; http://www.abyayala.org/"; tel 562633,
506247.

This is a great store with thousands of books on almost any subject on Ecuador, with a particular emphasis on ecology and the environment. (Interestingly, http://www.abyayala.com/ and http://abyayala.native web.org are also great web resources on Latin America. Funny how the word *abya-yala* caught the fancy of so many! This is a Kuna expression meaning ripe earth and the name the Kuna people gave to the Americas.)

Confederate Books
Calama 410 y Juan León Mera, Quito. tel 2527 890.
This is a pretty unique store that attracts mainly the expatriates and foreigners.

Liberia Cientifica
Boyaca 1317, Guayaquil. tel 322 901

Libri Mundi
Juan León Mera 851 y Wilson, Quito. tel 464 473, 234 791. http://www.librimundi.com/shop/home.asp
This carries a wide range of books on Ecuador in Spanish and English and a number of foreign newspapers. There's another store at Quicentro.

Gay Life
There is a considerable gay community in Ecuador. The year 1998 was a hallmark year for gays as the Ecuadorian constitution was amended to prevent any discrimination against any person for their sexual orientation. While this was a considerable step for gays, attitudes are still largely anti-gay in Ecuador. In 2001 a number of establishments that catered to gays in Guayaquil were closed down.

Quito has a number of nightclubs and services that cater to gays. In Guayaquil many gays meet in the area called Primero de Mayo y Esmeraldas. In Quito the Mariscal and Colon districts house many of the gay bars and meeting places. The best website for information on gay club life in Quito is http://gayquitoec.tripod.com/bars.htm. A gay-oriented tour company for Ecuador is **Zenith Travel** at: http://www.zenithecuador.com/.

Movies

There are a large number of movie chains throughout the major cities of Ecuador. Most of the major malls have cinemas. Listings can be found in the newspapers. Most are quite modern and the quality is good. **CineMark** is one of the largest chains here. Its Ecuadorian web page is http://www.cinemark.com.ec. Most cinemas have snack bars that look just like the ones in the United States.

Video Rentals

Quito
American Video Club: Avenida 10 de Agosto y Amazonas
Videoteca: Avenida República y Grecia

Television and Radio

Ecuador has a considerable number of radio and television stations. The systems used here are UHF and VHF. There are numerous radio stations in Ecuador. My favorite is Radio Cristal 860 AM in Guayaquil. Also known as the Voz del Pueblo, it broadcasts many programs on different topics. My favorite is an announcement program where anyone can place almost any type of announcement. For example, one can announce a lost cat or cow. In my case, my family was once worried about my whereabouts and were going to call Radio Cristal to announce my disappearance. They waited a few more hours before making a call to discover that I had been delayed at a *cantina* (bar) with a few of my friends having a few beers. Time certainly can slip away when you're enjoying yourself in Ecuador.

CULTURAL QUIZ

SITUATION ONE

You are standing in line at an airline counter in Guayaquil. You notice that fellow passengers are going to the counter past you, apparently just to ask a quick question. You also notice an elderly person cut straight to the front of the line and being served before the other passengers. Then you notice an agent acknowledge someone in the line and take him around the counter. He is furnished with a ticket and then escorted through the terminal and onto the plane before general boarding occurs. You become upset at the general lack of regard for queues.

A You start raising your voice and telling others to get back in line.

B When you get to the clerk you demand to see the manager in a loud voice and become quite irate. You begin thinking like a gringo might: "The squeaky wheel will get the grease." Yelling, you exclaim " I will never fly this airline again because you allow customers to cut the line ahead of others!"

C You smile and keep moving with the line but curse quietly to yourself. You keep reminding yourself how lucky you are to be in this unique and beautiful country.

Comments

A would be considered very rude by Ecuadorians, despite your desire for order. Ecuadorians have a much higher tolerance for queue-cutting than most North Americans or Europeans. You would be considered most rude if you started yelling at an older person, as they usually allowed to be served before others. However, in some cases, if you politely point out to the person who cut into the line that he/she has done so, the meeker people in the line might appreciate your attempt, even if that doesn't produce any results.

B is very similar to **A**. The clerk and manager will not argue with you. However, they will start to think of ways to make your life miserable. Challenging the manager will not change the situation. Getting angry will create the opposite effect. The person who received the preferential treatment was probably a friend of the agent or had connections in the airline.

C is the correct choice. Smiling and going with the flow is the best solution. Arriving at the airport as early as possible might reduce your stress.

SITUATION TWO

You meet an Ecuadorian friend for lunch at a restaurant. When the bill arrives you suggest that each of you pay for your meal. He wants to pay the bill but you insist that you pay your half.

A You continue to press the issue and insist you pay your part of the bill.

B You decide to pay for the bill as he has been very kind in the past and you know his funds are limited.

C You allow him to pay the bill. You comment that you will allow him to do so this time but you will treat for lunch the next time.

Comments

A would be considered very rude. Splitting bills or asking for separate bills at a public meal is not practiced by Ecuadorians. Being a host is considered an honor and you should be accept the hospitality graciously. The general rule in Ecuadorian society is that the inviting party is obligated to pay for any entertainment as well. Also, please don't negotiate in advance for separate bills.

B is acceptable unless your Ecuadorian friend asked you out for lunch.

C is also acceptable.

SITUATION THREE

While at the home of an Ecuadorian, he asks you about your children and how tall your son is. Not knowing his height measurements, you use your hand as a ruler for his height.

A You demonstrate the height of your son with your palm facing down.

B You demonstrate the height of your son by turning your hand in a 90-degree angle with the bottom of the hand being the ruler.

Comments

A is an extremely rude gesture to make in Ecuador. Measuring things with the palm down is only used for animals, not for people.

B is the correct answer and used to show the height of people.

SITUATION FOUR

An Ecuadorian friend has just visited your home in Quito. When he leaves, your appropriate gesture should be to:

A Shake his hand as he is leaving and see him off until he is in his car and well on his way, making sure you leave the front door open.

B Say goodbye at the front door and shut the door after he has left the house whilst waving to him.

Comments

A is the appropriate response. Ecuadorians shake hands a great deal both when meeting and parting with each other. Letting the friend leave the house and closing the door behind him would be considered rude. The door should be left open until you are sure he is well on his way.

SITUATION FIVE

While at a party you are drinking glasses of beer or whisky. You realize that you have had your limit.

A You finish the glass and tell your host you have had enough to drink.

B You accept one more glass but you continue to sip it and don't finish all of it.

Comments

A would not be appropriate. By finishing the beverage you are telling your host you would like some more. This is especially so among the lower classes. **B** is the appropriate response as you will be allowed to nurse your drink and will probably not be offered any more.

SITUATION SIX

You have a business appointment for four o'clock in the afternoon. Should you:

A Arrive exactly at four o'clock and expect to wait for your meeting.

B Arrive 15 minutes early and expect to wait for your meeting.

C Arrive ten minutes late and expect to wait for your meeting.

Comments

All answers are correct in this scenario. It is not considered rude to arrive a few minutes late for a business meeting, on time, or early. However, it is always best to be punctual and please be prepared to wait. (However, this is not the rule for a private party, arriving half an hour to 40 minutes late is fine.)

SITUATION SEVEN

You are the new country manager in Ecuador for a foreign major export company. One of your duties is to assign a manufacturing representative for Ecuador. You have found two qualified persons, one from Quito and the other from Guayaquil and your firm's practice in the past has been to assign only one representative.

A   You choose the agent from Quito because he has a little more technical experience than the agent in Guayaquil for your particular product.

B   The agent from Guayaquil is of Lebanese descent and has an excellent reputation in sales so you choose him.

C   You divide the territory up for the agents giving the Sierra region to the agent from Quito and the Costa market to the agent from Guayaquil.

COMMENTS

Choosing **A** may cause your firm to have representation problems, especially in the coast. The *serrano* will always be viewed as an outsider by many of the Guayaquil clients and not trusted.

B causes the same problem in reverse, although some businesspeople may disagree with me and decide to take the risk, given his expertise. The *costeño* will, however, have problems operating in the Sierra.

C is the best choice for market penetration, as numerous companies have found. This will also minimise travel expenses, resulting in a higher profit margin.

DO'S AND DONT'S APPENDIX

DO

• Speak as loudly as you like. Conversations here are often louder than what North Americans are accustomed to. Ecuadorians may also interrupt each other by using their hands. Loudness is not an indicator of confrontation or disagreement.

• Arrive at a party half an hour to 40 minutes after the stated time.

• Present your host/hostess a box of chocolates or flowers if you are invited to an Ecuadorian home.

• Defer to older persons in conversation or when entering or exiting a building. Age is openly respected in Ecuador.

• Feel free to display open affection for children in public.

• Laugh at jokes about Pastuzos. Pastuzo means from Pasto (Colombia) and this name is given to people from Tulcán, a town near the Ecuadorian–Colombian border who are considered naive. Many Ecuadorians use Pastuzo as the subject of jokes, much as Polacks are in the United States. An example of such a joke is: "How does a Pastuzo tie the shoelace on his right foot?" Answer: He puts his left foot on a chair and bends down to tie the shoelace on his right foot on the floor."

• Keep your hands above the table when you eat. Ecuadorians often rest their forearms on the table while they eat.

• Remember that women from Manabí are viewed by most Ecuadorian men as very attractive.

• Remember that women from the United States are often seen by Ecuadorian men as being sexually permissive.

• Feel free to breast-feed in public.

• Accept that begging is common in Ecuador. People just learn to ignore it or give a small amount.

• Remember that people from Europe or the United States are viewed by most Ecuadorians as being wealthy.

• Be aware that many Ecuadorians group people from Asia into one race, calling them "*chinos.*"

• Haggle or bargain in markets, this is an accepted practice.

• Open doors or get a female's chair for her.

• Get used to addressing people by their professions or titles as this is seen as a sign of respect. Men you are friendly with can be addressed as *Don*, followed by that person's first name. (In my first few months in Ecuador I actually believed people thought my name was Don.)

• Understand that elephants are seen as a sign of good luck in Ecuador. Many houses have a number of elephants. There is a phrase that says each home should have one elephant that was given, one bought, and one stolen. Many Ecuadorians will have the elephants facing a window or door for good luck.

• Allow women and older people to board the elevator first.

• Know that Tuesday the 13th is viewed as a day of bad omen.

• Give a light kiss on the cheek when greeting a female whose acquaintance you have made. Many women also kiss each other on the cheek.

• Remember that conduct in the workplace is generally more formal in Ecuador than in the United States.

DON'T

• Yawn in public. It is considered rude.

• Point at people.

• Arrive at a party at the designated hour.

• Discuss the border disputes with Peru or Colombia.

• "Go Dutch." If you invite a friend/s out you are expected to pay. This is especially true if you're a male and you have invited a female out.

• Give money openly to a female in public. This may have negative connotations.

• Finish all the food on your plate when eating as a guest in a lower-class home. If you clear the plate, the hostess may feel that the food wasn't sufficient.

- Spit in public.
- Clap your hands or hiss for service in a restaurant.
- Feel inhibited about urinating in public. It is a common practice.
- Be too direct or frank. The white lie is a practiced art in Ecuador. Ecuadorians will often tell you what you want to hear. This is especially true between a subordinate and a superior or between someone from a lower and higher social class.
- Ask someone not to smoke in public places as smoking is widely accepted here.
- Curse in public.
- Walk your pet in public places.
- Extravagantly flaunt your wealth. This is looked down upon.
- Walk barefooted in public.
- Bare all on public beaches.
- Use your cellular phones in banks. Do not forget that although cellular phones are used in many public places, they are seen as a sign of wealth.
- Laugh very loudly.
- Expect Ecuadorians to stand in a straight or orderly line. You will usually notice more of a circling or rounding of the group trying to get to the cash register or service counter.
- Forget that people of the middle and upper social classes view manual labor as below their station in life.
- Be offended if you are called a *hippy*. Hikers and campers are often called *hippies* here, especially if they have long hair.
- Forget that formalities and good manners is important to Ecuadorians, much more so than in the United States. Manners also are a sign of education to an Ecuadorian.
- Forget to shake the hand of the person you are greeting or parting from. Handshakes here are generally less firm but longer than in the United States.

GLOSSARY

LOWER-CLASS SLANG

A la johnny—Going to the United States

A precio de huevo—Cheap price (literally price of an egg)

Abreboca—Appetizer

Abrir cancha—Move out the way

Achumarse—To get drunk (Costa)

Afrecho—Crybaby (Cuenca)

Agringado—Refers to a local trying to act like someone from the United States

Aguatero—Water seller

Aguinaldo—Christmas gifts from employers

Aló—Hello when answering the phone

Ancheta—Good price

Ardilla—Poorly behaved child (literally means squirrel)

Arenilla—Small mosquito in the jungle

Atatay—Horrible! (Sierra)

Ayayay—Hurt, sore (Sierra)

Bacan—It's ok

Bachacha—Jail

Bambu—Cigarette from the United States

Biela—Beer

Boche—Fight

Botadero—City dump

Buena facha—Good dresser (Cuenca)

Buseta—Small bus that travels between the provinces

Cabeza de huevo—Bald man (literally means egghead)

Cacharrero—Seller of contraband along the borders with Peru and Colombia

Cachero or Maricón—Homosexual

Cachos—Jokes

Caído del petate—Fool

Caimán—Lazy person

Cajonera—Street salesperson (these operate off the sidewalks, especially in Quito)

Caleta—House

Calzonazo—Lazy man

Calzonudo—Fool (Costa)

Camarón—Inexperienced person (literally "shrimp")

Cana—Jail

Capillo—Loose coins (usually thrown by the bridegroom to children when leaving the church after the ceremony)

Cari—Macho (Cuenca)

Cháchara—Jokes

Chacra—Small garden plot outside the home

Chancho en bandeja—Fat (literally "pig in a tray")

Chanchullo—Bribe, usually between an individual and a public official

Chancleta—Baby (literally "sandal")

Chapudo—Cheeks/red face

Chevere—Good

Chimbo—Bounced check. Also refers to witchcraft. (Esmeraldas)

China—Maid

Chinear—To assault

Chiro—Broke

Chirona—Jail

Chocha—To be fond of someone or something new

Chompa—Jacket

Choza—Hut (Sierra)

Chuamarse—To get drunk (Sierra)

Chuchos—Breasts

Chupón—Baby pacifier

Conchudo—A person with no scruples

Cromo—Referring to a person's face

Cucaracha—Old car (literally "bug")

Cucayo—Lunch

Dar para la cola—Bribe (literally refers to providing someone a payment to purchase a Coca-Cola)

Domingo chiquita—Drunk or Monday morning hangover (literally refers to someone who continues drinking on Monday.)

Entrar de gancho—Two people admitted on one ticket

Estar con la leona—Hungry

Estar con la luna—Crazy (literally "with the moon")

Estar frito—Bad situation (literally "fried")

Estar limpio—Broke (literally "to be clean")

Fachosa—Badly dressed (Costa)

Farra—Party

Foco—Embarrassed

Gallada—Gang (literally refers to group of young people out having fun and raising a ruckus)

Hacer cola—Standing in line

Hacer dedo—Hitchhiking

Huasipungo—House (Sierra)

Jamar—Eat

Jeva—Girlfriend

La familia pavoni—Trying to get something for nothing, broke (literally "turkey family")

La llapa—Baker's dozen (Sierra)

Ladrar—Drunk (Literally "to bark" in Spanish)

Liga—To befriend

Mantel largel—Banquet in the house

Mario—Husband (Costa)

Matute—Contraband

Melindrosa—Picky eater

Michelin—Fat

Motoso—Curly hair

Mucha—Kiss (Sierra)

Ñaño—Brother or good friend

Nuevón—New employee

Papear—Eat

Palo grueso—Influential person with a lot of power

Pana—Friend

Pega—Work

Pelar el ojo—Alert, awake

Petate—Bed or straw mat used in the Costa

Pichón—Loan (Cuenca)

Pinganillo—Elegant

Pipón—Lazy person (literally a person who receives his pay every fifteen days but doesn't do any work)

Plana calles—Lazy person who levels the streets with his feet

Pleno—It's ok

Pluto—Drunk

Prenda el foco—Think (literally "let me turn the lightbulb on")

Ruquear—Sleep

Sambo—Person with curly hair

Ser del otro equipo—Homosexual

Soplar—To make love (literal Spanish meaning "to blow in the wind")

Sumercé—Your mercy (usually used in the Sierra between a person of indigenous origin and a white person or one of a higher social status)

Shunsho—Fool (Quichua)

Traguear—Drinking aguardiente

Trinche—Fork (Cuenca)

Turro—Broken, ugly, or of bad quality

X—Wife or husband (used "La X" or "El X")

Zorro—Homosexual or female prostitute

MEDICAL TERMS IN SPANISH

Alergia—Allergy
Amigdalitis—Tonsillitis
Ardentina—Fever
Arthritis—Arthritis
Asma—Asthma
Ataque al corazón—Heart attack
Bronquitis—Bronchitis
Diarrea—Diarrhea
Difteria—Diphtheria
Dolor de cabeza—Headache
Dolor de garganta—Sore throat
Dolor de oido—Ear ache
Conjuntivitis—Conjunctivitis
Erupción cutánea/salpullido—Rash
Fiebre—Fever
Fiebre amarilla—Yellow fever
Fiebre escarlatina—Scarlet fever
Fiebre tifoidea—Typhoid
Gripe—Cold/flu
Hepatitis—Hepatitis
Manchas rojas en la piel—Spots
Meningitis—Meningitis
Mordedura or picadura—Bite
Neumonia/pulmonia—Pneumonia
Paludismo—Malaria
Paperas/parotiditis—Mumps
Polio—Polio
Rabia—Rabies
Reumatismo—Rheumatism
Rubeola—German measles
Sarampión—Measles
Tétanos—Tetanus

Tos—Cough
Tosferina—Whooping cough
Varicela—Chicken pox
Viruela—Smallpox

CALENDAR OF FESTIVALS AND HOLIDAYS

PUBLIC HOLIDAYS

January 1	New Year's Day
May 1	Labor Day
May 24	Anniversary of the Battle of Pichincha
July 24	Simón Bolívar Day
August 10	Independence Day
October 9	Foundation of Guayaquil (Guayaquil only)
October 12	Dia de la Raza
November 2	Memorial Day/Dia de Difuntos (All Souls Day)
November 3	Foundation of Cuenca
November 6	Foundation of Quito
December 25	Christmas Day

HOLIDAYS WITH VARIABLE DATES

	2002	2003	2004
Carnaval	Feb. 11–12	Mar 3–4	Feb 23–24
Holy Thursday	Mar 28	Apr 17	Apr 8
Good Friday	Mar 29	Apr 18	Apr 9
Easter	Mar 31	Apr 20	Apr 11

RESOURCE GUIDE

Please note that telephone numbers are reflected in the old form here, since there is a gradual change of telephone numbers across Ecuador, as yet uncompleted at the time this book went to print. Please refer to the Settling In chapter for more information about the new prefixes to some telephone numbers. For the most current information on telephone numbers, http://www.ecuadorexplorer.com might be able to help. Please also note that the province codes have been left off the following telephone numbers. For international, province, and cellular phone numbers, please refer to Settling In chapter for more information.

EMERGENCY PHONE NUMBERS

Quito

Alcoholics Anonymous	309 023
Ambulance/Red Cross	131
Blood Bank	543 692, 280 777
Civil Defense	439 433
Criminal Investigations	554 236
Emergency	911
Fire Department	102
Police Radio Patrol	101
Police Regiment	459 811
Detention Center	950 250

Guayaquil

Airport	282 100
Alcoholics Anonymous	309 023, 448 212
Ambulance/Red Cross	560 674

Blood Bank	560 675
Civil Defense	321 111
Criminal Investigation	294 231
Fire Department	102
Police Radio Patrol	101
Transit/Vehicular Commission	103

TELEPHONES

If you have family calling you from Ecuador they can compare rates of numerous carriers at the following website: http://www.abelltolls.com/compare/international/longdistancerates/ecuador.htm. There are two major players in the cellular phone market in Ecuador—Bell South and Porta.

Bell South. Edificio Bell South, Avenida Republica y la Pradera Esquina, Quito. tel 593 222 7700; http://www.bellsouth.com.ec.

Porta. http://www.porta.net

For more information on telephone numbers in Ecuador, please refer to the Settling In chapter.

AIRLINES

Exito Travel: tel 1 800 655 4053; http://www.exito-travel.com
Intratours: tel 1 800 334 8069; http://www.intratours.com
Latin Cheap Tickets: tel 1 888 590 3152
Mill Avenue Travel: International tel 1 800 815 6455, U.S. tel 602 966 6300; sue.millave@wspan.comtel or sue.millave@wspan.com. I have used this agency for a number of years.
Safar International: tel 1 800 544 2369; safarinc@ameri tech.net;http://www.safarint.com

TAME: toll free tel inside Ecuador 1 800 555 999, http://www.tame.com.ec.

TOURIST OFFICES
Ecuador Government Tourist Office
• Reina Victoria 514 y Ramon Roca, Quito. tel 527 002
• Avenida Venezuela y Chile. tel 514 044 (smaller office)

Ecuador Government Tourist Corporation
Airport Executive Tower II, Suite 400, 7270 NW 12th Street, Miami, FL 33126. Tel 305 477 0041

http://www.ecuadorexplorer.com is a comprehensive website for anyone traveling or moving to Ecuador. While highly commercial in nature it does present good information.

CAB SERVICES
In Quito there is a radio taxicab company that you can call to your location—**Taxi Amigos** (tel 222 999). They often use cars that are not marked as cabs for security purposes, as thieves do think that foreigners who take cabs may have large amounts of cash. You can always ask for the identification of the driver. A cabdriver for local tours that I have found reliable and trustsworthy is Jorge, who has a marked cab and charges a rate of $3 an hour for local tours (in 2000). His home telephone number is 628 634. Another individual I have used for a trip from Quito to Guayaquil is Jorge Bonilla R. He is a metal worker who works part-time as a chauffeur. He uses his private vehicle (a Camry) and is very reliable (home tel 504 908).

Other cab companies in Quito
CCInmoquito: tel 441 183
Central Radio Taxi: tel 500 600
Teletaxi: tel 220 800

BANKING

Accountants
Price Waterhouse Coopers
• Carchi 702 2nd Floor, Guayaquil. tel 281 555
• Diego de Almagro N 32-48 y Whymper, Edificio IBM 1st Floor, Quito. tel 562 288

Taxes
The tax system is quite complicated and has changed significantly in the last several years in the government's attempt to increase revenues. The taxable rate for most foreigners who reside in Ecuador is usually about 25%. The government has a website on taxes: **http://www.sri.gov.ec**. The only catch is that it's in Spanish.

Bank Account
Opening up an account in Ecuador is pretty straightforward. A savings account will usually require a minimum of US$40 and for you to produce an identification card. Checking accounts require, in some cases, at least US$80 with a previous banking reference and two commercial references. Writing bad checks is serious business in Ecuador and can land you in jail. In 2000, at a certain bank, customers withdrawing money from its cash machines had the amount debited twice. Also, there have been several cases where money withdrawals were attempted but the machine didn't dispense the funds. However, the withdrawal showed on the statement. The banks involved then were Banco De Pichincha and Filanbanco.

Credit Cards
The most commonly accepted cards are **Diners Club**, **Mastercard**, **Visa**, and **American Express**.

American Express
<u>Quito</u>
Through Ecuadorian Tours at Avenida Río Amazonas, tel 560 488

<u>Guayaquil</u>
Through Ecuadorian Tours at Avebuda 9 de Octubre 1900, tel 287 111.

Diners Club
Edificio Diners at Avenidas de la Republica 710 y Eloy Alfaro, Quito. tel 221 372; http://www.dinersclub.com.ec. This is an excellent website with lots of information about upcoming events and special discounts. If you're moving to Ecuador for the long term, I would recommend that you obtain this card as it is considered prestigous and well accepted in Ecuador.

GAS COMPANIES
Cooking gas is delivered to most homes in Quito. One of the largest suppliers is through Sr. Marco Manosalvas. tel 400 519.

DOCTORS
<u>Quito</u>
• Dr Stephen Contag(Gynecologist)
Medico Medtropoli, Avenida Mariana de Jesus Suite 109. tel 267 972.
• Alvaro F. Davlos P. M.D.
La Colina 202 y San Ignacio, Quito, Ecuador. tel 500 267, 500 268; adavalos@pi.pro.ec.
• Dr Alba Sandoval M.D.
Ramirez Dávalos #117 y Avenid Amazonas, Edificio Turismundil 6th Floor #602. tel 523 974. HP 09 207 650.
• Dr Carlos Rojas (Dentist)
tel 462 741, 434 555. crcrdent@uio.telconet.net. Highly recommended and speaks English.

Guayaquil
• Dr Roberto Calderon. Clinic Alcivar Centro Medico, #2 2nd Floor. tel 343 575, 447 354.
• Dr Rafael Caputi. Clinica Kennedy Seccion Beta #21. tel 293 526.
• Dr Juan Cajas. Kennedy Norte Mig. H. Alcivar. tel 399 837.
• Dr. Federico Lebed. CEDIPE. FCO Boloña 610 y Decima. tel 287 624.
• Telmo Fernandez. L. Urdaneta 1401 y Garcia Moreno. tel 289 940.
• Dr. Gilberto R. Peñafiel, M.D. tel 285 886.
• Dr. Angel Serrano, M.D. 821 Boyacá. tel 561 785, 301 373, 301 362.

HOSPITALS

Quito
• Hospital Metropolitano. Avenida Mariana de Jesús y Nicolas Arteta y Calisto. tel 261 520, 269 030.
• Hospital Vozandes. 254 Villa Lengua, Quito. tel 262 142.

Guayaquil
• Clinica Alcivar. Coronel y Azuy Esquinas (Sur). tel 444 287, 580 030.
• Clinica Kennedy. Av. San Jorge entre 9a. y 10a. tel 286 963, 289 666. Ambulance 288 888.
• Clinica Kennedy – Alvorada. Guill. Pareja R. y Benj. Carrion. tel 247 900.

HEALTH SERVICES

Ambulances
Quito
• ADAMI. tel 265 020.
• UTIM. tel 562 613, 562 614. HP: 09 739 801

Air Ambulances/Evacuation

• Aeromedevac Inc. (U.S. Based). tel 1 800 462 0911 (from the U.S.) tel 1 800 832 5087 (from Mexico). http://www.aeromedevac.com.

• Ambulancias Aereas del Ecuador. tel 449 191 (Quito). International SOS (U.S. Based) 1 800 523 8930.

• Life Flight. tel 1 800 231 4357. http://www.lifeflightweb.com. webmaster@lifeflightweb.com. Non-emergency tel 713 704 4014. Emergency tel 713 704 HELP (4357).

• National Jets. tel 1 800 327 3710. www.nationalairambulance.com

International Health Insurance

• Access America. tel 1 800 284 8300. http://www.worldaccess.com, or, http://www.accessamerica.com. wasc@worldaccess.com. Carefree Travel Insurance. tel 1 800 645 2424.

• International SOS. www.internationalsos.com

• Wallach & Co. tel 1 800 237 6615, 540 687 3166. http://www.wallach.com. email: info@wallach.com.

Other Contacts

• **International Association for Medical Assistance to Travelers** (IAMAT). tel 716 754 4883 (Lewiston, New York). http://www.sentex.net/~iamat/. email: IAMAT@sentex.net or IAMAT @on.aibn.ca.

Free membership with listings of doctors who speak English. They have a set fee for the first visit. This is a very good organization that is funded by donations. Some donations include excellent climate and tropical disease charts for the world.

• **List of pharmacies in the Galápagos Islands:**

Santa Cruz
Farmacia Edith. tel 526 487
Farmacia Vanessa. tel 526 392

Farmacia Aida Maria. tel 526 117
Farmacia Sta. Cruz. tel 526 118

<u>San Cristobal</u>
Farmacia Jane. tel 520 242

<u>Isabela</u>
Botiquin Narcisa de Jesus. tel 529 153

• Another excellent service online for those travelling to Ecuador is **http://www.travmed.com**. It is a very good source of general and specific information on travelling around the world including Ecuador.

INTERNET SERVICES/CAFÉS
Access Internet. http://www.accessinter.net
AltesaNet. http://www.altesa.net
Ecuador Online. http://www.eolnet.net
Hoy.net. http://www.hoy.net
Satnet.net. http://www.satnet.net

Cybercafés
<u>Baños</u>
C@fe.com. 12 de Noviembre 500 y Oriente. tel 740309. http://www3.satnet.net/cafecom.

<u>Cotocachi</u>
Chito.Net. Gonzales Suarez 12-33 y 10 de Agosto. Chito@andinanet.net

<u>Cuenca</u>
Explore-Net Internet Café. Padre Aguirre 10-96 y Mariscal Lamar. http://www:explore-net.net. explore@explore-net.net. tel 844 473.

Guayaquil
• It@cybercafe. Cdla. Alborada, Av. G Pareja Rolando. tel 247 200.
• Cafeinat.com. La Garzota Mz 20 sol 7 Diag A. tel 279 714.

Otavalo
Internet Planet. Salinas 511 Modesto Jaramillo Plaza de Ponchas.

Quito
• Bluenet Café. Veintimilla 635 y Av. 6 de Diciembre. tel 557 746.
Without question this is my favorite internet café. A wonderful family
from Cuenca operates it. They have wonderful snacks and coffee and
fast internet connections. However, the smoking of patrons may be a
problem to some. Usually open until 2:00 am. silvabluenet@hot
mail.com
• Cafenet. Reina Victoria y Cordero, Local #14. tel 255 4005.
• Cafeweb.par. Avenida Amozonas #333 y Jorge Washington. tel 553
725. info@cafeweb.com.ec
• Interactive. Avenida 12 de Octubre y A. Lincoln, Edificio Torre
1492. tel 986 440. http://www.interactive.net.ec. email: ventasuio
@interactive.net.ec. Also has a branch on the third floor of Quicentro
next to Burger King
• Monkey Online. Juan León Mera n 21-10 y Jorge Washington. tel
500 979. http://www.altesa.net/monkeyonline/index.htm

POST OFFICES
Quito
• **Main Post Office**. Eloy Alfaro 354 and 9 de Octubre. Mon–Fri 7.30
am–7 pm, Sat 8 am–2 pm
• Branch Post Offices:
Reina Victoria and Colón (Edificio Torres de Almagro). Mon–Fri
7. 30 am–5.45 pm, Sat 8 am–11.45 am.
Espejo y Guayaquil (between Guayaquil and Venezuela). Mon–Fri
7.30 am–7 pm, Sat 8 am–2 pm.

Japón and Naciones Unidas. Mon–Fri 7.30 am–7 pm, Sat 8 am–2 pm.
Airport Mariscal Sucre (National Departures). Mon–Fri 7.30 am–7 pm, Sat 8 am–1 pm.

Guayaquil

The **main post office** is located at Pedro Carbo y Clemente Ballén. Another option for receiving your mail while you are overseas is by using a private company. **Personal Mail International** out of New Jersey offers such a service. tel 1 800 548 3622, 973 543 6001. http://www.pmipmi.com.

While in Ecuador I have found **Postnet** to be reliable for shipping and receiving mail and packages. While there are several branches throughout Ecuador, I have found the following branch particularly reliable and friendly: **Postnet Cetnro Piloto**, Coruña 1311 y San Ignacio Esq. tel 220 816, 220 817.

EMBASSY LIST

Most of the foreign embassies and consulate offices are in Quito. I have provided a list of foreign embassies and consulates in Quito and Guayaquil, their addresses and telephone numbers below but please take note that these are subject to change. To verify this information here are some related websites:
http://www.cee-mail.com/embassies/south_america/ecuador.php3;
http://www.ecuador-travel-guide.org/services/embassylist.htm;
http://www.embassyworld.com/embassy/ecuador.htm;
http://www.goabroad.com/embassy/embassy.cfm?embassy=home&fkcountry=23.

Quito

Argentina: Amazonas Ave. 477, 8th Floor. tel 562 2921
Austria: Veintimilla 878 y Amazonas Ave., 4th Floor. tel 524 811

Belgium: Juan LeónMera 863 y Wilson. tel 545 340

Brazil: Amazonas Ave. 1429 y Colón Ave. tel 563 086

Canada: 6 de Diciembre Avenida 2816 y Paul Rivet, Josueth Gonzales Bldg., 4th Floor. tel 232 114

Chile: Juan Pablo Saenz 3617 y Avenida Amazonas. tel 466 780

Colombia: Colón 1133 y Avenida Amazonas. tel 222 486

Costa Rica: Calle Rumipamba 692 entre Amazonas y Republic Ave. tel 254 945

Egypt: Baquedano 222 y Reina Victoria. tel 225 240

France: General Plaza 107 y Avenida Patrtia. tel 560 789

Germany: Avenida Naciones Unids y Avenida Repúbublica El Salvador. tel 970 822

Great Britain: Avenida Naciones Unidas y República El Salvador 14th Floor-City Plaz. tel 970800

Holland: Avenida 12 de Octubre 1942 y Cordero–World Trade Center, Tower 1 1st Floor. tel 525 461

Israel: Avenida 12 de Octubre y General Salazar. tel 562 152

Italy: La Isla y 111 y Humberto Albornoz. tel 561 077

Japan: Avenida Patria 130 y Juan Leon Mera. tel 561 899

Mexico: Avenida 6 de Deciembre N 36–165. tel 258 788

Peru: Avenida República de El Salvador 495 y Irlanda. tel 468 410/ 468 411

Russia: Reina Victoria 462 y Roca. tel 526 375

Spain: Avenida Amazonas y Pinta. tel 564 377

Switzerland: Avenida Amazonas Xerox Bldg. tel 434 949

United States: Avenida 12 de Octubre y Patria. tel 562 890. http://www.usembassy.org.ec

Uruguay: Avenida 6 de Diciembre 2816 y Daul Rivet 9 Piso. tel 544 228

Venezuela: Los Cabildos 115 y Hidalgo de Pinto. tel 268 635

Guayaquil
Australia: Edificio Techniseguros, Kennedy Norte y Calle San Roque. tel 298 823, 298 700
United States: 9 de Octubre y García Moreno. tel 323 570

BUSINESS CONTACTS

Ecuadorian–American Chamber of Commerce (Quito)
Edificio Multicentra 4 floor, La Nina y Avda. 6 de Diciembre, Quito. tel 507 450/451. http://www.ecamcham.com.

Ecuadorian–American Chamber of Commerce (Guayaquil)
Edificio Centrum 6th floor, Office 5, Francisco de Orellna Avenue, Kennedy Norte, Guayaquil. tel 693 470/71/72/73/74. http://www.caecam.org/amcham.html. caecam1@caecam.org.

Ecuadorian American Chamber of Commerce of Los Angeles
701 N. Alvarado Street, Los Angeles, CA 90026. tel 323 939 6568. franklinfigueroa@hotmail.com.

Ecuadorian-American Chamber of Commerce
4100 Westheimer, Suite 200, Houston, Texas 77027-4427. tel 713 877-8534. james@eacc.org. http://www.eacc.org.

Corporación Ecutoriana de Comercio Electrónico
Almagro N 32-349 y Shyris, Edificio Lorena, 3rd Floor. tel 509 595/509 578. http://www.corpece.net. This website has a tremendous amount of information about law dealing with electronics and intellectual property.

Export and Investment Promotion Corporation (CORPEI)
• Cdla. Kennedy Norte, Avda. Francisco de Orellana y Miguel H. Alcívar, Edificio Centro Empresarial Las Cámaras, Torre de Oficinas, 2nd Floor, Guayaquil. tel 681 550.

• Avenida 12 de Octubre y Cordero
World Trade Center Torre B office 1406. tel 236 506. http://www.corpei.org.

Federación Ecutoriana de la Pequeña y Mediana Industría (CAPEIPI) Avenida Amazones y Atahualpa, Centro de Exposiciones Quito 2nd Floor. tel 443 388. http://www.capeipi.com.

LAWYERS
Bermeo & Bermeo
World Trade Center, Bldg. Tower II, 12th Floor, 12 Octubre y Cordero, Quito, Ecuador. tel 545 871. http://www.bermeo-law.com. bblaw@andinanet.net.

Quevedo & Ponce
Torre 1492 Avenida 12 de Octubre y Lincoln 16th Floor, Quito, Ecuador. tel 986 570. http://www.quepon.com.ec.

MECHANICS
Quito
Miguel A. Taipe G. e Hijos. Ponteyedra 566 N 24-278 y Madrid, La Floresta. tel 236 640, 544 847.

Guayaquil
British Garage. tel 352 902.

REAL ESTATE BROKERS

Quito
Frave Real Estate. Corunia 1609 y Manuel Iturrey. tel 250 4156, 256 3346. http://www.ecuainternet.com.
Quito Real Estate Service. Calle Leonids Plza 353 y Roca.

If you're moving appliances or are going to purchase appliances for your move to Ecuador, there is a very good company in New York called **Appliances Overseas** where you can purchase items plus have them shipped overseas:

Appliances Overseas. 276 Fifth Avenue & 30th Street, Suite 407 New York, NY 10001-4509. tel 212 545 8001. help@appliances overseas.com. http://www.appliancesoverseas.com/

SCHOOLS
Quito
• **Academia Cotopaxi**. tel 467 410/467 411. http://www.coto paxi.k12.ec. Probably the best private school in Quito.
• **Alliance Academy**. Used primarily by Christian missionaries. http://www.alliance.k12.ec

Guayaquil
Inter-American Academy. tel 870 353. http://www.acig.k12.ec/ index.html. email: admin@acig.k12.ec.

STUDY ABROAD PROGRAMS
• Boston University. http://www.bu.edu/abroad
College credit languge and liberal arts program in Quito. Also offers a tropical ecology program with intensive fieldwork on the coast of Ecuador.
• Elderhostel. http://www.elderhostel.org
Offers numerous tours exploring Ecuador's history and culture. They also offer a Spanish language program.
• Marist College. http://www.marist.edu/international
Offers a program with Pontifica Catholic University of Ecuador in Quito. Semester and full year programs for variety of subjects including Ecuadorian studies.

• University of Minnesota. http://www.umabroad.umn.edu
Semester and year-long program offered in numerous subjects including agriculture, Andean studies, and anthropology.

RELIGIOUS & SOCIAL WORK

Quito
Baptist:
• First Baptist Church (English). El Telérapho 281 y Juan de Alcántara.
tel 249 482.

Catholic:
• El Girón Church. Avenida 12 de Octubre y Veintimilla
• El Batán Church. Av. Gaspar de Villareal y 6 de Deciembre

Christian:
• English Fellowship Church. Villalengua 884. tel 266 612.
• Presbyterian Church of Ecuador. Río Coca 1025. tel 435 548

Mormon:
• Iglesia de Jesuscristo de los Santos de los Ultimos Días. Av. Colón
706- y Almagro. tel 508 524.

Synagogue:
• Israelite Society Synagogue. 18 de Septiembre 954.

VOLUNTEER OPPORTUNITIES

• CEIBA – Foundation for Tropical Conservation. http://www.cei
ba.org/index.htm.
• Earthwatch Institute. http://www.earthwatch.org.
• Partners of the Americas. http://www.partners.net
• Global Volunteers. tel 1 800 487 1074. http://www.global
volunteers.com.

• HCBJ World Radio. http://www.hcjb.org

A number of Christian opportunities in technical fields and medicine.

• Reformed Church in America. http://www.rca.org/mission/volunteers/individuals/ecuador.html. This needs Doctors, Nurses, Construction and Agricultural Workers.

• United Nations Volunteers. http://www.unv.org

VOLCANO INFORMATION

Volcano information may be obtained at: http://www.ssd.noaa.gov/VAAC/guag.html.

WRITING NUMBERS

Dates are normally written as day-month-year (3-1-2002). Periods indicate thousand and millions, and commas are used for decimals, e.g. 1.101.800,10.

FURTHER READING

Reading as much as possible about Ecuador will enhance your understanding of this unique country. From fiction to scientific studies there is a substantial amount on Ecuador in print.

BOOKS

Business

Doing Business Guide: Ecuador (Pricewaterhouse Coopers, 1992). Much of the information here is dated but it does provide good information about the intricacies of operating a business in Ecuador.

Culture

Estrada, Jenny. *Del Tiempo De La Yapa*. (El Universo, Guayaquil: 1996. Second Edition)

Franklin, Albert B. *Ecuador Of A People*. (Doubleday Doran & Company Inc., Garden City, New York: 1943). Travel account that explores the culture of the Ecuadorians.

Fried, Michelle O. *Comidas Del Ecuador: Recetas Tradicionales Para Gente de Hoy*. (Impreseñal Cía Ltda, Quito: 1993).

Handelsman, Michael. *Culture and Customs of Ecuador* (Greenwood Publishing Group, Westport, Connecticut: 2000). Professor Handelsman writes in detail about many aspects of Ecuadorian society. A concise and well-written work, it contains seldom covered subjects in English about Ecuadorian culture. It provides excellent insights into a broad spectrum of Ecuadorian society that includes its media, music, and performing arts.

Miller, Tom. *The Panama Hat Trail: A Journey from South America*. (Vintage/Random House, New York: 1998). One of the best books on the unique Panama hat industry in Ecuador. Tom Miller really knows how to tell a story. If you have an interest in Ecuador, this is a very hard book to put down.

Von Hagen, Victor Wolfgang. *Ecuador and the Galápagos Islands* (University of Oklahoma Press, Norman: 1959). Very good description of the culture and geography of Ecuador.

Fiction

Aguilera Malta, Demetrio. *Don Goyo*. (Humana Press, Dlifton, New Jersey: 1980) Originally published in 1933 with a translation by John and Carolyn Brushwood. A mythical tale of the mestizos on the coast and their fight to keep the mangrove swamps from being torn down by the hated white class of Ecuador.

Enciclopedia del Ecuador (La Editorial "Océano" de Barcelona, Barcelona: 2000). Excellent reference work in Spanish covering all subjects about Ecuador.

Hassurek, Friedrich. *Four Years Among the Ecuadorians*. (Hurd & Houghton, New York: 1867). A frank account of Mr Hassurek's travels in Ecuador in the 1860s and his observations of Ecuadorian life.

Icaza, Jorge. *Huasipungo*. (Dennis Dobson, London: 1962). First published in 1934 with the 1962 edition translated by Mervyn Savill. This novel deals with the racism that the Indians suffered in a small mountain village.

Thomsen, Moritz. *The Farm on the River of Emeralds*. (Vintage/ Random House, New York: 1979). A crusty old codger writes about his attempts at farming in the province of Esmeraldas.

Poole, Richard. *The Inca Smiled: The Growing Pains of an Aid Worker in Ecuador*. (Oneworld Publications, England: 1994). Excellent accounts of a Peace Corps volunteer in Ecuador and his experience of the culture of Ecuador. This story is highly personal and examines in detail the problems of understanding another culture, its food, and its language.

Weismantel, Mary J. *Food, Gender, and Poverty in the Ecuadorian Andes*. (University of Pennsylvania Press, Philadelphia: 1989). This book is an indepth study of the role of food in the lives of the residents of Zumbagua, a small mountain village in the Andes.

Whymper, Edward. *Travels Amongst The Great Andes Of The Equator*. (Gibbs M. Smith Inc., Layton, Utah: 1987). Originally published in 1892, this is an account of Whymper's studies of the altitude and natural science.

History

Lowry, Walker. *Tumult at Dusk: Being an Account of Ecuador*. (The Grabhorn Press, San Francisco: 1963). This is a very unique book that covers both the culture and history of Ecuador. I highly recommend it. However, there are only 100 printed copies. There is one available at the UCLA special collections unit.

Phelan, John Leddy. *The Kingdom of Quito in the Seventeenth Century: Bureaucratic Politics in the Spanish Empire*. (University of Wisconsin, Madison: 1967). An excellent account of Ecuador in the 17th century with good material about graft and life in general.

Poetry

Cabiedes-Fink, Alicia, and Maier, Ted, ed. *Between the Silence of Voices: An Anthology of Contemporary Ecuadorian Women Poets.* (Associación Ecuatoriana de Ejecutivas de Empresas Turísticas, Cayambe, Ecuador: 1997). An excellent edition.

Travel

Pearson, David L., and Middleton, David. *The New Key to Ecuador and the Galápagos.* (Ulysses Press, Berkeley, California: 1999) One of the best travel guides about Ecuador with an emphasis on ecotourism. Dr Pearson has been traveling extensively to Ecuador since the early 1970s.

INTERNET SITES

Business

http://www.cig.org.ec (Association of Industry in Guayaquil)

Cities

http://www.quito.gov.ec (Quito)
http://www.guayaco.com (Guayaquil)

Culture

http://arts.ucsc.edu/faculty/Schechter (Dr Schechter is an expert on Ecuadorian music)
http://www.ecuadornostalgia.com (Very good site about Ecuadorian culture)
http://www.geocities.com/athens/styx/7165/1.html (Ecuadorian Poets)
http://www.lahora.com.ec/paginas/pint.htm (Ecuadorian Artists)

http://www.missecuador.com (Information about Miss Ecuador's beauty pageant)

General

http://www.ccm.net/~jsruiz/conflicto.htm (Ecuador/Peru Conflict)
http://www.cdc.gov/travel/diseases.htm (Center for Infectious Diseases)
http://www.derechos.org/nizkor/ecuador/ (Human Rights Group)
http://www.ecuanex.net.ec/lalinea/index.html (AIDS Organization)
http://www.elmilagrodemindo.com (Orphanage)
http://www.explored.com.ec (Massive collection of articles published about Ecuador –searchable database under Archivo Digital)
http://www.globalvolunteers.org/ecdrmain.htm (Volunteer Work in Ecuador)
http://www.paho.org/english/sha/prflecu.htm (Pan American Health Organization with excellent information about society and health in Ecuador)

Geography & Weather

http://www.cimas.edu.ec (Enviromental Groups)
http://www.gct.org/ (Galápagos Conservation Trust)
http://www.ecuadorciencia.com (Volcano Information)
http://www.jatunsacha.org (Conservation Project)
http://www.weatherhub.com/global/ec.htm (Links to weather reports on a number of cities in Ecuador)
http://www.weather.com

Government & Politics

http://www.bce.fin.ec/ (Central Bank of Ecuador)
http://www.britembquito.org.ec (British Embassy)
http://www.ccm.net/~jsruiz/presidents.htm

http://www.codenpe.gov.ec/index.html (Excellent site for indigenous information)

http://www.conaie.nativeweb.org (Site on indigenous issues)

http://www.ecuador.org (Ecuador Embassy in the U.S.)

http://www.ecuanex.net.ec/anticorrupcion/ (Anticorruption organization in Eucuador)

http://www.embassyworld.com/embassy/ecuador.htm (Lists many of the Ecuadorian embassies worldwide)

http://www.estade.org (Study of government organizations in Ecuador)

Internet Directories

http://www.bacan.com

http://www.ecua.net.ec

http://www.ecuaworld.com

http://www.mande.com

Magazines

El Agro http://www.elagro.com.ec/explorer/index.html (Agriculture in Ecuador)

El Financiero http://www.elfinanciero.com (Finance)

Gestión http://www.gestion.dinediciones.com

Revista Estadio http://www.revistaestadio.com (Sports)

Vistazo http://www.vistazo.com (Magazine covering the country)

Newspapers

El Comerico (Quito) http://www.elcomercio.com

El Hoy (Quito) http://www.hoy.com.ec

La Hora (Quito) http://www.lahora.com

Diario Expreso (Guayquil) http://www.diario-expreso.com

Diario El Extra (Guayaquil) http://www.diario-extra.com

El Universo (Guayaquil) http://www.eluniverso.com

El Telégrafo (Guayaquil) http://www.telegrafo.com.ec
Diaro El Tiempo (Cuenca) http://www.eltiempo.satnet.net
El Mercurio (Cuenca) http://www.elmercurio.com.ec
El Diario (Portoviejo) http://www.eldiario.com.ec
La Prensa http://www.laprensa.com
Yahoo http://fullcoverage.yahoo.com/fc/world/ecuador

Tourism

http://www.darwinfoundation.org (Galápagos Information)
http://www.discovergalapagos.com/default.html (Galápagos Tours)
http://www.ecuaventura.com
http://www.ecuadorexplorer.com
http://www.ecuaworld.com

THE AUTHOR

Nicholas Crowder is the webmaster of Latin America Traveler (http://www.latinamericatravel.com), which has more than 600 links covering Latin America. Nicholas is a contributing writer to *Honduras This Week* (a Central American weekly). Most importantly, he is married to a beautiful woman from Guayaquil and has lived in Ecuador for more than 20 years. Despite having traveled to almost every corner of Ecuador and interviewed thousands of Ecuadorians, his fascination for Ecuador continues.

INDEX